KU-115-950

BEN JONSON:
TO THE FIRST FOLIO

RICHARD DUTTON
School of English, University of Lancaster

2970

CAMBRIDGE UNIVERSITY PRESS

CAMBRIDGE

LONDON   NEW YORK   NEW ROCHELLE

MELBOURNE   SYDNEY

Published by the Press Syndicate of the University of Cambridge
The Pitt Building, Trumpington Street, Cambridge CB2 1RP
32 East 57th Street, New York, NY 10022, USA
296 Beaconsfield Parade, Middle Park, Melbourne 3206, Australia

© Cambridge University Press 1983

First published 1983

Printed in Great Britain at The Pitman Press, Bath

Library of Congress catalogue card number: 83–1819

British Library Cataloguing in Publication Data
Dutton, Richard
Ben Jonson. – (British and Irish authors)
1. Jonson, Ben – Criticism and interpretation
I. Title   II. Series
822'.3   PR2638

ISBN 0 521 24313 0 hard covers
ISBN 0 521 28596 8 paperback

For
MAURA

Contents

Preface

This book has been a long time in the making. I first discovered Jonson at school where, unusually, we were given *The Alchemist* to study for 'A' Level. This led to a production of the play, which made me a devoted Jonsonian; I played Sir Epicure Mammon, which may help readers to understand some of the extravangances of the following pages. I studied Jonson again at King's College, Cambridge, and for a doctoral dissertation at the University of Nottingham. I should like to take this opportunity of thanking all my teachers, and particularly Dr George Parfitt, who supervised my dissertation.

Over the past ten years I have published a number of articles on Jonson, and I should like to thank the editors for their permission to re-use material (usually in somewhat altered form) which first appeared in the following journals: 'The significance of Jonson's revision of *Every Man In His Humour*', *The Modern Language Review*, 69 (1974); '*Volpone* and *The Alchemist*: a comparison in satiric techniques', *Renaissance and Modern Studies*, 18 (1974); 'The sources, text and readers of *Sejanus*: Jonson's "integrity in the story"', *Studies in Philology*, 75 (1978); '"What ministers men must, for practice, use": Ben Jonson's Cicero', *English Studies*, 59 (1978). More recently, I have had the pleasure of editing Jonson's *Epigrams* and *The Forest* for Carcanet Press and selections of *Jacobean and Caroline Court Masques and Civic Entertainments* (including many by Jonson) for Nottingham Drama Texts. I am grateful to the publishers of the former and the general editors of the latter for permission to re-use some of my introductory material in those volumes.

For the past eight years my students and colleagues at the University of Lancaster have borne patiently with my obsession, and I want to put my gratitude on record here, together with a general acknowledgement of all the comments and criticisms which have made this book a better one than it would otherwise have been. My apologies, finally, to my wife, daughter and cats, whose lives have been continually disrupted by the writing of this book.

August 1982. Lancaster   Richard Dutton

A note on texts

Quotations from, and references to, the works of Jonson are based on the definitive Clarendon *Ben Jonson*, 11 vols. (Oxford, 1925–51), edited by C. H. Herford and Percy and Evelyn Simpson (cited in the notes as H & S). I have modernised the spelling throughout, but I have retained Jonson's characteristic punctuation because it is often the key to his sense; when Groom Idiot is told

> And so my sharpness thou no less dis-joints,
> Than thou did'st late, losing my points
> (*Epigrams* 58)

Jonson means by 'points' both his punctuation and his argument. It is useful to bear in mind that Jonson usually punctuates for the speaking voice, and that apparent difficulties often disappear when the phrase is read out loud.

Quotations from Shakespeare are taken from the single-volume *Pelican Shakespeare* (revised edition, Baltimore, 1969), general editor, Alfred Harbage, except that quotations from *The Two Noble Kinsmen* are taken from the edition by N. W. Bawcutt (Harmondsworth, 1977).

The Catalogue.

The 1616 folio and its place in Jonson's career

> Pray thee, take care, that tak'st my book in hand,
> To read it well: that is, to understand.
>
> (*Epigrams* 1)

Ben Jonson suffers from being at once too well known and too little read or understood. He is the sort of author with whom we are immediately on first-name terms, 'rare Ben' with his 'mountain belly, and . . . rocky face', [1] the 'Spanish great galleon' of the famous wit-battles with the 'English man-of-war', Shakespeare.[2] The vivid and convincing portrait in the National Picture Gallery and the fortuitous survival of his racy *Conversations* with William Drummond of Hawthornden have both contributed to our sense of his being a colourful character in a colourful age. On the other hand, his works (with one or two notable exceptions) have not commonly inspired the same kind of enthusiasm; their characteristics – classicism, 'humours', realism, satire, moral earnestness, occasional lyric grace – are commonly acknowledged and as commonly taken for granted.

Despite prodigious scholarly efforts in recent years, T. S. Eliot's summary of Jonson's reputation is as true today as when first written, sixty years ago: 'To be universally accepted; to be damned by the praise that quenches all desire to read the book; to be afflicted by the imputation of the virtues which excite the least pleasure; and to be read only by historians and antiquaries – this is the most perfect conspiracy of approval.'[3] Sometimes the approval shades into boredom, as when eminent scholars dismiss Jonson's masques as 'of small literary value'[4] or remark coolly of essays on his poems that 'as could be expected of their subject, they do not offer any surprising revelations or startling new insights'.[5]

There is, in short, a familiarity about Jonson, a familiarity which has bred not contempt but complacency, a feeling that he is known, weighed up, comprehended – a colourful character, perhaps, but not the most exciting of writers. I wish in this book to question the general estimate of Jonson as a writer that I have just outlined and, if possible, to rediscover the challenging *literary* figure that he clearly was for his contemporaries. It was as a writer, not as a colourful personality, that Jonson continually found himself in conflict with the Privy Council, in danger on at least one occasion of having his ears and nose cut (see p. 8, below). It was at least as much his beliefs about the importance of literature as his fiery temper that led to heated altercations with such men as John Marston, Inigo Jones and George Chapman and to his notorious differences with Shakespeare, as well as to those quarrels with the world in general in the odes 'To Himself'[6] provoked by the reception both of *Poetaster* and of *The New Inn*. And it was first and foremost as a writer that Jonson earned the accolade 'rare' that was later carved on his tombstone, attracting around him in his later years a 'tribe' of aspiring younger writers who were proud to be known as his 'sons'.

This is not the place to rehearse the history of Jonson's declining reputation,[7] but rather to ask why all the scholarship devoted to Jonson in recent years has done little to reverse the process, to replace the familiar Jonson with what his contemporaries saw – something less predictable and more challenging. The fact is that the best scholarship *has* done something of this; books like Jonas Barish's *Ben Jonson and the Language of Prose Comedy*, for example, or Stephen Orgel's *The Jonsonian Masque*,[8] have helped us to see Jonson as a more complex and stimulating artist than many people suspected. But it is noticeable that such works have tended to focus on relatively limited areas of Jonson's achievement and have been for the specialist rather than the general reader. It has been when writers have attempted to confront Jonson's career as a whole that it has proved difficult to generate the same kind of excitement, to keep before us the same kind of challenging figure: it is easier to keep reproducing the old familiar Ben.

The reasons for this are not hard to find. The length of Jonson's career, together with the sheer quantity and variety of his output, poses intimidating problems: an attempt to confront everything he wrote almost inevitably degenerates into a bland survey, while any attempt to select the best or most representative of his work inevitably loses touch with the real scope and complexity of the subject. Jonson's literary career lasted some forty years, longer than that of any of his major contemporaries. His earliest surviving works date from the last years of Elizabeth's reign, yet he was still writing virtually up to his death in 1637, only a few years short of the Civil War. He outlived all his notable friends and rivals, including Shakespeare, Donne, Bacon, Chapman, Webster, Middleton, Beaumont and Fletcher. He started writing while Spenser was still alive and died just as Milton was emerging as the major poet of the mid seventeenth century (and Dryden, the major poet of the end of the century, was preparing to go to Jonson's old school, Westminster). During this long and varied career, beset alike with triumphs and catastrophes, Jonson produced a wide diversity of works – comedies, tragedies, masques, entertainments, non-dramatic verse (lyrics, satires, poems of praise, remembrance, piety and self-justification), translations and critical prose.

No wonder it is difficult to keep all this in the same challenging focus. Certain threads may, of course, be traced through most of what he wrote, adding up to what we might call his vision or his philosophy of literature. In the Prologue to *Volpone* (1606), for ex-ample, we find the declaration:

> In all his poems, still, hath been this measure,
> To mix profit, with your pleasure.   (7–8)

Twenty-five years and several reiterations later, he is still rehearsing the same formula in the text of one of the last of his Court masques: 'all representations . . . either have been, or ought to be the mirrors of man's life, whose ends . . . ought always to carry a mixture of profit, with them, no less than delight'.[9] But the idea of literature mixing 'profit' (or moral instruction) with the delight or entertainment of the reader/audience is only a stock formula. It derived ultimately from the Roman poet and critic, Horace, with whom Jonson felt an affinity, but was widely reiterated by Renaissance writers, notably Sir Philip Sidney in his *Apology for Poetry* (published 1595). Such a formula imposes no real restraints, either of style or subject-matter, upon an author, and in itself it tells us nothing about the peculiar qualities of Jonson's writing. To focus on such a theme inevitably runs the risk of reinforcing Jonson's reputation as an unimaginative classicist, while telling us nothing about the real variety and complexity of his work.

My own answer to the problem of doing proper justice to the diversity of Jonson's career in the compass of a single book may not be perfect, but it has the virtue of being Jonson's own answer. I have chosen to focus not on themes or on my own selection of the 'best' of Jonson, but on the great first folio of his *Works*, which Jonson himself saw through the press in 1616. Such a decision involves making many sacrifices, of course; I am effectively excluding those works written before 1616 which Jonson chose not to print in the folio, and every-thing printed after that date, including more than half of the non-dramatic verse, some of the most interesting masques, all the critical prose and some unduly neglected plays. I particularly regret not being able to find room to discuss *The Devil is an Ass* (1616), *The*

Gypsies Metamorphos'd (1621), *The Staple of News* (1625) and the lyric sequence, ' A Celebration of Charis in Ten Lyric Pieces', printed in *The Underwood* (published 1640) – the more so if my decision gives further credence to the unwarranted myth that the second half of Jonson's career was a long, slow falling off from the triumphs enshrined in the 1616 folio.

Given, however, that a choice *had* to be made, I would defend this one on two grounds. Firstly, the folio does contain most of the works which have attracted modern attention and are likely to be familiar to readers of this book – *Every Man In His Humour*, *Sejanus*, *Volpone*, *Epicoene*, *The Alchemist*, the earliest and most heavily annotated masques, and poems such as 'On My First Son', 'To Penshurst' and those 'To Celia'. The most unfortunate omission in this respect is *Bartholomew Fair*, the most ambitious single work that Jonson seems ever to have attempted, and in many people's view his finest achievement, even if it has never enjoyed the popularity of *Volpone* or *The Alchemist*. It was written two years before the folio was printed, may be said (as I shall argue later) to encapsulate the principles that inform the folio as a whole, and was only omitted from it for lack of space. For all these reasons, I have therefore seen fit to break my own rule to the extent of including a chapter on *Bartholomew Fair*. The second argument with which I would defend my decision is the more important one: the very fact that the 1616 folio is not a complete record of Jonson's career to that date, but his own deliberate selection from it, gives that volume a value which many people have overlooked. It points to various connections between the different facets of his career which Jonson himself wished to emphasise. When the folio was first published it was scorned by many as a piece of pretentiousness, in the main because it printed plays alongside poems in a prestige volume, and play-scripts had not hitherto been regarded as serious literature. In retrospect, we can see Jonson's decision as a brave and important moment in the history of literature, redefining the significance of drama and paving the way for the Shakespeare first folio of 1623 (as well as the publication of many other Jacobean plays which might otherwise have been lost). Unfortunately today Jonson's folio has little more than this archaeological interest; its; historical significance seems in some perverse way to have obscured its intrinsic value as a statement by Jonson himself about the nature of his career. The mixture of plays, poems, masques and entertainments that Jonson put together was deliberate and artful, the whole amounting to more than the sum of the parts. Failure to observe this fact has helped to maintain the serious modern undervaluation of Jonson as a living and challenging writer. By returning to Jonson's own view of what was vital in his own career up to that point we may put ourselves in a better position to appreciate why his contemporaries thought so much of him and what he still has to offer today.

The significance of the 1616 folio will be easier to grasp if we place it in the context of Jonson's life and times. He was born, either in 1572 or 1573, probably on 11 June and very probably in London. He was thus nearly ten years younger than the Warwickshire-born Shakespeare, but almost an exact contemporary of John Donne, who was born in Bread Street, London, in the first half of 1572. Jonson's father, a clergyman, died about a month before Ben (as he chose usually to be called) was born, and his mother was soon remarried, to a Westminster bricklayer. Jonson was later to tell William Drummond of Hawthornden how he was 'brought up poorly, put to school by a friend (his master Camden), after taken from it, and put to another craft'[10] – almost certainly that of bricklaying. In later years his enemies taunted him for his association with this 'demeaning' occupation.[11] The school was Westminster, and it was clearly here that Jonson laid the foundation of the classical scholarship which was to underpin his entire career.

It was presumably to escape the bricklaying that Jonson joined the army in the Low Countries that was fighting the Spanish; the Counter-Reformation was at its height and the European struggle between Catholics and Protestants was an important back-drop to Jonson's early life. A characteristic anecdote tells how 'in the face of both the camps (he) killed an enemy and (took) *opima spolia*[12] from him' (244–6). He shortly returned 'to his wonted studies', however, and to a marriage in 1594 to Anne Lewis, of whom little is known beyond Jonson's memorable testimony that she was 'a shrew yet honest'. The precise number of their children is not known, though they included the daughter, Mary, and the son, Benjamin, whose early deaths are movingly recorded in *Epigrams* 22 and 45. We may surmise that the marriage was sometimes a stormy one from the fact that they were once separated for a period of five years, during which time Jonson 'remained with my lord Aubigny' (255),[13] though against that must be set the testimony: 'In his youth given to venery. He thought the use of a maid nothing in comparison to the wantonness of a wife' (287–8).

By the mid 1590s Jonson was already associated with the theatre. He seems to have acted briefly with a 'strolling company', one of the parts with which he was associated being Hieronimo in Kyd's phenomenally popular *The Spanish Tragedy*; eventually he was employed as an actor–writer by the theatrical entrepreneur, Philip Henslowe. In 1597 Jonson first came to the attention of the authorities for acting in, and apparently part-writing, the lost satirical play, *The Isle of Dogs* (the principal author was Thomas Nashe); he was arrested and imprisoned for his part in the production – not the most auspicious of débuts on the stage of history, but typical of the man. This is an early indication of how strict the theatrical censorship of the day was. Various other plays which have survived in one form or another seem to belong to this period, notably *A Tale of a Tub* (which was only belatedly published in the form that Jonson revised for production in 1633),[14] and *The Case Is Altered*, which was not published until 1609, and then probably without Jonson's help or approval. *Every Man In His Humour*, performed by the Lord Chamberlain's Men (Shakespeare's Company) in 1598, seems to have been Jonson's first *major* theatrical success; it was the first work which, albeit in a much-revised form, he was to include in the 1616 folio.

The year 1598 also had a less pleasant side for Jonson. He killed a fellow-actor, Gabriel Spencer, in a duel and only escaped hanging by pleading benefit of clergy[15] – one of the last men in England to do so. As he told Drummond, 'being appealed to the fields he had killed his adversary, which had hurt him in the arm, and whose sword was ten inches longer than his: for the which he was imprisoned, and almost at the gallows. Then took he his religion by trust of a priest who visited him in prison. Thereafter he was twelve years a papist' (246–51). The conversion to Roman Catholicism was just as dangerous in its way as the manslaughter, since Catholics were looked on with dark suspicion by the Elizabethan authorities, who always assumed that their loyalties might lie with the Pope and Spain rather than with Queen and country. This probably explains the following mysterious episode: 'In the time of his close imprisonment, under Queen Elizabeth, his judges could get nothing of him to all their demands but "aye" and "no". They placed two damned villains to catch advantage of him, with him, but he was advertised by his keeper; of the spies he hath an epigram' (256–60).[16]

Every Man·Out of His Humour, apparently a sequel to *Every Man In His Humour* but actually a very different, more openly satirical style of play, was performed by the Lord Chamberlain's Men at their new theatre, The Globe, in 1599. Jonson followed this up with two satires, *Cynthia's Revels* (1600) and *Poetaster* (1601); these were written for one of the new children's companies, the Children of the Chapel Royal, who performed in an indoor or 'private' theatre, and these two works seem to have comprised Jonson's contribution to the so-called War of the Theatres. Playwrights employed by the various acting companies always seem to have made comic milage out of poking fun at each other, but for a time – perhaps inspired by the competition from the new children's companies[17] – it developed into an all-out 'war'. Jonson's particular targets were Dekker, who replied in kind with *Satiromastix* (1602), and Marston: 'He had many quarrels with Marston, beat him, and took his pistol from him, wrote his *Poetaster* on him; the beginning of them were that Marston represented him in the stage' (284–6). It is difficult to know how seriously to take any of this; certainly the quarrels did not preclude Marston and Jonson from collaborating on a play a few years later. Jonson's 'comicall satyres' were all reprinted, with some alterations, in the 1616 folio, but a number of other works, like *Page of Plymouth*, *King Robert II of Scotland* and *Richard Crookback* (for all of which he was paid by Henslowe between 1599 and 1602) were not to be included and have not survived at all.

The year 1603 was another traumatic one in Jonson's life, firstly because it saw the death of his eldest son:

When the King came in England, at that time the pest was in London, he being in the country at Sir Robert Cotton's house with old Camden, he saw in a vision his eldest son (then a child and at London) appear unto him with the mark of a bloody cross on his forehead as if it had been cutted with a sword, at which amazed he prayed unto God, and in the morning he came to Mr. Camden's chamber to tell him, who persuaded him it was but an apprehension of his fantasy at which he should not be dejected; in the mean time comes there letters from his wife of the death of the boy in the plague. He appeared to him he said of a manly shape and of that growth that he thinks he shall be at the resurrection. (261–72)

That year also saw at least one further altercation with the authorities: 'Northampton was his mortal enemy for brawling on a St. George's day one of his attenders, he was called before the Council for his *Sejanus* and accused both of popery and treason by him' (325–7). It is not clear whether it was *Sejanus* – the first of his extant tragedies, but not well received on its first performance – or the brawling that elicited the charges of popery and treason, but Henry Howard, Earl of Northampton, was a dangerous man to choose for an enemy, being one of the closest advisors of the new King. That was the other notable development of 1603: the death of the old Queen and the accession of her cousin of Scotland,

James VI and I – a development of crucial importance in Jonson's career.

Jonson and Dekker between them were entrusted by the city authorities with devising the dramatic pageants which were to greet King James on his ceremonial entry into the City of London (an event actually delayed by the plague until March 1604).[18] Jonson also created a charming entertainment at Althorpe for the new Queen, Anne, on her journey south. These may have led to his eventually being given the commission to write *The Masque of Blackness*, which was performed at Court on Twelfth Night 1605, with Queen Anne and her ladies in the leading roles. It seems to have been a success since Jonson and his stage-designer collaborator, Inigo Jones, were regularly employed on such masques at Court thereafter. Jonson composed on average about a masque a year throughout the reign of King James, usually for performance about the Christmas and Twelfth Night celebrations. These gorgeous and costly entertainments, so long neglected until recent scholarship began to rediscover their significance, were of very practical importance to Jonson. He complained to Drummond that 'of all his plays he never gained two hundred pounds' (566) and it was clearly the case that no playwright could support himself comfortably just by producing playscripts (unless, like Shakespeare, he also happened to be an actor and shareholder in the company that produced them). The regular masque commissions were well rewarded and helped enable Jonson to escape the treadmill of hack-writing for the likes of Henslowe in a way that writers like Dekker, Webster and Heywood never really managed. Unlike Shakespeare, Jonson never achieved real financial security, perhaps because he was not the most provident of men with his money – 'Sundry times he hath devoured his books; once sold them all for necessity' (328–9) – but at least he enjoyed a relative freedom, which allowed him to think of his writing as an art and not merely a craft. This was clearly a significant factor in the evolution of the 'pretentious' 1616 folio.

The fact that Jonson was writing regularly for the Court did not, however, protect him from the authorities; nor does it seem to have inclined him to avoid contentious material in the plays he wrote for the public stage.

He was delated by Sir James Murray to the King for writing something against the Scots in a play *Eastward Ho* and voluntarily imprisoned himself with Chapman and Marston,[19] who had written it amongst them. The report was that they should then have their ears cut and noses. After their delivery he banqueted all his friends, there was Camden, Selden and others.

At the midst of the feast his old mother drank to him and show(ed) him a paper which she had [if the sentence had taken execution] to have mixed in the prison among his drink, which was full of lusty strong poison and that she was no churl she told she minded first to have drunk of it herself. (273–83)

It had been a close shave, and Jonson was properly alarmed; he had written to Sir Robert Cecil – the King's first minister and a key figure in Jonson's life, as we shall see[20] – asking him to intercede on behalf of Chapman and himself. In this letter[21] Jonson confesses to his 'first error' (*The Isle of Dogs? Sejanus?*) but protests that since then 'I have so attempered my style, that I have given no cause to any good man of grief.'

This appeal, or one like it, must have secured Jonson's release, but he appears not to have escaped the authorities' net. Around Michaelmas Term (October) of 1605 one 'Benjamin Johnson' was noted as having been seen in the company of a group of disaffected Catholic gentry who were to go down to history as the Gunpowder Plotters. On 7 November, moreover, two days after the infamous Plot was discovered, he was given a warrant by the Privy Council to act as a go-between from themselves to an unnamed Catholic priest 'that offered to do good service to the state'. Nothing came of this because, as Jonson reported to Salisbury, 'that party will not be found, (for so he returns answer)'.[22] He concludes, however, with protestations of loyalty to the state, to the King and to Salisbury himself (as Cecil had now become). We must assume that the Privy Council chose Jonson for this mission because he was known to be Catholic, with access to underground Catholic circles, but thought to be trustworthy. It is possible, however, that it was not as straightforward as that. We know that, within the period of May to November 1605, Jonson was imprisoned and under threat of severe penalty for *Eastward Ho*, released – perhaps through the intercession, certainly with the knowledge, of Salisbury – associated with the Gunpowder Plotters and then used by Salisbury in the efforts to track the Plotters down. The possibility that Jonson was for some of this time, either willingly or unwillingly, a double-agent, working for Salisbury under the cloak of his Catholicism, is difficult to discount. It is a possibility we shall have cause to consider further in relation to *Volpone*, the *Epigrams* and *Catiline*.

None of this seems to have interfered with Jonson's devising of his next Court masque, *Hymenaei*, which was given early in 1606 to celebrate the wedding of the young Earl of Essex and Lady Frances Howard. Nor did it impede the writing of *Volpone*, of which he claimed 'five weeks fully penned it' (Prologue, 16) before it was presented by the King's Men (as the Lord Chamberlain's Men had now become), some time prior to March of that year. That spring, however, Jonson and his wife were arraigned for failing to attend the Church of England, as required by law; he was let off fairly lightly, perhaps in view of his services to the government, but it was a reminder of his precarious position. This was, nevertheless, the beginning of what many would see as the most fruitful decade of Jonson's career; the four comedies – *Volpone* (1606), *Epicoene* (1609), *The Alchemist* (1610) and *Bartholomew Fair* (1614) – are generally regarded as his finest achievements; the one 'failure', *Catiline* (1611), survived its disastrous first performance to become perhaps the most respected tragedy of the seventeenth century; the masques of the period show an inventive flair equal to Inigo Jones's remarkable innovations in the staging; and Jonson was able to display the best of his non-dramatic verse in carefully devised selections: *Epigrams* (which he planned to publish as an independent volume in 1612 but apparently did not) and *The Forest*.

These were also the years of the Mermaid Tavern, nostalgically recalled by Francis Beaumont in his 'Letter from the Country' (1616):

> What things have we seen,
> Done at the Mermaid! heard words that have been
> So nimble, and so full of subtle flame,
> As if that every one from whence they came,
> Had meant to put his whole wit in a jest,
> And had resolv'd to live a fool, the rest
> Of his dull life.

Later ages have shamelessly romanticised this piece of hyperbole,[23] making the Mermaid the setting for Jonson's 'wit-battles' with Shakespeare, surrounded by all the great names of Jacobean literature – Donne, Bacon, Raleigh, Beaumont and Fletcher. Sadly, there is little corroborative evidence for this. Jonson probably met there with young admirers like Beaumont, and there is a possibility that Donne was there on at least one occasion. But the closest that Shakespeare has been traced to the Mermaid is in the fact that its landlord was a party to his last known property transaction,[24] while Bacon was probably too much of a politician for such conviviality and Raleigh could not possibly have been there (see the next paragraph). It is perhaps sufficient to note that there is ample evidence, particularly in *Epigrams* and the posthumous commonplace book, *Timber, or Discoveries*, that Jonson was on terms of strong mutual respect, and possibly of friendship, with all these men,[25] as he was with such discerning patrons as Lucy, Countess of Bedford and William, Earl of Pembroke, from whom 'every first day of the New Year he had £20 sent him . . . to buy books' (312–13).

Jonson's private life in this period was marked by two characteristic episodes. Some time around 1610 he returned to the Church of England: 'After he was reconciled with the Church and left off to be a recusant at his first communion in token of true reconciliation, he drank out all the full cup of wine' (314–16). Drink, as Drummond drily remarked, 'is one of the elements in which he liveth' (683–4), and drink was his undoing in the other memorable episode:

S[ir] W[alter] Raleigh sent him governor with his son anno 1613 to France. This youth being knavishly inclined, among other pastimes (as the setting of the favour of damsels on a cod-piece) caused him to be drunken and dead drunk, so that he knew not where he was, thereafter laid him on a car which he made to be drawn by pioneers through the streets, at every corner showing his governor stretched out and telling them that was a more lively image of the crucifix than any they had, at which sport young Raleigh's mother delighted much (saying his father young was so inclined) though the father abhorred it. (295–305)

Sir Walter Raleigh, who had fallen foul of Northampton and Salisbury at the beginning of the reign, was at this time confined to the Tower of London; Jonson was one of those who visited him there, collaborating on his *The History of the World*: 'The best wits of England were employed for making of his *History*. Ben himself had written a piece to him of the Punic War which he altered and set in his book' (198–201). He also contributed a poem, 'The Mind of the Frontispiece to a Book' (also printed as *The Underwood* 24). The printers were eventually so overwhelmed by Raleigh's monumental work, published in 1614, that they had to delay the printing of Jonson's folio.

However disreputable Jonson's private life might occasionally be, his literary reputation was clearly in the ascendant in the years 1612–16, during which he put together the folio; this was formally recognised in 1616 by the award of a royal pension which made Jonson in fact, though not in name, Poet Laureate. It is against this background that the nature of the folio becomes intelligible: it is not simply a record of his career to date, but a deliberate and selective account of that career, emphasising those elements which the eminent man-of-letters wished to commemorate and quietly expunging those he did not.[26] This is a monument to a Poet Laureate, not to a former bricklayer. We cannot be sure, in fact, just how much Jonson did leave out. As early as 1598, Francis Meres included Jonson in his list of 'our best for tragedy',[27] but we know nothing of the works on which he based that judgement, even the titles; certainly none of them is included in the folio. Nor is the putative original version of *A Tale of a Tub*. We know at least the titles of *Page of Plymouth*, *King Robert II of Scotland* and *Richard Crookback*, from the period 1599–1602, but none of these is preserved either. *The Case Is Altered* and at least one collaborative work, *Eastward Ho*, have survived, but neither appears in the folio. Of the non-dramatic verse, only *Epigrams* and *The Forest* are included, though it is clear that they represent nothing like his total output to 1616. Only the run of Court masques is, so far as we can tell, complete (and even there the chronological order of the last two has been reversed so as to provide a more polished ending to the volume – further emphasising that this is not a simple 'collected works'); of the other specially commissioned 'entertainments' at least one – the Lord Mayor's Show for 1604, for which Jonson was certainly paid – is not included.

A major principle behind this selection was certainly the promotion of the image of himself as a serious poet – something very different from a mere playwright (a term Jonson despised; see *Epigrams* 49, 68, 100). The clearest indication of this is his choice of a revised version of *Every Man In His Humour*, with a totally new prologue, to stand at the head of the volume. Even in its revised form, the play is self-consciously new in style and format, with a clear ancestry in Roman comedy, in ways that are not true – for example – of *The Case Is Altered* or, significantly, of Shakespeare's comedies. Jonson offers it as the beginning of his 'real' career, the career of the Horatian poet. He emphasises the point by dedicating the play to William Camden, his master at Westminster School (the play that 'begins' his career is the first fruit of his classical education), and by adding a prologue which decries such styles of drama as chronicle histories and spectacular romances: he advocates an austere neo-classicism, such as will be found in all the plays in his own folio and first found its true voice in this play.[28] The survival of titles like *Richard Crookback* (suggesting old-fashioned chronicle history) from the period after 1598 should remind us that two careers – Horatian poet and mere playwright – must have overlapped for a time, if indeed Jonson was aware of the distinction at the time; the dedication to Camden did not appear in the original 1601 quarto of *Every Man In His Humour*. Jonson's claim to be a serious artist, even in works written for the public stage, must to some extent have been a retrospective invention.

It is difficult to discount the suspicion that Jonson's first folio is a piece of self-promotion, the proud advertisement of a poet now patronised by the highest in the land, determined to lay the ghosts of his past as a bricklayer and playwright. But we should not let this possibility blind us to the fact that it is also much more than that; the principles behind its selection and arrangement are positive as well as negative. The most impressive feature of the 1616 folio is not actually its promotion of a particular self-image (undeniable though that is) but its homogeneity. Its parts add up to a whole and speak to each other across their generic boundaries. Over the last few years there has been a growing recognition that the organisation of the *Epigrams*[29] – like that of *Bartholomew Fair* – is far more subtle, sophisticated and significant than at first meets the eye; behind the apparent randomness or spontaneity, there is a careful and deliberate structure. In different, though related ways we may now begin to appreciate that the same is true of the first folio as a whole. As I mentioned before, the tendency of modern scholarship has been to deal separately with the different facets of Jonson's career – 'humours' and 'comicall satyres'; the best comedies; the tragedies; the 'dotages' (Dryden's indiscriminate dismissal of the later plays); the masques, which are generally thought of as existing in a different sphere altogether; and the poems, which are treated as independent pieces, with scant regard given to which selection, if any, they belong. The result of this has been to make us lose sight of something that the organisation of the first folio is surely intended to impress upon us – the essential interrelatedness of the items within it, inviting us to read it as a unified volume, across generic boundaries. All this has diminished Jonson's status as an artist; the sum of his parts is an unknown quantity, because it is so rarely contemplated. To his contemporaries, it was clearly most impressive.

An attempt, therefore, to come to terms with the 1616 folio as a whole should help us to rediscover some of the challenge he made to his contemporaries – and so become less complacent about him ourselves. Apart from the claims this volume implicitly makes about Jonson's status as a poet, it actually spells out a far more outrageous claim: that the different facets of his career all contribute to the same essential endeavour, which we can only describe as the entertainment and education of the age. He is not only the author of a number of individually impressive works, but the poet who has most rigorously and conscientiously confronted the issues of his age as they manifest themselves at the heart of the nation, in London and Westminster. It is an enormous claim, of course, and one which seems almost inconceivable if we persist in thinking of Jonson as primarily a writer of comedies; for us, on the whole, comedy is so much less a form than, say, epic or tragedy (though perhaps we ought to ask ourselves whether it should be). But Jonson's great comedies constitute only a part of the folio, albeit an important one, and when we survey the volume as a whole, the claim is not so easily dismissed.

If we probe behind the generic differences of Jonson's works (presented in the order: plays, poems, entertainments and masques – from public forum, through select private readership to the aristocratic patrons, Court and King) it is not difficult to identify a consistent set of attitudes, a 'vision', humanist and conservative on the whole (though there is room for debate on how genial or pessimistic he is). The aims of Jonson's art change very little in his first folio. What do change, and change in ways as challenging as the claims of the volume as a whole, are the tactics by which Jonson prosecutes those aims. I use the military metaphor advisedly. Jonson is essentially a satirist, by which I mean here a poet measuring reality against an unrealised set of ideals; the difficulty for the satirist is not to be 'truthful' or even how to be 'entertaining' but how to do so in a way which brings home to the reader/audience how and why the ideals are not being realised, and why it matters – in short, *involving* the reader/audience in the satire, not alienating them by being too virulent or holier-and-wiser-than-thou. As a satirist, Jonson is the supreme tactician, an unusually inventive strategist: it is only when we contemplate the folio as a whole that we can appreciate just how inventive.

In the theatre, the most striking evidence of his developing tactics is the increasing sureness with which he constructs a play as an event to occur in a certain time and place, before a particular audience, often with an intensely topical theme – culminating in the precision of *Bartholomew Fair* being performed 'at the Hope on the Bankside, in the County of Surrey . . . the one and thirtieth day of Octob. 1614' (Induction, 65–8). Paradoxically, in being so exact and specific, he makes us see that the contemporary moment is not unique but typical of many similar moments, both past (this is the special significance of his Roman tragedies) and probably also future. This is why the plays work not only for a live audience but also on the printed page: Jonson was the first English dramatist to appreciate this possibility. They work because he has perceived (certainly in the plays from *Sejanus* on) that the real objects of his satire are not the literary creations which people his plays, but the creatures they mirror among his audience and readers. Increasingly, his plays involve audience and readers in a process of *self*-examination. Similarly in the masques, we see Jonson exploiting the possibilities opened up by Jones's revolutionary staging and inherent in the antimasque (the comic preliminaries to the main action): with the same intention of finding the most effective ways of involving the spectators in the whole experience. As for the poems, the crucial step is the organisation into deliberate selections; *Epigrams* and *The Forest* have careful but unobtrusive structures, such that the poems carry more weight in context than they do individually. The unobtrusiveness is important; it is not something all readers will see and appreciate. As so often in Jonson, it amounts to a challenge, a way of sorting sheep from goats. The preface to the quarto text of *The Alchemist* is addressed 'To the Reader' and begins: 'If thou beest more, thou art an understander, and then I trust thee.' The distinction between 'the Reader in Ordinary' and 'the Reader Extraordinary' (as he puts it in the prefaces to the quarto *Catiline*) is one which Jonson draws constantly and is a key to his most pervasive and fundamental tactics.

It is often assumed that the distinction between true understanders and everyone else is fundamentally a snobbish one, Jonson allying himself with the educated upper classes against the ignorance and prejudice of those (literally) 'understanding gentlemen o' the ground' – the groundlings who can only afford to stand in the pit and will not appreciate his sophistication. There may be some truth in this, particularly when (as with *Catiline*) Jonson was determined to defend a play which had failed in the theatre. But there is an important sense in which the distinction goes much deeper, cutting clean across class boundaries. At bottom, we are all understanders in *both* the complimentary *and* the sarcastic senses (or have the capacity to be); we are all capable of comprehension but are beset by qualities which hinder it – laziness, inattention, prejudice, lack of judgement. Jonson's literary tactics, then, are always aimed at mocking, or challenging, or circumventing our weaknesses; he is looking for the real understander in each of us. This makes the business of reading Jonson neither easy nor comfortable; he is merciless on our penchant for simple answers and pleasures. But it does make him immensely challenging and rewarding – far more so than the 'known' Jonson I described earlier.

The structure of the 1616 folio thus embodies a search for 'understanding'. In later chapters, I offer my own 'understandings' of some of the issues which have commonly been thought central to Jonson's works – 'humours', classical borrowings, covert allusions to contemporaries, flattery of the Court etc.; in each case I approach these through detailed examinations of individual texts, rather than fall back on broad generalisations. I think this is the best way of elucidating the 'tactical' element in Jonson's satire. But I have sometimes made unusual or unconventional collocations – linking *The Forest* with *The Alchemist* and *Catiline*, for example, or *Epicoene* with the masques – because such cross-references seem to me to be essentially in keeping with the spirit of the folio as a whole. Each single 'understanding', each satiric tactic divined, leads to a deeper appreciation of the volume as a whole, the whole being more than the sum of the parts.

A sad measure of the truth of this last statement is to be found in a comparison of the 1616 folio with its continuation, the second part of the two-volume folio *Works* which Jonson did not live to complete, and which was brought out in 1640 by one of his 'sons', Sir Kenelm Digby. We should look at this before continuing our study of the 1616 folio because it too has had an insidious effect on Jonson's long-term reputation, and we will only rediscover the challenging figure that he was to his contemporaries if we rid ourselves of all the misconceptions that posterity has pinned upon him. To understand Digby's volume, we need to know how Jonson's career developed after 1616.

In 1616 itself, *The Devil is an Ass* was performed by the King's Men; it is apparent from what he told Drummond that it got Jonson into trouble, though it is not clear exactly why:

a play of his upon which he was accused, *The Devil is an Ass*; according to *comedia vetus*, in England the devil was brought in either with one Vice or other, the play done the devil carried away the Vice; he brings in the devil so overcome with the wickedness of this age that (he) thought himself an ass. *parergos* is discoursed of the Duke of Drownland. The King desired him to conceal it. (409–15)

Whether because of this problem or not we do not know, but Jonson now gave up the public stage for eight years – a fact which has had a profound effect on his long-term reputation. His plays, and particularly his comedies, have long been seen as the most substantial and accessible parts of his achievement; the fact that he abandoned this form of writing at the height of his career has often been construed either as snobbishness, perversity or as an admission of his failing powers. There is no evidence for any of these; the fact is that Jonson simply chose to channel his still prodigious energies in other directions. Certainly, the retirement from the public stage had no such immediate effect upon his reputation. He continued to write masques and, in 1618, was awarded an Honorary M.A. by the University of Oxford, which was conferred upon him in person the following year.[30] It was also in 1618 that he undertook a remarkable journey to Scotland, on foot; it may be that Jonson was naturally curious about the King's other realm, or that he felt the need of sustained exercise (he had grown to be a great barrel of a man, nearly twenty stone in weight), or that he had some ancestral connection with that country.[31] At all events, it was a great success; he was warmly received by Edinburgh society, being made a burgess of the city that September.

Towards the end of the year he spent some time at the house of the Petrarchan poet, William Drummond of Hawthornden, whose record of their conversation helps us so remarkably to flesh out Jonson's biography and personality. It is worth quoting the Scotsman's rather disenchanted verdict on his guest:

He is a great lover and praiser of himself, a contemner and scorner of others, given rather to lose a friend, than a jest, jealous of every word and action of those about him (especially after drink, which is one of the elements in which he liveth); a dissembler of ill parts which reign in him, a bragger of some good that he wanteth, thinketh nothing well but what either he himself, or some of his friends and countrymen hath said or done. He is passionately kind and angry, careless either to gain or keep, vindictive, but if he be well answered, at himself.

Of any religion as being versed in both.

Interpreteth best sayings and deeds often to the worst: oppressed with fantasy, which hath ever mastered his reason, a general disease of many poets. (680–93)

It is only too clear that there were temperamental differences between the two men, and that we need to be very circumspect about taking anything Drummond recorded too seriously; at times one suspects that Jonson may even have been joking in ways that his host did not appreciate. One side of Jonson that was apparent to Drummond, however, and which is apt to be forgotten when modern readers concentrate on the classicism or moral earnestness of his works, was his exuberant imagination or 'fantasy'. Drummond quotes a notable example, besides the strange premonition of his son's death: 'He hath consumed a whole night in lying looking to his great toe, about which he hath seen Tartars and Turks, Romans and Carthaginians fight in his imagination' (322–4).

The Jonson in Drummond's *Conversations* is, whatever reservations we have about them, essentially the Jonson of the 1616 folio. The absence of similarly vivid biographical details about the latter half of his career is another factor which, quite unwarrantably, has given rise to the impression that the later Jonson was a less vital or challenging figure than the earlier one. It is a measure of his continued standing at Court that, when he returned home ('He went from Leith homeward the 25 of January, 1619', 637), he found that his absence had been 'regretted' and the masque that had been devised without him 'not liked'. He had no trouble renewing his regular commission the following year. The King later showed his general appreciation of Jonson by granting him the reversion of the Mastership of the Rolls;[32] it was even rumoured that the King planned to knight Jonson, but that the poet's more prudent friends at Court disuaded him – presumably fearing the ridicule that might ensue.

In 1621, Jonson produced the most successful of all his masques, *The Gypsies Metamorphos'd*, performed an unprecedented three times, with subtle modifications for the three different settings.[33] Some of its popularity with the King undoubtedly lay in its providing a perfect vehicle for the histrionic talents of his last and most powerful favourite, the Duke of Buckingham; but even that, in its way, is a compliment to Jonson's professional skills – within such restraints he still managed to produce a lively and attractive entertainment. It was a further compliment to Jonson that, when the usual venue for Court masques (the Banqueting House at Whitehall) burned down in 1619, one of his pieces – *The Masque of Augurs* – was chosen to inaugurate Inigo Jones's splendid new Banqueting House (which still survives), on Twelfth Night 1622.

But then fire struck more cruelly at his career. In 1623, a fire at his lodgings destroyed his extensive library, together with a number of his own unpublished works. 'An Execration Upon Vulcan' (*The Underwood* 43) ruefully tries to come to terms with the loss and describes the works lost: 'my journey into Scotland song / With all th'adventures' (94–5); an almost completed history of the reign of Henry V; the story of Argenis in three books (perhaps a translation of Buchanan's Latin romance of that name); 'humble gleanings in divinity' (102); a translation of Horace's *Art of Poetry* and a Grammar. The last two pieces were rewritten and finally included in the 1640 folio, though sadly not the preface to the former, which Jonson had read to Drummond; it was apparently written in the form of a dialogue and contained 'an apology of a play of his *St Bartholomew's Fair*; by Criticus is understood Donne' (82–5). What a significant addition that would have been to the history of literary criticism. The loss of all these works has inevitably dealt a further heavy blow to his posthumous reputation, particularly since they included pieces very different from anything he had attempted before – a history, an account of his journey to Scotland (he told Drummond he was going to call it a 'discovery'), and a romance; these might, so to speak, have filled the gap left by his retirement from the public stage. At the time, however, the loss must have been made more bearable by the company of a younger generation of poets and dramatists, who looked to him as an elder statesman – the so-called Sons or Tribe of Ben.[34] These included, at various times, the poets Herrick, Suckling and Cleveland, and the dramatists Randolph, Brome and Field; they seem to have met regularly at various taverns – Herrick later looked back nostalgically to their 'lyric feasts' at 'the Sun, the Dog, the Triple Tun'[35] – but most famously in the Apollo room at the Devil, for which Jonson devised rules of conduct.

With the death of James I in 1625, troubles began to accumulate around Jonson. Charles I had tastes very different from those of his father, and Jonson lost the regular commissions for Court masques which he had enjoyed throughout the previous reign. We must assume that it was this loss of income which drove him back to the stage. *The Staple of News* was acted, quite successfully, by the King's Men in 1626. Following the death of Thomas Middleton, Jonson was made Chronologer of the City of London in 1628, but he wrote nothing to justify the appointment and in 1631 the City refused to pay the fee that went with it; it is not clear whether Jonson regarded the post as an honorary one or whether he was simply incapacitated by a stroke he suffered around the time he was appointed, and which left him partially paralysed. He had recovered sufficiently by January 1629 to see his new play, *The New Inn*, performed, but this proved to be the worst disaster of his career; in the printed text, he presented the play to the public 'as it was never acted, but most negligently play'd, by some, the King's Servants. And more squeamishly beheld, and censured by others, the King's subjects.'[36] The failure of the play, which the audience did not even allow to finish, prompted Jonson's furious 'Ode to Himself'; that in turn provoked a number of replies, some of them unkindly satirical about the ageing poet and his self-conceit.

Money troubles also increasingly beset him, as we may gauge from a number of poems written to both the King and Queen, angling either for more money or renewed patronage. He was successful to the extent of having his royal pension raised from a hundred marks to a hundred pounds, with the additional favour of an annual tierce of canary wine (which is still a perquisite of the Poet Laureate) – though 'An Epigram to the Household. 1630' (*The Underwood* 68) suggests that the royal staff were less prompt in such matters than their master. Jonson was also called upon to write two further Court masques, *Love's Triumph Through Callipolis* and *Chloridia*, but the consequences were unfortunate; when he came to publish the texts, there was a public altercation with Inigo Jones over whose name should appear first as their 'deviser'. Relations between the two men had clearly been edgy for many years; even in 1618, Jonson had told Drummond: 'he said to Prince Charles of Inigo Jones, that when he wanted words to express the greatest villain in the world he would call him an Inigo' (467–9). But this public falling-out, over the relative status of the poetry and the spectacle in masques,[37] did Jonson no good at all. The King and the Court sided with Jones, who had made himself indispensable both as an architect and as a stage-designer; Jonson received no further royal commissions.

In 1631 Jonson set about a second folio of his works, to complement the 1616 volume. But the incompetence of his printer, John Beale, and perhaps his own continuing ill-health caused him to abandon the project, with only *Bartholomew Fair*, *The Devil is an Ass* and *The Staple of News* set up in print. The following year he produced his last original play, *The Magnetic Lady: or Humours Reconciled*. In the Induction, he speaks of how 'the Author, beginning his studies of this kind, with *Every Man In His Humour*; and after, *Every Man Out of His Humour* . . . finding himself now near the close, or shutting up of his circle, hath phant'sied to himself, in *idaea*, this *Magnetic Mistress*' (99–106). The old man was trying to round things off neatly, perhaps with a touch of nostalgia for the great Elizabethan era which now seemed so far in the past. In fact his very last work for the public stage may have been a revision of a play he had written all those years ago, *A Tale of a Tub* (1597? 1633; but see note 14); if so, he recast it with the obvious intention of making one character, Vitruvius Hoop, a satirical squib against Inigo Jones. This was spotted by the censors, who insisted that all the offending material be removed; the text as it has survived is an uneasy mixture of the early play, some elements of the revision and belated attempts to preserve some of the venom aimed at Jones by transferring it to another character. It is a sad addendum to Jonson's career as a dramatist; when it was performed, it was 'not liked'.

Happilly, Jonson was not completely abandoned in his final years. The Duke of Newcastle, for one, continued to patronise him, and it was for him that Jonson wrote his last two masques, *Love's Welcome at Welbeck* (1633) and *Love's Welcome at Bolsover* (1634). But as the last of his contemporaries died off – Donne in 1631, Chapman (with whom he had latterly quarrelled) around 1634 – Jonson must have seemed increasingly the relic of a bygone age. His death, on 6 August 1637, caused no great stir; his friends and 'sons' contributed to a memorial volume, *Jonsonus Virbius* (1638), but it contained nothing to equal the elegy, 'Lycidas', written by Milton for a rival volume in memory of the virtually unknown Edward King. Jonson was buried in Poet's Corner, Westminster Abbey, and there were plans for a splendid monument, but these fell through, perhaps because of the deteriorating political situation in the country. According to the great gossip, John Aubrey (quoting Isaac Walton), it was a casual visitor to the Abbey, Sir John Young, who caused the epitaph, 'O Rare Ben Jonson' to be carved on a bare slab of marble over the grave.

Given the pattern of Jonson's last twenty years – the interrupted career as a dramatist, the 1623 fire, the loss of royal patronage, ill-health – it is not difficult to see why the second volume of the 1640 folios should be so much less impressive than the 1616 volume. It opens well enough with the three plays Jonson prepared for the press in 1631, omits *The New Inn*, but includes *The Magnetic Lady* and the most unsatisfactory text of *A Tale of a Tub*. It also contains all the masques written after 1616. The non-dramatic verse is collected together as *The Underwood*: 'I am bold to entitle these lesser poems, of later growth, by this of *Underwood*, out of the analogy they hold to *The Forest*, in my former book, and no otherwise' (To the Reader). It is clear that Jonson had done some preliminary work, perhaps in 1631, towards selecting and arranging these poems, but evidence of critical organisation diminishes the further one reads, and it seems likely that Sir Kenelm Digby simply included whatever was to hand, in something approximating to chronological order (though the omission of some poems openly attacking Inigo Jones may indicate that he exercised *some* discretion). Jonson's commonplace book-cum-critical anthology, *Timber, or Discoveries*, is similarly patchy; some passages have the ring of being polished, considered statements, while others seem to be random jottings, and there are only intermittent signs of an overall plan or structure to the book as a whole.

Digby's aim, in short, seems to have been to salvage what he could of what Jonson left, including such scraps as the fragment of *Mortimer's Fall* and the half-finished pastoral, *The Sad Shepherd*; he was not concerned to select on merit or to offer (by careful arrangement) any deliberate view of Jonson and his writing in the later years. On top of this, he was far less meticulous about his proof-reading than Jonson had been. We must be grateful that so much has survived as a result of his efforts, but there is no denying that the effect on Jonson's long-term reputation has been unfortunate. Digby's volume en-shrines the image of a long, slow falling-off from the triumphs of 1616. The truth of the matter is that Jonson flourished and diversified (if not always on the public stage, where many assume that he *ought* to have been) until his serious incapacity in the late 1620s. If the 1623 fire had not happened, or if Jonson had brought out the second folio as he planned, in 1631, edited as selectively as the first, his long-term reputation would have been very different.

As it is, this lingering image of the long, slow falling-off casts retrospective shadows even on the earlier triumphs: as we contem-plate the ageing poet among his young admirers we are more inclined to feel pity for him than to appreciate just how impressive a mentor he must have seemed to them, how substantial and challenging in his achievements. There is a danger that what we perceive as the later 'failure' may somehow call into question the earlier success, adding to whatever doubts we may already have about Jonson's extrava-gant, but probably justifiable claim to be the most *central* poet of his generation, the one who has most fully and consistently confronted his age. It is that claim we shall be testing as we undertake our 'understanding' of his most substantial achievement, the 1616 folio.

1

The early plays

Invest me in my motley, give me leave
To speak my mind, and I will through and through
Cleanse the foul body of th'infected world,
If they will patiently receive my medicine.
(Jaques, *As You Like It*, II. vii. 58–61)

I

There is a charming old story, first related in 1709 by Nicholas Rowe, of how *Every Man In His Humour* came to be performed by the Lord Chamberlain's Men:

[Shakespeare's] acquaintance with Ben Jonson began with a remarkable piece of humanity and good nature; Mr. Jonson, who was at that time altogether unknown to the world, had offer'd one of his plays to the players, in order to have it acted; and the persons into whose hands it was put, after having turn'd it carelessly and superciliously over, were just upon returning it to him with an ill-natur'd answer, that it would be of no service to their company, when Shakespeare luckily cast his eye upon it, and found something so well in it as to engage him first to read it through, and afterwards to recommend Mr. Jonson and his writings to the public. After this they were profess'd friends; though I don't know whether the other ever made him an equal return of gentleness and sincerity.[1]

There may be a grain of truth in this; Shakespeare may have helped persuade the company to accept the play, in which he certainly acted. But it is remarkable how many myths, or at least unsubstantiated traditions, are enshrined in this brief anecdote less than a century after the deaths of the two men: one is of 'gentle' Shakespeare, here displaying 'humanity and good nature', 'gentleness and sincerity'; this may be based on fact but it is remarkable and unfortunate that it is so often linked with malicious imputations of Jonson's being a grudging friend, ungrateful and ungracious ('I don't know whether the other ever made him an equal return'). The eighteenth century was full of such attempts to polish Shakespeare's reputation by tarnishing Jonson's, so that even today it is difficult to discuss the literary differences between the two men, without raising spectres of a personal antagonism between them, at least on Jonson's part. It is worth repeating that there is no reliable evidence for this, while Jonson's own testimony makes it clear that he had the greatest respect for the older poet, even where he differed from him on questions of poetry and drama.[2] The indisputable flaw in Rowe's story, however, is that of making Jonson in 1598 'altogether unknown to the world'. This is to swallow the myth of Jonson's own making that *Every Man In His Humour* was his first play, the beginning of his career.

As we have already seen (though Rowe could not have known) by 1598 Jonson was sufficiently well known in theatrical circles to have been imprisoned for his part in *The Isle of Dogs* affair and to have been noted by Francis Meres as among 'our best for tragedy'. It is most unlikely that any players would turn a new work of his 'carelessly and superciliously over'. We can only really guess at why Jonson chose to set *Every Man In His Humour* at the head of his folio, as if it were his first play; but Rowe's anecdote, for all its bias and palpable inaccuracies, does suggest a likely factor in his thinking. By 1598 Shakespeare was already the most successful dramatist of his generation, author of a steady stream of English histories, romantic comedies and occasional tragedies, all staged by the foremost acting company of the day, in which he was also both an actor and a shareholder. For an ambitious man in the theatre, Shakespeare was the example to emulate; but, for a man of independent spirit and intelligence, his was also the example to challenge, to react against. This was what Jonson was doing in the earliest of those plays he chose to preserve – perhaps tentatively in the first instance, but with increasing assurance as he found his style. Certainly this was how he looked back on it when he came to write his Prologue for the folio *Every Man In His Humour*, which begins a process that is to continue throughout the volume: that of educating an audience brought up on Shakespeare as a 'norm' in different theatrical forms and values. Today, when Shakespeare's classic status is assured, it is still a lesson worth attending to; genius is not restricted to a single mode, nor is it ever beyond legitimate criticism. Jonson rejects the example of those who

> with three rusty swords,
> And help of some few foot-and-half-foot words,
> Fight over York, and Lancaster's long jars:
> And in the tiring-house bring wounds, to scars.
>
> (Prologue, 9–12)

He offers instead:

One such, to day, as other plays should be.
Where neither Chorus wafts you o'er the seas;
No creaking throne comes down, the boys to please . . .

But deeds, and language, such as men do use:
And persons, such as comedy would choose,
When she would show an image of the times,
And sport with human follies, not with crimes.
(Prologue, 14–16; 21–4)

These are not personal slurs on Shakespeare, but the manifesto of a younger man who has found a different and (he will insist) better way of doing things. He rejects the implausibilities of chronicle history plays (and if he still had to write *Robert II* and *Richard Crookback* for Henslowe, he will prefer not to remember the fact); he does not mention Aristotle by name, but it is clear that he favours a style of drama which abides by the unities of time, place and action;[3] he prefers to focus on 'deeds, and language, such as men do use' rather than on the 'creaking throne', 'nimble squib', 'roll'd bullet' or 'tempestuous drum' – the paraphernalia of romantic theatre. It is a recipe for a kind of realism, a kind of theatrical experience in which the members of the audience are not taken imaginatively *out* of themselves but are engaged by the truthfulness of the play.

In this, as in so much else, Jonson is declaring his adherence to certain neo-classical principles which were alien to Shakespeare. We can see, for example, how closely Jonson was to follow the model of Roman comedy if we compare his plays with the typical pattern of a work by Plautus or Terence, such as that offered rather tongue-in-cheek by Dryden in his *Essay of Dramatic Poesy*:

In their Comedies, the Romans generally borrow'd their Plots from the Greek Poets; and theirs was commonly a little Girl stollen or wandred from her Parents, brought back unknown to the City, there got with child by some lewd young fellow; who, by the help of his servant, cheats his father, and when her time comes, to cry *Juno Lucina fer opem*; one or other sees a little Box or Cabinet which was carried away with her, and so discovers her to her friends . . . By the Plot you may guess much of the Characters of the Persons. An Old Father who would willingly before he dies, see his Son well married; his Debauch'd Son, kind in his Nature to his Mistres, but miserably in want of Money; a Servant or Slave, who has so much wit to strike in with him, and help to dupe his Father, A braggadochio Captain, a Parasite, and a Lady of Pleasure.

As for the poor honest Maid, on whom the Story is built, and who ought to be one of the principal Actors in the Play, she is commonly a Mute in it: She has the breeding of the Old Elizabeth way, which was for Maids to be seen and not to be heard; and it is enough you know she is willing to be married, when the Fifth Act requires it.[4]

While none of them follows quite that plot, plays like *Every Man In His Humour*, *Volpone* and *The Alchemist* all preserve the general characteristics: the unsentimental tone, the rather mechanical plot (oiled by a witty 'servant'), the clearly defined character 'types', even the relative insignificance of the female characters. Shakespeare might borrow a particular plot or character from Roman comedy (indeed, he did so at least as often as Jonson),[5] but he never does so with Jonson's thorough-going spirit, which preserves a good deal of the original style and flavour. Shakespeare generally makes the love-interest the central focus of his comedies, often promoting a female character to the principal (and far from 'mute') role and setting the action in some fanciful royal court or pastoral landscape; Jonsonian comedy generally revolves around intrigues over money or power, set firmly in the urban (and predominantly masculine) world of cheaters and cheated (or, in Jacobean terms, cozeners and cozened). Most of Shakespeare's comedies end on the festive note of marriage, however much qualified by unharmonious elements like Jaques or Malvolio; even where marriage may be in the offing, Jonson's comedies pointedly do not end on such a genial note at all. Shakespeare's comedies are peculiarly timeless, set in the never-never worlds of Illyria or the Forest of Arden; Jonson's always attempt to show 'an image of the times', reflecting the contemporary scene as his Roman models had done. Shakespearean comedy is never at a far remove from the incredible or the magical – the fairies in *A Midsummer Night's Dream*, Hymen in *As You Like It*, the strange happenings in plays like *Cymbeline* or *The Tempest*; Jonsonian comedy is always resolutely plausible and unfanciful about the things that guide human destinies.

This, I think, takes us to the heart of the matter. Jonson's adherence to neo-classical principles, his more faithful adaptation of classical models, is not merely pedantry or an insistence on 'art' where Shakespeare relies on 'nature'. It is a reflection of Jonson's profoundly held views both on the nature of drama and on the human condition. All of Jonson's plays, comedies and tragedies alike, try to examine what human beings do and have done to them credibly, in terms of their definable strengths and weaknesses. Two of Jonson's comments to Drummond are revealing in this context: 'he had an intention to have made a play like Plautus's *Amphitrio*, but left it off, for that he could never find two so like others that he could persuade the spectators they were one' (420–3); 'Shakespeare in a play brought in a number of men saying they had suffered shipwreck in Bohemia, where there is no sea near by some 100 miles' (208–10). Shakespeare had, of course, adapted Plautus's *Amphitrio* for *The Comedy of Errors*, apparently happy to let costumes, make-up and make-believe dispel the implausibility; he had also rather carelessly given Bohemia a sea-coast in *The Winter's Tale*. Jonson fiercely resists both kinds of implausibility, just as he resists fanciful settings, supernatural phenomena and theatrical gimmicks, because they are distractions from the reality that concerns him: the reality of men and women in a social context, faced with making moral choices about their personal conduct and their treatment of other people. It is a different reality from that which Shakespeare explores, but an equally important one, and it requires different styles and conventions. For Jonson, 'understanding' is more important than 'suspension of disbelief'.

The fact that Jonson left behind two versions of *Every Man In His Humour*, the play which he singled out as the beginning of his 'true' career, offers us a unique opportunity to observe the development and definition of Jonson's personal style. The quarto text is the play as the Lord Chamberlain's Men performed it in 1598, while the folio text is a later revision, made some time between 1606 and 1613, possibly just for that volume.[6] It is a pity that we cannot date it with greater precision, but at least we know that the revision was made between *Volpone* (1606) and *Bartholomew Fair* (1614), when Jonson was at the height of his powers and his style was distinctively his own. *Every Man In His Humour* is clearly based on Roman comedy, though it is rather more diffuse, with a whole array of 'extraneous' characters, than classical precedent would warrant. It is essentially a play in which the suspicion and jealousy of the older generation (Lorenzo Senior and Thorello in the quarto, Kno'well and Kitely in the folio) are ridiculed and exploited by the somewhat supercilious younger generation (Lorenzo Junior and Prospero in the quarto, Edward Kno'well and Wellbred in the folio), with the help of a devious and witty servant, Musco/Brainworm. Edward Kno'well's love for Hesperida/Bridget, Kitely's younger sister, never becomes as central as we would expect in romantic comedy and is effectively only one more intrigue on which to hang a sequence of foolish and affected characters, notably the 'gulls' Stephano/Stephen and Matheo/Matthew, the apoplectic Guiliano/Downright and the braggart soldier Bobadillo/Bobadill; all the complications are eventually resolved by the morally sound but eccentric Doctor (later Justice) Clement.

Jonson's most obvious alterations to the original involve a whole change of setting from a rather nominal Florence to a quite specific London, which inevitably also means having to change most of the characters' names. The London 'colouring' is neither casual nor incidental, but comes in strategic bursts, where it is most telling, notably in the opening scene. For example, the idiotic Stephen grows pompous: 'Because I dwell at Hogsden, I shall keep company with none but the archers of Finsbury? or the citizens, that come a ducking to Islington ponds?' (I. i. 47–50, folio) and 'mine uncle here is a man of a thousand a year, Middlesex land' (I. ii. 3–4, folio). The former passage is a completely original insertion; in the latter, the word 'Middlesex' is inserted into a line of the quarto. One effect is precisely to define Stephen's milieu and the nature of his pretensions to the London audience, familiarity making for greater clarity. On a very basic level, the local insertions act as clearer strokes of the pen in a blurred original picture: 'Over the fields to Moregate' was obviously easier for Jonson's audience to conceptualise than a bare 'to Florence', and in this sense they are no more significant that Jonson's obvious efforts to clarify the sister/sister-in-law/brother/half-brother relationships complex, which is needlessly confusing in the quarto, or than the tightening-up of the denouement in the last act. We expect this kind of care from an experienced professional.

But Jonson goes much further than this, merging details of the new setting with a thorough revision affecting even word-style. Well-bred's intercepted letter, for instance, the mainspring of the action, is almost completely rewritten; there is less in the grandiose manner about Apollo and the Muses, which is part of a general toning-down of references to poets and poetry throughout the play, including the excision of the much-praised and often-quoted speech by Lorenzo Junior (v. iii. 312–43, quarto). The early play smells very much of Jonson the young Renaissance poet, flexing his new-found muscles and glorying in the traditional powers through his young poet-character. The role of the poet as both a critic and kind of spiritual physician for society is implicitly a key issue in all Jonson's works, but it has little direct bearing on the action of this play, and it is properly played-down in the revision. It is perhaps the surest sign of Jonson's maturity in the revising that he had the heart to cut out such a major speech on 'the state of poesy . . . blessed, eternal, and most true divine', despite its intrinsic merit. To return to the letter: in place of the sententiousness of the original, the folio version captures more exactly the bantering wit of the young man-about-town, revealing a closer attention on Jonson's part to the type-veracity of his characters: 'Do not conceive that antipathy between us, and Hogs-den; as was between Jews, and hog's-flesh' (i. ii. 74–5, folio). The style is still affected and 'clever' (this is part of Wellbred), but the idiom is snappier and more convincingly spontaneous (less 'literary') in its flow of ideas than the original, and this makes old Kno'well's suspicious misunderstandings all the more credible. 'Leave thy vigilant father, alone, to number over his green apricots, evening, and morning, o'the north-west wall' (i. ii. 75–7, folio). This is taken up by the slow-witted, literal-minded Kno'well: 'Why should he think, I tell my apricots?' (i. ii. 103, folio). The effect of such tiny details is a neat and credible demonstration of old and young minds working on different wave-lengths – one of the central themes of the play. It sets old Kno'well off on the chase.

It is notable how integrated the improvements are; the local and verbal realism – familiar settings, topical allusions and colloquial idioms (for example, the pun on Hogsden) – all contribute to what we might call an increased psychological realism, defining the characters more closely. But it is also notable that this represents technical improvement on Jonson's part – doing better what he had tried to do earlier – rather than a fundamental change of style; there is no suggestion, for example, of any attempt to create a Shakespearean 'roundness' in the characters. On the contrary, what we see is a more precise definition of Jonson's personal idiom, a refinement of something already there in the quarto. The change in old Kno'well's lines, for example, reveal Jonson's closer attention to the character's 'type', his eccentric, even deranged personality; there is a greater terseness to imply his suspicious and impatient mind. His lines are recast to seem less studied or balanced; his rebuke to Stephano, 'Go to, you are a prodigal, and self-wild fool' (i. i. 46, quarto) becomes 'You are a prodigal absurd cocks-comb: go to' (i. i. 54, folio), with a real crescendo of impatience which gives a genuine stab to the 'go to' at the end. Stilted and artificial formulae, like the following advice to Stephano, are simply omitted from the folio:

> Cousin, lay by such superficial forms,
> And entertain a perfect real substance.
> (i. i. 73–4, quarto)

(One suspects that this is Jonson talking, rather than the old man.) Kno'well's reaction to the letter, pathetically tame in the quarto ('Well, it is the strangest letter that ever I read . . .' i. i. 176), becomes an explosion in the folio, at the signature 'from the Windmill':

> From the Bordello, it might come as well;
> The Spital: or Pict-hatch.
>
> (I. ii. 91–2)

Once again, the psychological actualisation and the London setting
merge perfectly. Old Kno'well is not simply an abstract 'humorous'
character; he is a manifestation of the London in the play, where
suspicious and cynical old age is out of tune with regenerative forces
represented here by the playful vitality of the young men (though
that in turn is not beyond criticism; it is marred by self-conceit).

We find parallel developments in the transposition of Thorello/
Kitely, whose predominant characteristic is obsessive jealousy, reflected in the nervous, erratic qualities of his speech. Interestingly,
he describes the way in which his own mind works; in the earlier
version there is a mellifluous Shakespearean metaphor:

> my imaginations like the sands,
> Run dribbling forth to fill the mouth of time.
>
> (III. i. 43–4)

But in the later text smoothness is sacrificed for a more anxious:

> my imaginations run, like sands,
> Filling up time
>
> (III. iii. 50–1)

– genuinely expressive of his inner tensions. Kitely's anxiety is acted
out at length in this ludicrous scene, when he debates with himself
whether to confide or not in Thomas Cash, his man. In the quarto
everything is left to the actor to convey the comedy of his wild logic;
in the folio, the insight becomes clearer, shrewder and more explicit.
When, for instance, he imagines some prevarication on Cash's part
about taking an oath of secrecy, he reflects:

> He is no puritan, that I am certain of.
> What should I think of it?
>
> (III. i. 80–1)

In the folio this rather sober, abstracted reflection takes on more
definition with an infusion of realistic detail and disjointed rhythm:

> H'is no precisian, that I am certain of.
> Nor rigid Roman-Catholic. He'll play,
> At fayles, and tick-tack, I have heard him swear.
> What should I think of it?
>
> (III. iii. 88–91)

The deranged running together of ideas adds far more weight to the question, while the urgency of the style (down even to elisions) evokes the jealous man more convincingly.

By every criterion in fact, the revised *Every Man In His Humour* improves on the original, making it a fine play if not one of Jonson's very best works. The diffuse plot is made clearer, the denouement is shortened and made more intelligible, while the characterisation and setting are far more closely realised. The commitment behind Jonson's writing and the assurance of his mature style are both fully engaged. The difficulty, however, is that the improvements are improvements within Jonson's own terms; anyone brought up on Shakespeare as a model of Elizabethan drama may initially find these terms baffling. It was Swinburne, who had a love–hate relationship with Jonson's writing, who best expressed the most commonly felt objection: 'it is difficult to believe that Ben Jonson can have believed, even with some half-sympathetic and half-sardonic belief, in all the leading figures of his invention'.[7] However true the characters are to their age, however laboriously accurate Jonson is in their delineation, they lack 'the sympathetic faith of the creator in his creatures', 'the vital impulse of the infallible imagination' – in short, they are not Shakespearean. The problem is most apparent at the end of the folio version of *Every Man In His Humour*, where Justice Clement – a relatively uncomplicated *deus ex machina* of perspicacity and common sense – arraigns old Kno'well and Kitely and bids them put off: 'you, Master Kno'well, your cares; master Kitely, and his wife, their jealousy' (v. v. 71–2). At this point, in complete reversal of the care which we have seen Jonson taking to make them vivid and credible, they cease to have any significance; without their respective cares and jealousies, they cease to have any existence, dramatic or otherwise.

In fact this has nothing to do with any lack of 'the sympathetic faith of the creator in his creatures'; it is the working out of the moral and humane principle that lies at the heart of Jonson's drama. It may be different from Shakespeare's, but it is no less cogent. The act of creation for Jonson is also an act of judgement: just as he measures the play (or poem, or masque) he writes against his concept of what a work of art should be, so he measures his characters against a human standard. Not to do either would be, for Jonson, irresponsible. This is a paradox that lies behind all his plays: on the one hand the patient effort that goes towards the solid depiction of the characters, on the other the structural logic of the drama which is invariably bent on questioning, reducing, even 'exploding' what he depicts. The characters Kitely and old Kno'well are manifestations in their different ways of folly, embodiments of a diseased condition which cannot simply be explained away in modern psychological terms. It is a moral condition as much as a mental one, reducing their full status as human beings. In their folly they have lost touch with reality, creating for themselves private worlds of fantasy and illusion which, however comic, are not harmless; they attack the fabric of social harmony, creating the friction and mistrust which run through the play. It is in the tension between these private illusions and actual reality that Jonsonian drama is generated (it is no accident that so many of his plays hinge on disguisings), but also that he manifests a genuine concern for humanity, in a sane and rational society. This is the basis for his notorious theory of humours, but since Jonson did not spell out that theory until his next play, *Every Man Out of His Humour*, I shall not pursue it further for a moment.

A detailed comparison of the two texts of *Every Man In His Humour* demonstrates that neither of the qualities for which Jonson's comedy is best known, its detailed depictions of London life and its minute observation of obsessive psychology, came to the author as naive instinct: they are things he worked on and developed as his art matured. People sometimes think of Jonson as an artless reporter of the picturesque low-life of London and its eccentric characters, but nothing could be further from the truth. The realism of his urban scenes and of his characterisations are both subsumed to an overriding criterion, which we may describe as 'moral realism'. So, for example, we find that the familiar London settings of this play may act as a point of reference for distinguishing between folly and illusion on the one hand, truth and reality on the other; when Bobadill lets the ease of his braggart façade get the better of him, he inadvertently mentions 'Turnbull, Whitechapel, Shoreditch, which were then my quarters, and since upon the Exchange' (iv. vii. 44–6, folio). The sordid reality of brothels and doss-houses suddenly invades his fanciful bravado and the result is a laughable incongruity which 'explodes' his pretensions. It has to be said, however, that this is only a small example and that the superimposed London setting does not work consistently or cohesively enough in this way to make this one of Jonson's best plays. In his finest works, the balance between the characters and their setting – Volpone's Venice, the Rome of the tragedies, Lovewit's house in *The Alchemist*, Bartholomew Fair – is so handled that it helps us not only to judge individual follies and vices but also to see each one, perhaps relatively harmless in itself, as part of a wider malaise, a corporate insanity. Old Kno'well, Kitely, Bobadill and the others are well-executed cameos, but they never take on such collective significance.

This is linked with another problem in *Every Man In His Humour* which Jonson is unable to solve for all his careful revision. I have spoken of Jonson's art being one of judgement, calling for distinctions between illusion and reality. Ultimately judgement must lie with the audience, but it is a brave author who will leave his audience to reach their judgements unaided – it is one of the marks of Jonson's maturity that, in his best plays, he allows us to do just that. In earlier works, such as this, Jonson feels the need to play safe and include someone within the play – someone both authoritative and acceptable to the audience – to help us to the proper conclusions. In the quotation from *As You Like It* (1599) at the head of this chapter, Jaques – glancing at the likes of Jonson – voices the universal dilemma of the satirist in his attempts to guide the audience; he promises to 'Cleanse the foul body of th'infected world, / *If they will patiently receive my medicine*' (my italics). Why should any audience 'patiently receive' the medicine either of the satirist himself or of his thinly disguised spokesman within a play? Almost invariably the satirist falls into one of two traps: either purporting to be holier-than-thou, and so effectively preaching to an audience who would doubtless, at best, prefer such matters to be reserved for the Sunday pulpit; or displaying such an understanding and affinity for vice in denouncing it that we suspect his secret sympathy and so discount the satire. So the Duke denies Jaques's right to moralise: 'For thou thyself hast been a libertine, / As sensual as the brutish sting itself' (II. vii. 65–6). Similarly, we may have doubts about Surly's credentials in *The Alchemist* when we learn that he deals 'with the hollow die' and 'the frail card' (II. i. 9, 10). In *Every Man In His Humour* Jonson tries to solve the problem by separating the mechanical revelation of folly from the passing of judgement upon it. Brainworm largely performs the first function, and there is no real effort to explain or motivate his witty scheming beyond giving him the traditional ironic role (from Roman comedy) of a servant more clever and resourceful than his masters. Justice Clement, who finally passes judgement, recognises his dependence on Brainworm's schemes when he announces at the end: 'Here is my mistress. Brainworm! to whom all my addresses of courtship shall have their reference' (v. v. 86–8). The pun on 'courtship' – courting a mistress and a court of law – is an addition in the folio and perhaps reflects Jonson's mature recognition that a wise magistrate (such as Clement purports to be), who is somehow above the fray, able to be both authoritative and humane after the chicanery, is really too good to be true. If the Justice needs his Brainworm, can he really be above suspicion? For the purposes of the play, Jonson chooses to pretend that he can – to choose otherwise would entail a far more radical re-write – hoping to carry the audience's approval with Clement's bluff good sense. But for a committed satirist like Jonson, the solution could hardly be satisfactory: Brainworm is too much of a mechanical contrivance, Clement patently a convenient device for bringing the play to a conclusion. Worst of all, this definitive 'exploding' of follies leaves the audience with nothing to do (except applaud); they remain passive observers of a process which is self-contained on stage, for all Jonson's efforts in the revision to imply that his characters belong to the real world of London. Satire which does not involve its audience, but erects butts for the apparent satisfaction of simply knocking them down, is apt to fall into self-congratulation. It takes all of Clement's hearty madcap manner to avert the suspicion of self-congratulation from this play.

II

In many respects the development of Jonson's career as it is reflected in his first folio can be seen as a series of attempts to resolve the problems posed by *Every Man In His Humour*, which not even a thorough revision of the play was able to eradicate: how to build a play around the satirising of foolish characters, how to give such a play unity, how to make it a convincing mirror of the real world and, above all, how to do it without either preaching on the one hand or compromising moral integrity on the other, which must in some way mean involving the audience in the judgement, making it a communal process rather than a matter of individual taste and assertion. In the drama it was not until *Sejanus*, or possibly even *Volpone*, that Jonson really began to find the answers to these questions. The three plays that intervene, *Every Man Out of His Humour* (1599), *Cynthia's Revels* (1600) and *Poetaster* (c. 1601) are frankly experimental works in which Jonson, having achieved something of a popular success with *Every Man In His Humour*, strove to define and develop the personal idiom he had carved out for himself with that play. Even more than that first 'humour' play, these 'comicall satyres' (to use a contemporary term) run defiantly against the mould of Elizabethan drama established by Shakespeare, helping to break it forever. It must largely have been in response to new spirits like Jonson, Chapman and Marston that, around the turn of the century, Shakespeare himself abandoned chronicle history plays and romantic comedies,

turning triumphantly to tragedy with *Hamlet* but also prob-
lematically to darker comedy such as *Troilus and Cressida* and *Measure
for Measure*.

From its title, one would expect *Every Man Out of His Humour* to be a
straightforward companion piece to its predecessor. In fact it is a
very different kind of play, which takes the business of 'humours' far
more seriously and bases its structure squarely on the need to expose
and 'explode' them, largely to the exclusion of entertaining intrigues
and coherent plot. Its presiding figure is a man in two parts – Asper,
'of an ingenious and free spirit, eager and constant in reproof, without fear controlling the world's abuses' (Characters, 2–3) and
Macilente, an envy archetype, described as 'a man well parted' but
'his judgement is so dazzled, and distasted, that he grows violently
impatient of any opposite happiness in another' (*ibid.* 8, 11–13).
Asper is the supposed presenter of the play that is to follow, who
appears 'After the second sounding', or just before the performance,
in conversation with Mitis and Cordatus, who will remain on stage
throughout as a 'Grex or Chorus'; it is to them that he explains the
proper definition of a 'humour':

> Why, humour (as 'tis *ens*) we thus define it
> To be a quality of air or water,
> And in itself holds these two properties,
> Moisture, and fluxure: as, for demonstration,
> Pour water on the floor, 'twill wet and run:
> Likewise the air (forc'd through a horn, or trumpet)
> Flows instantly away, and leaves behind
> A kind of dew; and hence we do conclude,
> That what soe'er hath fluxure, and humidity,
> As wanting power to contain itself,
> Is humour. So in every human body
> The choler, melancholy, phlegm, and blood,
> By reason that they flow continually
> In some one part, and are not continent,
> Receive the name of humours. Now thus far
> It may, by metaphor, apply itself
> Unto the general disposition:
> As when some one peculiar quality
> Doth so possess a man, that it doth draw
> All his affects, his spirits, and his powers,
> In their confluctions, all to run one way,
> This may be truly said to be a humour.
> But that a rook, in wearing a pied feather,
> The cable hat-band, or the three-pil'd ruff,

A yard of shoe-tie, or the Switzer's knot
On his French garters, should affect a humour!
O, 'tis more than most ridiculous.
                        (After the second sounding, 88–114)

It is worth quoting the definition at this length, so that we may be sure what we are dealing with. Asper starts with what we might call the standard textbook scientific/medical terminology of the day, defining humour literally ('as 'tis *ens*') as a property of two of the four elements, air and water. This property is naturally ascribed to the supposed four bodily fluids: choler, melancholy, phlegm and blood; these are held to be responsible for our dominant personality traits, depending on the balance within us (so even today we may be described as choleric, melancholic, phlegmatic or sanguine). At this point, however, the definition becomes blurred: Asper does not actually say that the 'general disposition' of an individual is caused by a humorous imbalance of the bodily fluids, as we might suppose. He merely says that the terminology he has been using may be applied 'by metaphor' to the 'general disposition', skirting the issue of whether this is a physiological or a psychological disorder. But a disorder it certainly is, as if the man were 'possessed'. He then goes on to scorn the voguish affectation of humour in the wearing of outlandish fashions; what he does not explain here, since the audience might be expected to know, is that the affectation of a humorous personality (particularly a melancholic one) had become almost fashionable, because one theory held that it betokened a person of exceptional gifts and talents – which would naturally be reflected in the wearing of eccentric clothes. We thus have two possible types of humorous character: the genuinely 'possessed' man, in an almost clinical sense, and the foolish person who merely affects to be like that. Unfortunately, when Asper carries on, after a brief interruption by Cordatus, it is not really clear whether he is referring just to the latter type, or to both:

Well I will scourge those apes;
And to these courteous eyes oppose a mirror,
As large as is the stage, whereon we act:
Where they shall see the time's deformity
Anatomiz'd in every nerve, and sinew,
With constant courage, and contempt of fear.
                        (*ibid.* 117–22)

In fact, *Every Man Out of His Humour* is almost exclusively concerned with the affectation of humour (though a case might be made for the wretched Sordido as a genuine 'humour') and this is what Asper's satire attempts to 'scourge' – not pathological conditions but egos too much in love with their own fantasies, ridiculously out of touch with reality and their responsibilities. This is substantially true also of the next play, *Cynthia's Revels*, though from *Poetaster* on (by which time Jonson had ceased to talk so openly about humours) his comedies tend to deal substantially with something like real humours: Morose in *Epicoene*, for example, is not simply affected in his abhorrence of noise but has real character problems. This is one reason why the best comedies are so much more substantial than the early works; they deal with more serious and less tractable conditions. But one thing remains constant: Jonson never turns his satire merely on what we would think of as a medical condition. All his humorous characters, of whatever type, have this in common, that they are too much in love with themselves and that, as such, they have lost touch with reality and their responsibilities as human beings to the rest of the world. If this is merely whim or affectation on their part, it may be laughed away; if it lies deeper, the remedy may not be so simple: we may be dealing with vice and tragedy rather than folly and comedy.

Asper may be able to define humours and convince us that it is important they be eradicated, but it does not necessarily follow that he is the man to do it. From the start, in fact, Asper's satiric zeal might be described as 'over the top':

> I'll strip the ragged follies of the time,
> Naked, as at their birth . . .
>
> . . . and with a whip of steel,
> Print wounding lashes in their iron ribs.
> (*ibid.* 17–18; 19–20)

This brings warnings from Cordatus ('Be not too bold') and Mitis ('be not thus transported with the violence / Of your strong thoughts'). Asper's 'sharpness' is not dropped, however, merely transmuted when he takes on the role of Macilente in the play proper. Macilente is so far from being a balanced critic as to be the most truly humorous character in the play. He is distinctly more repulsive than any of those he rails against; his poisoning of Puntarvolo's dog, for example, is the least sympathetic action in the entire play. But it is clear that Jonson never expects him to engage the audience's sympathy; his function is to act as a critic, but never one with whom we laugh easily or indulgently. He is motivated by envy, not by moral rectitude, and this offers the audience an unusual pespective on his fellow characters – one that invites reaction rather than acquiescence. So, for example, Macilente squirms at the sight of Fungoso in one of his Brisk-suits:

> I fain would know of heaven now, why yond fool
> Should wear a suit of satin? he? that rook?
>
> (II. v. 40–1)

This is not righteous indignation; he is only concerned with the inequities of the world: why hasn't he got such a suit himself? But Jonson thus obliquely raises the question of what ridiculous affectation causes Fungoso to ape the Court fashion – why should he (or Macilente, come to that) *want* to wear such things? To a large extent we are able to discount Macilente's prejudices, being so crudely obvious, but the virulence of his concern does oblige us to take note and judge the objects of his envy more objectively ourselves. This is most evident at the point where Sordido, the miserly speculator in bad weather, is introduced (I. iii); Macilente mocks him in a series of asides, but leaves without pressing home the attack, and Mitis objects:

me thinks, Macilente went hence too soon, he might have been made to stay, and speak somewhat in reproof of Sordido's wretchedness, now at the last.

> (I. iii. 149–52)

But Cordatus points out his mistake:

O, no, that had been extremely improper ... you must understand, signior, he envies him not as he is a villain, a wolf i'the commonwealth, but as he is rich, and fortunate; for the true condition of envy is, *Dolor alienae faelicitatis* [grief at another man's felicity].

> (I. iii. 153; 162–5)

All the humorous characters are guilty of wanting to be, or pretending to be, something they are not, and this makes Envy their natural foil; Jonson's chief problem, then, is how best to use Macilente so that his role does not become merely repetitive and predictable. Mitis – who acts throughout as a convenient stooge, voicing the wrong attitude so that Cordatus can put him (and us) right – suggests at one point that Asper/Jonson (as the playright) might have 'altered the shape of his argument, and explicated 'hem better in single scenes' (II. iii. 293–4), but Cordatus insists that it is 'an object of more state, to behold the scene full, and reliev'd with variety of speakers to the end' (297–8). It is this variety which infuses the play with life, the various humours playing off one against another, and not requiring Macilente's diatribes to expose them one at a time. For instance, Brisk's pretensions to be a manly courtier act as a yardstick to measure Sogliardo's attempts to become a gentleman, which in turn parallel Fungoso's vain wish to imitate Brisk; similarly, Fallace's doting upon Brisk would not be quite so ridiculous if we did not see Brisk himself being so casually mocked by his professed mistress, Saviolina. This principle of suggestive juxtaposition becomes very important in Jonson's art, particularly in contexts such as his collections of poetry and *Bartholomew Fair*, where there is no immediately obvious structure or plot holding things together.

The most interesting character in this respect in *Every Man Out of His Humour* is Carlo Buffone, the only one who is not actually envied by Macilente (damnation indeed):

> 'Tis strange! of all the creatures I have seen,
> I envy not this Buffon, for indeed
> Neither his fortunes, nor his parts deserve it:
> But I do hate him . . .
>
> (I. ii. 226–9)

In fact, in their mutual hatred they complement one another. Buffone is one who 'with absurd similes will transform any person into deformity' (Characters, 26–7), though it would be more accurate to say that his foul-mouthed jesting does not so much transform them as give them the names they truly deserve. Like Macilente's envy, though less thoroughly, his obscenity creates a perspective for identifying true 'deformity':

BRISK: What a silly jest's that? whither should I ride, but to the court?
BUFFONE: O, pardon me, sir, twenty places more: your hot-house, or your whore-house –

(II. i. 13–16)

The identification of courtly affectation with whoring is richly suggestive. When Macilente and Buffone combine in their envy/abuse, the effect is really to 'strip the ragged follies of the time / Naked as at their birth':

SOGLIARDO: Nay look you Carlo: this is my humour now! . . . I will be a gentleman, whatsoever it cost me.

(I. ii. 1–3)

Buffone borrows a metaphor from alchemy to express his contempt: 'I'll make admirable use i'the projection of my medicine upon this lump of copper here' (26–7). In other words, Sogliardo is an ignorant piece of base metal wanting to become gold – but the profit will really come to Buffone. Macilente's reaction is similarly in character:

> 'Sblood, why should such a prick-ear'd hine as this
> Be rich? ha? a fool?

$$(32–3)$$

'Prick-ear'd' = alert or pricket (a young male deer) or something altogether more vulgar; 'hine' = hind, a female deer; the imputation of sexual ambiguity, for all Sogliardo's apparent virility, cuts to the heart of his 'humour', adding another dimension to his 'baseness'.

There are times when this kind of commentary on the characters becomes redundant, inventive as it can be; a case might be made, for example, for letting Puntarvolo's Quixotic homecoming unroll itself. It is significant that the 'wretch' Sordido is literally left to his own salvation, which he finds in a failed attempt at suicide (III. vii; viii); this is on a different plane from the major untrussing of humours that takes place in the last act – indeed, the possibility of spiritual redemption is a rare theme in any of Jonson's works, and it is not well integrated here with the rest of the play. Perhaps Jonson wanted to counterpoint the exposure of folly with the discovery of true grace, but it is an uneasy mixture. Nevertheless, when Asper/Macilente wishes to bring the main strands of the play to a 'catastrophe', it is appropriate that he should do so by urging Buffone to be nothing but himself, a kind of make-shift satirist: 'mary, Carlo (as thou lov'st me) run over 'hem all freely tonight, and especially the knight; spare no sulphurous jest that may come out of that sweaty forge of thine' (v. v. 26–9).

This precipitates the crisis in which all remaining humours are 'exploded', including effectively Macilente's own, since there is nothing left to be envious of – the pat mathematical solution; the action simply stops when Macilente becomes Asper again, with nothing left to do. *Every Man Out of His Humour* is an inventive work in many respects, but it does not really solve the satirist's dilemma which I outlined in respect of its predecessor; indeed it makes it more apparent. We are offered a chinese-box of perspectives on the action, with Cordatus and Mitis commenting on the actions of Asper, who in turn transmutes his own role by taking on the attributes of Macilente. In some ways this distances Jonson from his satiric agents, with whom we are never expected to sympathise, and places the final onus of judgement on the audience. There is, however, an unmistakable aura of self-congraulation about the neat conclusion Asper/Macilente brings about, from which it would be difficult to divorce Jonson, the real author; the conclusion is all the more disturbing in its self-confidence, its apparent conviction that any and all follies can be eradicated by the satirist's pen. Much of this might be more acceptable were it not for the fact that Jonson felt it necessary to include the Cordatus/Mitis dialogues throughout the play, with the evident function of making sure that the audience appreciates the kind of play that he is writing. After the scene in which Sordido tried to commit suicide, for example, Mitis is ready to object to such serious matter in a comedy, but Cordatus has an answer: 'Ay? what think you of Plautus, in his comedy, called *Cistellaria*, there? where he brings in Alcesimarchus with a drawn sword ready to kill himself? . . . is not his authority of power to give our scene approbation?' (III. viii. 86–9; 91–2). The rights and wrongs of the argument are less germane here than the question of whether an author should interrupt the action of the play, with no apparent hint of irony, to lecture his audience on classical precedents. What this betrays is Jonson's fundamental lack of confidence in the audience's ability to judge for themselves, which in turn perhaps reflects his own lack of confidence in the new style of drama he was experimenting with. It is, in the end, a nervous work, trying to make up in over-assertion for what it lacks in real confidence and conviction. And this is as true of its satiric judgements as of its style.

We should perhaps expect such problems in a work so avowedly experimental. It is unfortunate, however, that Jonson was not then able to consolidate and grow in confidence by building directly upon the experience of the two 'Humour' plays. Instead we find that the next two plays preserved in the folio were written for performance, not in the public theatre (*Every Man Out of His Humour* had been given at the Lord Chamberlain's Men's new Globe Theatre), but in the so-called private theatres used by the children's companies. This called for further experimentation rather than consolidation. Moreover, if not by *Cynthia's Revels* certainly by *Poetaster*, Jonson became involved in what is grandly known as the War of the Theatres, when a number of dramatists – certainly Jonson, Marston and Dekker, possibly Shakespeare and others – intensified what had always been a habit, alluding to and parodying each other's works, conducting open debates on their relative merits. On this occasion the bickering seems to have taken on an unusually personal edge and so we find Jonson – still not securely settled into a personal idiom, but never one to take criticism quietly – experimenting if anything even more radically and justifying himself with a stridency which it is very easy to mistake for arrogance.

Cynthia's Revels is, of all the plays in the first folio, the one modern readers find most difficult to come to terms with. The reasons for this are numerous: it was written for performance by the Children of the Queen's Chapel (one troupe of the 'little eyases' Hamlet's players complain of) at the indoor Blackfriars Theatre; unfortunately we know very little about how the children acted and to what extent their style differed from that of the adult companies (did they consistently parody their elders, for instance?), nor can we be certain what effect playing indoors had – though the auditorium was considerably smaller than that of the public playhouses, and the audiences were prepared to pay a good deal more (perhaps six times as much) to get in. What did they get for their money? It is generally assumed that the children, with their grammar-school educations, would have made use of their training in rhetorical delivery, and of music and dancing in which they were also instructed, while indoor lighting – difficult though it was to localise – would have encouraged the use of impressive scenic effects, enhanced possibly by mirrors: very little of this can be recovered from a reading of the play as Jonson printed it and, as with the masques (which in many respects this play resembles – it actually contains the first masque Jonson wrote) we are obliged to make a considerable effort of the imagination to appreciate what it might be like in performance.

Nevertheless, it is unfair to dismiss the play, as one standard reference work does, with the words: 'The plot is extremely slight, and the play is tedious and of little interest at the present day.'[8] *Cynthia's Revels* is essentially pageant drama of a type which has links not only with the exclusive Court masque but also with the most widely seen drama of the Renaissance period, the street shows which accompanied major civic events such as royal processions and, in London, the annual installation of the Lord Mayor. The principal feature of these pageants was not plot or action, but an appropriate symbolic motif around which a sequence of *exempla* would be organised, with a presenter to point up their significance. So, for example, the ceremonial entry of King James into his new capital city (delayed by plague until March 1604) was celebrated by Dekker and Jonson, who between them were commissioned to devise seven triumphal arches, each demonstrating different features of the city and people's welcome for their new monarch. Jonson's own arches (the first, at Fenchurch Street, and the last, at Temple Bar – the texts for them are included in the folio) depicted respectively London as the Royal Chamber and the Temple of Janus, 'translated' from its role in worshipping the mythical gods to do honour to the tangible virtues of the new King. For both pageants the principal presenter was the Genius, or presiding spirit, of London, played at the former – and also very probably at the latter – by the great actor, Edward Alleyn, which indicates that there was less distinction between such tableaux-drama and what we now consider more 'legitimate' theatre for the Elizabethans than there is for us.

For *Cynthia's Revels*, Jonson's motif is The Court (or 'The Fountain of Self-Love', as the sub-title introduces it). In advance of the play proper, one of the child actors – to all appearances not acting, but really motivated by jealousy – outlines such plot as there is to the audience before his fellows can stop him, effectively removing the what-comes-next element that we normally think crucial in a dramatic performance. But this is appropriate in a work in which Jonson promises (in the Prologue) 'Words, above action: matter, above words' (20); where there is to be no significant intrigue it is surely right to forestall expectations before they become positively distracting. In all this Jonson is implicitly trying to flatter his audience, insisting that those

> Who can both censure, understand, define
> What merit is
>
> (Prologue, 16–17)

do not need the vulgar trappings which keep the attention of more popular audiences, and that they will appreciate his play all the more for its being confined to essential 'matter'. So the play proper opens with Cupid and Mercury revealing what little divine intrigue is afoot, and they lead into Echo's lament for Narcissus, lost in the Pool of Self-Love; these extremely formal verses do not relate materially to the main body of the action, but serve symbolic warning of the danger of self-love, which is the play's theme. It is typical of the entire mode of the play that we should be offered this lament as a kind of second prologue, a caution always to look for the deeper meaning, the truth behind the artifice.

These various 'introductions' finally give way to a series of loosely linked vignettes designed to point up the vanities of the creatures who flutter about the Court, and their dubious mistresses; these are described in exhaustive detail by Mercury and Cupid. Against the likes of Amorphus, Asotus and Philautia, however, we are also introduced to Crites and his guiding-spirit, Arete (i.e. virtue). To the vain Amorphus 'this is a trivial fellow, too mean, too cheap, too coarse for you [Asotus] to converse with' (I. iv. 176–7) but to Mercury he is 'a creature of a most perfect and divine temper' (II. iii. 123–4) and 'I

could leave my place in heaven, to live among mortals, so I were sure
to be no other than he' (148–9). This is the hallmark of Crites, to be
maligned by the vicious and adored by the gods, to stand above the
tide of human frailty, secure in his unflagging virtue. When Hedon
and Anaides plot to defame him, he laughs it off:

> Do, good detraction, do, and I the while
> Shall shake thy spite off with a careless smile.
>
> (III. iii. 1–2)

In his moment of final triumph he reflects that he must act so as not
to:

> appear vindicative,
> Or mindful of contempts, which I contemn'd
> As done of impotence.
>
> (v. xi. 123–5)

Crites is the focus of the play's judgements and its satire, a position
reflected in his confident use of asides to the audience (e.g. 'would
any discreet person hazard his wit so?' v. iv. 202–3) and formally
recognised when Arete commands him, at Cynthia's behest, to write
the masques which will ritually purge the vices which have crept into
the Court, and so restore its proper harmony: 'A virtuous Court a
world to virtue draws' (v. xi. 173). The corrective implications of his
masques are far more explicit and personal than anything Jonson
himself was to be able to write for the Court: the foolish characters
perform as their antithetical virtues, are revealed before Cynthia, and
obliged to recant. Crites himself is finally vindicated and showered
with praise.

It will be apparent even in my résumé of his role that Crites poses
problems for a modern reader just as much as the tableau-style of the
play: he is just too perfect, priggish to the point of self-righteousness
and indeed only too often redundant. Scenes such as those in which
Amorphus coaches Asotus in the more absurd Court mannerisms are
acutely observed in themselves and really require no further under-
scoring, while the games of 'substantives and adjectives' and 'a thing
done and who did it' fully make the point of their own inanity (like
the game of vapours in *Bartholomew Fair*) without the need of any
'knowing' commentator. Jonson's detractors, then and since, have
suggested that the problem is simply that he identifies far too
completely with Crites, that he really believes himself to be the one
man of taste and judgement divinely appointed to show benighted
fools the light of day. What I think is missing in this account is the

element of the play-as-play to which Jonson constantly draws our attention; when the boys appear initially *in propria persona* they underline the fact that they are indeed only children, with very plausible childish squabbling (a plaintive voice calls from within 'Why Children, are you not asham'd? come in there' Induction, 11), and that, when they act in Jonson's play, they can never *become* the characters they impersonate, but will always be little caricatures, mocking their elders and betters.[9] As I said at the outset, we do not know to what extent this was a regular feature of the acting of the children's companies, but it must certainly be a feature here, since Jonson draws attention to it during the play itself; for example, as Mercury is introducing Crites with what may seem extravagant praise, Cupid says:

> S'light, I believe he is your minion, you seem to be so ravish'd with him.
> MERCURY: He's one, I would not have a wry thought darted against, willingly.
> CUPID: No, but a straight shaft in his bosom, I'll promise him, if I am Cytherea's son.

> (II. iii. 150–5)

This bawdy talk ('minion', 'ravish'd', 'willingly', 'straight shaft') would surely be out of place and distasteful if these were adult actors playing gods admiring a youthful Crites, but the whole point is that they are boys joking about adult things, pretending to a knowingness they do not really have. This needs to be taken into account when assessing the role of Crites throughout: the disdainful superiority he adopts towards most of the other characters is in some respects only an extension of the childish squabble at the beginning about who is to recite the Prologue. The boy playing Crites glories in having the virtuous leading role while those, like Amorphus, who do not, lose no opportunity to voice their sour grapes. There must always be an element of make-believe about the one virtuous man exposing the follies of the world, as there is about children pretending to be adults.

When set against the tradition of pageant-drama and the special circumstances of performance by boy actors, much that initially seems perverse or unpalatable about *Cynthia's Revels* becomes explicable, though difficult to translate into modern terms and it is almost impossible to imagine its being revived satisfactorily today. Even in its own time it must have worked much better on stage than on the printed page – it is difficult to keep making allowances for the arch and comic effects of performance by children when reading it privately. It is for this reason that the play does not constitute an advance in Jonson's attempts to solve the satirist's dilemma: an all-virtuous Crites, beloved by the gods, may be possible within this very special kind of performance, and may even find the

> gracious silence, sweet attention,
> Quicker sight, and quicker apprehension
> (Prologue, 1–2)

that Jonson was looking for in his audience, but he will not be credible elsewhere. There are limits to how far we can expect an audience to look through the 'playings' of children to a true understanding of the danger of vanity in the real world, where there is no Crites to put them right. The play itself comes near to admitting this when Cynthia (a thinly disguised version of the semi-mythic Queen Elizabeth, approaching the end of her reign) mentions

> Actaeon (who), by presuming far,
> Did (to our grief) incur a fatal doom.
> (v. xi. 14–15)

This surely glances at the fate of the Earl of Essex who, like Actaeon, presumptuously burst in upon his Virgin Goddess at an inopportune moment and paid a dreadful penalty. This is as close as the play can come to dealing with the real world: what power would a Crites be able to wield against the vanities of real men?

The next play, *Poetaster*, shows Jonson already taking stock of the brief selective career so far that he was later to enshrine in the first folio; of all his plays, it is the one which deals most explicitly with the issues of poetry and the state, the targets and tactics of satire. To some extent this may have been forced upon him by the developing War of the Theatres, in which it is clear that Jonson's pretensions as a poet and satirist met with scepticism and scorn from some of his fellow dramatists, notably those like Dekker and Marston who were also writing for the children's companies. We do not know exactly what of Marston's Jonson took offence to, but we may get some idea of the general tone of disagreement from Dekker's *Satiromastix*, in which the accusation is levelled at 'Jonson': 'You must be called Asper, and Criticus [quarto form of the folio Crites], and Horace' – in other words, that the self-righteous satirist figures in his plays were only a mouthpiece for his own self-important views. Yet it is surely a mistake to read *Poetaster* too narrowly as a reply to such personal criticisms; Jonson doubtless derived satisfaction from bestowing on Demetrius (Dekker) and Crispinus (Marston) a taste of poetic justice, but he does so in a context which is wider and more thoughtful than mere personal animosity.

This is clear from the opening of the play, where Jonson lays a kind of trap for the audience. Ovid is completing a poem:

> Then, when this body falls in funeral fire,
> My name shall live, and my best part aspire.
>
> (I. i. 1–2)

His name did, of course, live; Ovid was the most popular classical poet of medieval and Renaissance times, and we might have good reason to suppose that he would be Jonson's hero or mouthpiece in this play – an expectation apparently confirmed when we see him mocked and bullied by his philistine father and other narrow-minded materialists, who want him to study law at the expense of his poetry. But there is an unexpected irony in Ovid Sr's outburst: 'Your name shall live indeed, sir; you say true: but how infamously, how scorn'd and contemn'd in the eyes and ears of the best and gravest Romans, that you think not on . . .' (I. ii. 1–4). All of which actually comes to pass in the course of the play, though not for the sorts of reasons he supposes. Ovid is made the object of crass and vulgar attacks on poetry as a whole ('they will rob us, us, that are magistrates, of our respect, bring us upon their stages, and make us ridiculous to the plebeians' I. ii. 39–41; Tucca dismisses Homer as 'a poor, blind, rhyming rascal . . . the whoreson hungry beggar' 84–7). An audience, who are after all patrons of the arts, might be expected to sympathise with his brave defence:

> O sacred poesy, thou spirit of arts,
> The soul of science, and the queen of souls . . .
>
> (I. ii. 231–2)

But sympathy for a character must not blind us to his faults, as Jonson was to insist time after time in his later plays: it becomes almost a hallmark of Jonson's technique, probing the uneasy ground between our emotional responses and our rational apprehensions. When Ovid pretends to make poetry of the law, even as a joke, he commits a kind of blasphemy, because true poetry is itself a law, a divine gift; such thoughtless versifying cheapens it. Before the act is out we see Ovid's true nature:

> Julia's love
> Shall be a law, and that sweet law I'll study,
> The law, and art of sacred Julia's love.
>
> (I . iii. 55–7)

47

It is not that love itself is wrong, but that Ovid's love is sensual adulation rather than virtuous affection, knowing no proper bounds; it is this which compromises Ovid in his pretensions to be a poet. He has the ability but no true sense of values, and this effectively makes him a traitor. The issue is widened in the second act by the introduction of Crispinus, who turns out to be the comic obverse to Ovid's tragedy: where Ovid squanders true talent, Crispinus never has it to lose. When Ovid says of Chloe, 'I see, even in her looks, gentry, and general worthiness' (II. ii. 29–30), he is wrong in a disturbing way; even if he is joking, his judgement of this silly woman lacks taste and discretion – qualities essential in a poet. But that Chloe should think herself gentry, and Crispinus concur, is merely pathetic, as are their views on poetry:

CHLOE: . . . Could not one get the Emperor to make my husband a poet, think you?
CRISPINUS: No, lady, 'tis love, and beauty make poets: and since you like poets so well, your love, and beauties shall make me a poet.

(II. ii. 73–7)

Crispinus uses his pretensions as a poet to make advances to Chloe, who may be gullible but is not averse to this sort of thing. It is a low parody of Ovid's great romance and points to the essential worthlessness of both affairs. Crispinus is never the real threat to poetry that Ovid is, however, for the simple reason that there is never a real threat of his ever being a poet. At his very worst in the play he is only a nuisance when he turns his hand to satire – another branch of poetry he totally misunderstands; for him it has no ethical basis and is merely spiteful caricature. This may help to give poetry a bad name among those who know nothing about it, but true poets and understanders will shrug off such misrepresentations.

It is only when he has spent two acts establishing the broad question, 'what is a true poet?' in his comparisons of Ovid and Crispinus, that Jonson introduces Horace, whom Dekker and others have taken to be his true spokesman in the play. There can be no doubt but that in the scenes where Horace leads in the 'purging' of Demetrius and Crispinus, Jonson virtually invites this identification. But this is an inadequate account of the Horace we see in the play as a whole, who is something of an inconsistent character and does not have the easy superiority we might expect of an author's mouthpiece. When we first encounter him, he is comically trapped by Crispinus in a trivial and inane conversation, from which he is too polite to extricate himself abruptly and which Crispinus is too thick-skinned to see that he has no interest in.[10] This establishes Horace as a humane, sensitive and long-suffering individual, but also as someone slightly ineffectual, incapable of dealing on the spot with the rampant inanity Crispinus represents; the scene helps to justify the revenge he will wreak at the end of the play, but it hardly convinces us that he has the resources to do it. Nor does the scene really prepare us for the totally serious Horace who will expound on the true moral basis of satire (in the Apologetical Dialogue originally printed at the end of the quarto, but inserted at the end of act III in the folio) or the man who enjoys the confidence of Augustus Caesar and is able to denounce the Lupus 'plot'. Horace in fact fluctuates between being an idealised portrait of a rational man of action, a serious poet, and something of a comic butt; the inconsistency may be deliberate on Jonson's part, since it would help to explain one of the most striking features of the play – Horace's reaction to the banishment of Ovid – but it can hardly be described as very satisfactory.[11] When Augustus Caesar banishes Ovid, Horace tries to intervene on his behalf, arguing that his crime was only tasteless high spirits which deserve clemency. This is humane and courageous but, the final emphasis of the play suggests, an inadequate response to the severity of the offence; if the audience have thought of Horace as Jonson's own spokesman, and therefore the voice of right reason in the play, this must come as another moment when they will have to re-think their judgements.

The crime of Ovid and his followers is a kind of hubris; forgetting the deep obligations and responsibilities that come with the divine gift of poetry, they abuse it, substitute vanity and sensuality for true virtue, and believe themselves to be above the laws of both gods and men. 'Who knows not (Cytheris)', says Gallus, 'that the sacred breath of a true poet, can blow any virtuous humanity, up to deity?' (IV. ii. 34–6). Horace argues that this is just a joke in poor taste, but Caesar sees it as a complete betrayal of the trust with which the power of the poet is granted. In Ovid, graced with the greatest share of that power, it amounts to treason:

> Are you, that first the deities inspir'd
> With skill of their high natures and their powers,
> The first abusers of their useful light?
>
> (IV. vi. 34–6)

Poetry is not merely a private pastime, but a 'useful' art, a social responsibility, and it is the abuse of this which provokes Caesar's severity. Ovid's refusal to repent and his continuing unseemly passion for Julia ('Ay me, there is no stay / In amorous pleasures: if both stay, both die' IV. ix. 95–6) underline the justice of the sentence.

The canonical rectitude of Caesar's action is finally established in the last act, which incorporates an appeal to ultimate judgement in the person of Virgil. Horace may be a good man, with more than adequate poetic talent, but Virgil is something more:

EQUES: Virgil is now at hand, imperial Caesar.
CAESAR: Rome's honour is at hand then.

(v. i. 68–9)

Horace notes, with an approval that implicitly questions his own qualities (or at least puts them in perspective), that Virgil is 'refin'd / From all the tartarous moods of common men' (102–3) and Tibullus is moved to make a formal definition of his virtues:

> That, which he hath writ,
> Is with such judgement, labour'd, and distill'd
> Through all the needful uses of our lives,
> That could a man remember but his lines,
> He should not touch at any serious point,
> But he might breathe his spirit out of him.

(118–23)

Once again we see the stress on poetry as a useful, social art ('the needful uses of our lives') and implicitly Ovid is dragged to an ever-lower region of hell. The reading from the *Aeneid*, on the sins of Dido and Aeneas, who abandoned duty for love, puts an almost biblical seal of approval on Ovid's banishment. This is the climax of judgement in the play; all the errors perpetrated in the play are placed in a calm and absolute perspective by Virgil's divine meditations; there is no room for doubt – for mere human error – in the face of purity and authority of this order.

Significantly, only Caesar and a small, select group are allowed to be present at the reading, which is held behind guarded doors. These are the solid core of right-thinking men, equivalent perhaps to the true 'understanders', upon whom the spiritual well-being of the state depends; poetry and politics go hand in hand since, as Jonson put it in the *Discoveries*, 'A prince without letters, is a pilot without eyes' (1234). This ideal of poetry as a pilot for the state, appealing always to the most discriminating audience, is one that lies behind the whole conception of the first folio. It is nowhere else spelled out quite so baldly, though the Court masques were to give Jonson his own opportunity to address the highest in the land directly. Unfortunately, there is no evidence that the audiences of his masques were any more inclined to accord him the solemn reverence that Virgil receives than were those who attended his dramatic satires. Perhaps even by *Poetaster* Jonson was realist enough to appreciate that what we might call such undiluted poetic seriousness could only be effective in a very limited – if important – context, and that something more entertainingly rough-and-ready was necessary for dealing with the everyday follies of the world. So in an interesting foreshadowing of the interruption of Prospero's solemn masque in *The Tempest*, Virgil's grand oration is disturbed by Asinius Lupus's absurd accusations against Horace; from the etymology of his name he identifies himself with an ass and a wolf in one of Horace's poems. Horace's urbane irony (rather than Virgil's refined eloquence) proves to be the proper response for this asinine reasoning: 'If you will needs take it, I cannot with modesty give it from you' (v. iii. 99–100). This translation of poetic wisdom into practical action is carried a step further in the 'Arraignment' of Crispinus, where Horace's medicinal purgative is almost a parody of the 'useful light' with which poets are credited. Crispinus is beyond Virgil's scope on the inverse of the principle by which Ovid is beyond Horace's; the satirist must meet his subject on equal terms if he really wishes to 'explode' the folly – Crispinus would not begin to understand Virgil while Ovid could not be so conveniently purged. The true satirist, such as Horace, will gain his inspiration from high wisdom such as Virgil's, and so avoid the vindictive lampoons of which he is always accused, but his method will have to be altogether more pragmatic if he is to breach the vain and self-centred thinking which allows folly to flourish.

No one would pretend that *Poetaster* is a wholly satisfactory play; the mixture of high seriousness and satiric farce is not always convincing, even though they are linked thematically, and the inconsistencies in Horace's role are a serious flaw since, even if he is not in a simple sense Jonson's spokesman, he is very much the focal character. Nevertheless there are signs that Jonson is on the way here to mastering the new dramatic mode he has so contentiously made his own. For one thing he has assembled a cast of characters and permutated them through a sequence of plots in a way that does not immediately smack of 'humours' assembled merely to be exploded; two acts go by before Horace appears as a kind of commentator and this allows the likes of Ovid, Crispinus and Tucca to develop and go about the business of damning themselves for some time without the audience receiving any heavy prompting from the author. This suggests a greater confidence on Jonson's part, largely reflected in a new relationship with the audience; not only is there no character in the early part of the play to help us interpret the action, but there are signs of deliberate attempts to mislead (or at least test) us. In the cases of both Ovid and Horace, albeit in different ways, our sympathy is at first encouraged, but we are obliged to adjust our initial judgements in the light of limitations that appear later. In effect it is not until the appearance of Virgil in the last act that we can feel the play to have delivered its ultimate judgements, and up to that point we have been involved in a succession of incomplete perspectives which allow us only partial judgements. That being so, the audience are not merely passive spectators (if, that is, they are alert at all) but participants in the whole process of evaluation. This is to be a cornerstone of Jonson's method in his best plays, and has analogies with his use of perspective in the masques.

There is a further earnest of Jonson's more mature accomplishments in his handling of those features of the play which comment, more or less explicitly, on the contemporary scene; before the play begins, Envy 'arising in the midst of the stage' hopes

> To blast your pleasures, and destroy your sports,
> With wrestings, comments, applications
>
> (23–4)

but is dumbfounded to discover that the scene is set in Rome:

> What should I do? Rome? Rome? O my vex'd soul,
> How might I force this to the present state?
>
> (33–4)

This is clearly a delightful double-bluff on Jonson's part, since there can be little doubt that Demetrius and Crispinus are lampoons of Dekker and Marston and meant to be appreciated as such. The setting of a play can be as remote as you like without making any of its 'applications' any the less valid. Time and again Jonson was to protest that he intended no such direct allusions to contemporary persons and events, and each time we may take it with a pinch of salt – may even suspect that it is an oblique invitation to the audience to discover in the work precisely what he is disowning. In this case, for all Jonson's care to make Demetrius and Crispinus part of a much wider discussion than mere personal spite would warrant, we may feel that the element of personal animosity calls the integrity of the satire in question here. But it is important to get this in perspective: the attacks on Dekker and Marston are not, finally, the meaning or purpose of the play. They only deal with immediate facets of a problem (in this case the uses and abuses of poetry) which Jonson's satire pursues on many different levels. Perhaps they titillate or intrigue an audience which feels privileged when it perceives a 'private' allusion, but their ultimate value is to stimulate the audience to enter further into the wider process of evaluation and understanding.

At least, in retrospect I think we can take this to be their function; to judge from the 'Apologetical Dialogue' Jonson appended to his text, 'which was only once spoken upon the stage', a good part of the original audience did not appreciate such fine distinctions and attacked him with 'sundry impotent libels'. Bloodied but unbowed, Jonson determines to write a tragedy:

> There's something come into my thought,
> That must, and shall be sung, high, and aloof,
> Safe from the wolves' black jaw, and the dull asses' hoof.
> (To the Reader, 237–9)

– a clear snub to the Asinius Lupuses in his audience. The 'something' is *Sejanus*. Jonson's apprenticeship is now over; he is on the point of finding answers to all the problems we touched on in respect of his earliest plays. Even though he is temporarily forsaking comedy for a tragedy set in classical Rome, he will not forget anything of the business of the satirist he has learned in the first four plays he will place in his folio.

> Rome? Rome? O my vex'd soul,
> How might I force this to the present state?

2

Sejanus and *Volpone*: the defence of virtue

Sejanus, an account of the ambitious rise and dramatically sudden fall of a lieutenant of the Roman Emperor, Tiberius, was not a success when it was first performed in 1603. We do not know the reason for this, though it has often been assumed that its fastidiously classical style and manner would not have appealed to an audience brought up on the liberal imaginative flair of Kyd, Marlowe and Shakespeare. But it is just as likely that the audience took offence at what they deemed to be the play's covert allusions to contemporary political events.[1] Whatever the problem was, Jonson remained unabashed; he not only published the play in 1605, but rewrote parts that had been by an unknown collaborator, so that the whole work was unmistakably his own. In several important respects, this 1605 quarto represents an aggressive defence both of the style and of the content of what Jonson had written, consistently upbraiding his audience for failing to understand and appreciate the play. In particular, Jonson liberally annotated the text with precise historical sources for the scenes, characters and speeches he presents, often mentioning the specific editions he had consulted. This may smack of pedantry, but Jonson defends the practice in his typically truculent address 'To the Readers': 'lest in some nice nostril, the quotations might savour affected, I do let you know, that I abhor nothing more; and have only done it to show my integrity in the story, and save myself in those common torturers, that bring all wit to the rack' (26–30). The notes are firstly, then, a defence against misinterpretation and misapplication. At the same time, however, the determination to show his 'integrity in the story' is of a piece with what he had earlier described as the 'offices of a tragic writer', which he lists as 'truth of argument, dignity of persons, gravity and height of elocution, fulness and frequency of sentence'[2] (18–20). Most of these 'offices' relate to what we might call the technical or stylistic requirements of tragedy, but 'truth of argument' and 'integrity in the story' focus on a further significant consideration which is central to Jonson's 'tactics' in this play; it was an established neo-classical principle that tragedies must be based on true historical facts if they are to be convincing and effective,[3] and Jonson's citing of his sources is an ostentatious demonstration of how faithful he has been to that principle. He admits that *Sejanus* is not absolutely faithful to the form of neo-classical tragedy 'in the strict laws of time' (7) and 'in the want of a proper chorus' (8), but he insists that its contents are unimpeach-able.

Equally clear and unimpeachable, Jonson insists, is the general moral or meaning of the play. 'This do we advance as a mark of terror to all traitors, and treasons; to show how just the Heavens are in pouring and thundering down a weighty vengeance on their unnatural intents, even to the worst princes: much more to those, for guard of whose piety and virtue, the angels are in continual watch, and God himself miraculously working' (The Argument, after line 38). When Jonson came to revise the text for his folio, he omitted the whole of 'To the Readers', the marginal annotations of his sources, and this last paragraph of 'The Argument': perhaps he felt that the whole context of the folio volume made these points for him, without special pleading. Conversely, by concentrating on the terms of reference that Jonson expressly set for the play in the quarto text – a reasonable approximation to neo-classical tragic form, a strict adherence to the historical truth, a high moral tone – I hope to explain its place in the folio and in Jonson's career as a whole.

Both in the adherence to verifiable sources and in the generally neo-classical style – eschewing the 'mixed' comic and tragic action of most Elizabethan tragedy, and its portrayal of violence – Jonson aims to convince the reader of a particular kind of realism in the play: not so much simple verisimilitude as a sober rendering of the 'truth' and 'integrity' of known historical facts. Just as his comedies avoid fantasy, demanding judgement of their audiences rather than imaginative surrender, Jonson's tragedies insist on the unvarnished reality of the action they depict. It is this truthfulness which will give the play living dramatic force and relevance to any audience – not sensational action or comic by-play. In doing this, Jonson does not regard the truth as an end in itself; it is a means to the end of understanding – in this instance, of understanding how an evil man both rose and fell, a lesson which may be of relevance at any time. So Jonson aims to combine the roles of historian and dramatic poet; Sir Philip Sidney and others had deemed these roles to be incompatible,[4] on the grounds that the historian merely records what happens and what human nature is actually like, while the poet's role is to instruct men in how they *should* live, to inform them (as Jonson himself put it) 'in the best reason of living'.[5] The whole strategy of *Sejanus* can be seen as an attempt to reconcile these two roles.

An admirer, writing after Jonson's death, praised his tragedies in these terms:

> When I respect thy argument, I see
>   An image of those times: but when I view
> The wit, the workmanship, so rich, so true,
>   The times themselves do seem retriev'd to me.[6]

The distinction is not profoundly expressed, but it is significant: however true Jonson is to his argument (the bare outline of the known facts), there will inevitably be a qualitative difference between that and the finished play. The difference lies in 'the wit, the workmanship'; Jonson is not merely a transparent medium but a craftsman (he would say, a poet), who remodels his basic material. The marginal notes, acknowledging Tacitus and Dio Cassius, Suetonius and Plutarch (among others), may distract our attention from the fact but they do not obscure it altogether. Wherever possible, of course, Jonson is punctilious about retaining the flavour and texture of his sources, to a degree which is little short of obsessive – no rabble fling their anachronistic caps in the air here, as they do in Shakespeare's *Julius Caesar*. It was obviously with some pride that he recalled to Drummond how 'in *Sejanus* he hath translated a whole oration of Tacitus' (602) – preserving the original without recourse to wit or workmanship. Similarly, Roman sacrificial ritual is rendered with exact detail, and one suspects that only Jonson would have changed a quarto reading like:

> POMPONIUS: By Castor, that's the worst.
> ARRUNTIUS: By Pollux, best.

to an insipid folio:

> POMPONIUS: By Pollux, that's the worst.
> ARRUNTIUS: By Hercules, best.
>
>   (IV. 438)

The pointed balance of the original is sacrificed to Jonson's late discovery that only women swore 'by Castor' – an obscure detail which it could only have given Jonson himself pleasure in the rectifying.[7]

Beneath this surface punctiliousness, however, we find that Jonson's use of his sources in *Sejanus* is far less staid and predictable than we might have been led to expect. The wit and workmanship have taken liberties which the strict marginal notes do not hint at. Take this speech, for example:

> SEJANUS: Our city's now
>   Divided, as in the time o'the civil war,

And men forbear not to declare themselves
Of Agrippina's party.

(II. 369–72)

The source is certainly in Tacitus,[8] but there Sejanus speaks directly to Tiberius – a soldier to his emperor; in the play, Sejanus is speaking to Postumus, who will relate it to Augusta, Tiberius's domineering mother, and in this way it will finally reach the emperor. The change is slight, but significant, like that of having Tiberius hire Macro before retiring to Capreae (Capri), rather than – as in the sources – after. Both changes contribute to the mood of intrigue, of political deviousness, which is the norm of the play. Through such touches Sejanus emerges as a sly Machiavel, by indirections probing, stirring, hinting, but avoiding personal implication; in Tacitus, he is more of a blunt soldier, albeit an ambitious one. Both changes also add to the aura of remote and malign authority which Tiberius wields in the play. Tacitus, who has no time for either Tiberius or Sejanus, does at least concede that the emperor was essentially well-meaning, if weak and influenced by his mother, early in his reign; later, corrupted by absolute power and in virtual retirement so that he could indulge his vices at will, his sudden outbursts of cruelty are interpreted as signs of mental instability and a pathological fear of assassination. The play ignores these mitigating factors throughout, and presents Tiberius simply as a master of cold, premeditated *real-politik*.

It may be argued that Jonson's dramatic method disposed him to concentrate on what he saw as the essential aspects of a character, at the expense of confusing and contradictory details – a tragic equivalent of the comic 'humours'; nevertheless, such 'concentration' seriously affects the emphases of what purports to be authentic history. Jonson's handling of the lesser characters, similarly, is marked by what can only be described as sins of omission: there is no mention in the play of the favour shown in actuality by Tiberius to Lepidus (whom both Jonson and Tacitus project as a good, honest man); the scheme of the drama does not allow for such an alliance of honesty and vice. Sabinus in the play is a model of Stoic reserve and rectitude where, in Tacitus, he is given to whining and bitterness: Jonson does not compromise his virtue with such facts. If these are sins of omission, there are times when he is guilty of obscuring the truth even when he sticks to the letter of history. For instance, the trial of Silius in the play is clearly stage-managed, and the accusation of treason is palpably false, so that his suicide is portrayed as the desperate expedient of a virtuous man; the prosecution also accuses

Silius of connivance with an enemy chieftain, of rapacity and extortion. Tacitus seems to believe these charges, only suggesting that the treason charge is fabricated; the context of the play, where we have no cause to believe the prosecutors, gives the impression that the prosecution is a *complete* fabrication, and that Silius is the innocent, unwitting victim of malign forces. The difference here between Jonson and his sources is that between the truth and the whole truth; he does not tamper with the facts, but only with the sense those facts make. This is a difference seen at its most extreme in the handling of Agrippina and the Germanicans; the memory of the dead Germanicus is an important theme in the play, and it is noticeable that Jonson expands and enlivens Tacitus's praise of the hero,[9] giving it greater prominence. He also places Tacitus's reservations about Agrippina in the mouth of Sejanus, where an audience – who know him for what he is – readily discount them. For Jonson, but not for Tacitus, she is the focus for the forces of virtue in Tiberius's Rome.

Apart from these subtle modifications and half-truths about the characters, there are a number of occasions when Jonson compresses or re-arranges the sequence of events; at times this may simply be the 'workmanship' of dramatic construction – for instance, the running together of three distinct meetings of the Senate to create the extended trial-scene in act III (though even this has the added effect of making matters seem more cataclysmic than they were). Other examples are less easy to account for: Caligula's expedient decision to join Tiberius on Capreae and the affair hinted at between Caligula and Macro's wife are both in the sources allright – but not until several years after Sejanus's death and the end of the play. Such alterations have been seen by some critics as evidence that Jonson's reading of history is one of grim pessimism, stressing the irreversible progress of Machiavellian evil and lamenting the inevitable demise of virtue in its wake. Against this, it must be objected that Jonson went just as far out of his way to 'create' the virtues ascribed to the Germanicans and others who resist tyranny in Rome as he did to 're-arrange' the vices that destroyed them. This includes the virtual invention of their leading spokesman, Arruntius; such a character does exist in Tacitus, but very sketchily, and not in Sejanus's lifetime.

Rather than construing Jonson's revisions of the historical record (which, of course, no casual reader would be in a position to appreciate) as signs either of pessimism or of optimism, what I think we should appreciate is how they unmistakably bring about a much clearer confrontation than occurs in any of the sources between the forces of evil (in their various manifestations: Tiberius, Sejanus, Macro, Caligula) and the forces of virtue (mainly the Germanicans and Stoics). The confrontation is hardly shaded at all – as it is in the sources – by the unpredictability of human affairs or by the complex vagaries of human nature. The shift is just enough, in fact, for Jonson to be able to address the question of how men *should* have behaved in such a confrontation without losing touch with how the record says they actually *did* behave: and to do it in quintessentially dramatic terms. History has been adapted to provide vivid and (as we shall see) *provocative* contrasts of outlook, which are the stuff of Jonsonian drama. The 'truth' of the argument and the 'integrity' of the story of this play are not simply a matter of dead history, but relate to moral choices which are still essentially with us.

It is a commonplace to think of *Sejanus* as a tragedy of civic decadence – a warning against the evils of Machiavellianism and a lament for the destruction of traditional virtues. At best, this is only a partial account of the play. The fact of the matter is that, in terms of astuteness and clear-sighted policy, Tiberius *deserves* to triumph as he does. Sejanus, his nearest rival, finally destroys himself with 'the incredible blindness of clear-sighted policy, the fundamental unrealism of Machiavellian realism'[10] – though some might say that, in sacrificing to Fortuna, he had forsaken the Machiavellian creed of self-help by which he had achieved so much. The Germanicans and their supporters, meanwhile, undo themselves through their sheer inactivity, but nothing in the play suggests that their fate was inevitable. In fact, Jonson goes out of his way to demonstrate that the helplessness of the Germanicans is, to an appreciable extent, of their own making. Arruntius is often proved wrong by events and the pious fortitude which prompts (in particular) Silius's 'honourable' suicide plays directly into the hands of such as Sejanus. The play continually points out that political success – whether it be in a virtuous or a vicious cause – demands a positive conjunction of judgement and action; this is a fact that the Germanicans conspicuously fail to appreciate. The play is not, in short, a tract upon the inexorable progress of political 'realism' but a dynamic examination of vice in action, and of the failure of virtuous men to construct a viable alternative.

Arruntius's smug detachment points to the heart of the problem: 'We / That are the good-dull-noble lookers on' is how he describes himself and his fellows. Well aware of the decay of the state, his criticisms – though heated – never suggest any positive alternative:

> Times? the men,
> The men are not the same: 'tis we are base,
> Poor, and degenerate from th'exalted strain
> Of our great fathers.
>
> (I. 86–9)

Such breast-beating, a form of masochistic nostalgia, takes the place both of action and of constructive thought; it creates an impediment, blocking any real attempt to emulate the past or improve the future, and it rightly earns Sejanus's contempt: 'And there's Arruntius too, he only talks' (II. 299). Lepidus's solution is 'plain, and passive fortitude, / To suffer, and be silent' (IV. 294–5) – which is virtuous in its way, but suicidal. It is in fact the memory of Germanicus in the play which, with a fine irony, implicitly condemns his latter-day admirers:

> He was a man most like to virtue; in all,
> And every action, nearer to the gods,
> Than men, in nature.
>
> (I. 124–6)

So Germanicus aligned 'virtue' with action; while Arruntius only appeals to the gods (e.g. IV. 259–71), Germanicus himself had wrought god-like deeds. Sabinus characterises him as having 'The innocence of Cato, Caesar's spirit' (I. 151) – a telling combination of integrity and initiative. Agrippina shows that spirit when she argues that 'Virtue's forces / Show ever noblest in conspicuous courses' (II. 456–7) but Silius over-cautiously urges 'providence'; it is also Agrippina, however, who advises the surviving Germanicans to separate: 'Let us fall apart: / Not, in our ruins, sepulchre our friends' (IV. 34–5). This proves disastrous: the whole logic of the play demonstrates the insufficiency of individual responses to an evil which threatens society as a whole. She exhorts her children: 'then stand upright; / And though you do not act, yet suffer nobly' (IV. 73–4). The outcome of this advice is that, of Germanicus's three children who take their separate, passive courses, only Caligula ominously survives. Without collective security, virtue is defenceless.[11]

Significantly, no one actually spells out these deficiencies to the audience. They are something inferred, something we have to work for – to notice the ironic difference between Germanicus and his latter-day followers; to appreciate the validity of Sejanus's *judgements* ('he only talks') even though there is no question of sympathising with him; to recognise that judgements made and actions taken by the most laudable (and sympathetic) men consistently operate in their own, and virtue's, worst interests. Jonson's presentation of history, in other words, is not dogmatic but provocative, designed in a way that will engage the audience's own discrimination as actively as possible. For example, it is the spy, Latiaris, insidiously trying to elicit an admission of treason, who spells out most clearly to the Germanicans how mistaken they are. Romans, he argues, should:

> not sit like spent, and patient fools,
> Still puffing in the dark, at one poor coal,
> Held on by hope, till the last spark is out.
> The cause is public, and the honour, name,
> The immortality of every soul
> That is not bastard, or a slave in Rome,
> Therein concern'd . . .
> It must be active valour must redeem
> Our loss, or none.
>
> (IV. 146–52; 157–8)

The advice is sound, but the Germanicans and Stoics are so entrenched in their private virtues, dissociating themselves from a known spy, that they fail to recognise its value: Sabinus can only counter with an ultra-cautious 'A good man should, and must / Sit down rather with loss, than rise unjust' (IV. 165–6). This proves to be a suicidal doctrine, but who is to say that he is not right too, in his way? The argument is not black and white, and it is the audience which is left with the responsibility of weighing the political and ethical 'truths' of a confrontation where the issues (as distinct, perhaps, from our sympathies) are not easily resolved. It is a peculiarly *dramatic* technique – a conflict of personalities and philosophies in which the members of the audience are arbitrators, positively involved in the issues themselves (unless, that is, they are lazy and inattentive, and remain 'good-dull-noble lookers on' themselves).

In both of his tragedies Jonson concentrates significant parts of the action in the Senate House, effectively making the audience additional ranks of senators, responsibly involved in the issues that are debated there. The whole manner of the play is, in fact, what we have come to call Brechtian, endlessly confronting and provoking the audience, cutting across their likely sympathies and expectations; so, for example, we are likely to be perplexed by a continual discrepancy between moral *sententiae* voiced in the play from time to time and the reality of the experience to which they relate:

> It is an argument the times are sore,
> When virtue cannot safely be advanc'd;
> Nor vice reprov'd . . .
>
> (III. 481–3)

Lepidus's observation is so bland as to become a part of the malady he purports to diagnose, in the same way as evocations of Germanicus invariably mock the speaker. What raises *Sejanus* above being merely an observation on the soreness of the times is precisely this uncomfortable balancing of virtue and judgement, integrity and success. One of the play's ostensible morals is that voiced by Lepidus:

> Fortune, thou hadst no deity, if men
> Had wisdom: we have placed thee so high,
> By fond belief in thy felicity.
>
> (v. 733–5)

This is a direct reflection on the fall of Sejanus, who had sacrificed to the Goddess Fortune, but it is clearly more than that: it suggests that men have the power to shape their own fortunes, if they will apply it – a lesson demonstrated by Tiberius and (in memory) by Germanicus, half-learned by Macro, learned and forgotten by Sejanus, and never really understood by the play's virtuous characters, including Lepidus himself, however sententiously they may declaim on the point. When news of Sejanus's heightened influence over Tiberius is announced, after he has saved the emperor's life on Capreae, Agrippina reflects to her children that it is 'a fortune sent to exercise / Your virtue, as the wind doth try strong trees' (IV. 68–9). Fate teaches them only fortitude, and not the need for action. Arruntius complacently regards the rise of Macro and the overthrow of Sejanus as the inevitable work of the wheel of fortune (v. 701–4), discounting the very tangible intervention of Tiberius. The irony of the emperor's 'modest' refusal of divine honours (I. 375–541) is that his grasp of human affairs is such that without the title, he already wields the effective power of a god.

So the play continually calls upon the audience to discriminate between sense and folly, words and deeds, sympathy and judgement. In Tacitus (though not in the play) Lepidus asks: 'may not our personalities play some part, enabling us to steer a way, safe from intrigues and hazards, between perilous insubordination and degrading servility?'[12] The play is in many ways a searching examination of that question. Is no acceptable form of resistance available to a virtuous man in a vicious society? Is the price of political success inevitably a compromise of personal integrity? It is not, after all, in the nature of *Sejanus* to offer direct answers to such questions:[13] the whole shape and presentation of the play are such as to oblige the reader/spectator to think for himself, to appreciate the ironies and regard the problems with a proper scepticism and respect for their complexity. Failure to do that at the time is what led to tragedy in that chapter of the history of Rome, and Jonson is implicitly asking what each member of his audience would have done to avoid that. It is, of course, only another way of putting the same question to ask them what they are doing to guard against the same thing *now*.

These issues may seem a long way removed from the follies and inflated egos which Jonson had attacked in his earlier comedies, but they are in essence the same: his prime concern is always to promote rational and virtuous conduct, whether in the personal, social or political sphere. In as much as *Sejanus* depicts the failure of any single individual to act *both* rationally and virtuously it is, in effect, a satire, measuring all its characters against an ideal – in this case, not an Asper or a Crites present in the action, but the dead Germanicus. It is a tragic satire precisely because it depicts a society which fails to live up to his memory, however much they pay lip-service to it. The element of hope in such a satire lies in the possibility that the modern audience – rather than the characters in the drama – may learn from that failure; Jonson will not spell out to them exactly how they should act and think, but it is implicit in the whole provocative structure of his drama that they must see themselves as free and rational beings, not creatures of fortune, and able to defend virtue if they have the resolution. All the subsequent plays in Jonson's 1616 folio are based on these assumptions – comedies and tragedies alike.

Jonson's 'integrity in the story' of *Sejanus* is thus the very antithesis of academic (i.e. disinterested) pedantry. One would not have to be much of a cynic to suggest that the ostentatious fidelity to known sources – while having its effect in making the drama exceptionally credible – is also a bluff, a disguise, a way of raising political questions that would otherwise be barred to him.[14] But Jonson makes a virtue of necessity and capitalises on the restriction: by raising the question of what history is, and what the limits of 'truth' are, he engages the 'understanders' for whom he writes in a judgement not only on the play as a work of art, but also on the moral issues it raises and on its relevance to contemporary conditions. It is this insistence on a dialectical process, on the extra dimension added by the involvement of the audience, that gives Jonsonian tragedy its real life, in contrast with the more emotive and more obviously 'imaginative' mirrors to life held up by Shakespeare and other contemporary tragedians.[15]

At first sight, nothing could be further removed from the strict historical accuracy of *Sejanus* than the flamboyant theatricality of *Volpone*; in place of the discipline of known facts we have the freedom of a beast fable, and in place of actual historical persons, characters identified by appropriate animal labels: Volpone (the fox), Mosca (the fly), Corbaccio (the raven), Corvino (the crow), Voltore (the vulture), etc. On closer examination, however, the two plays have more in common than divides them: both are concerned with the central question of how virtue may be preserved or defended in an immoral or amoral world; and both depend crucially on the involvement of the 'understanders' of the audience *within* the play's discussion of that question. But where *Sejanus* made 'truth of argument' and 'integrity in the story' the leading edge of its challenge to the audience, *Volpone* confronts us directly with its artifice, with its theatricality, teasing us about the strange, ambivalent experience of being entertained by 'make-believe'. Since the play itself is about a whole succession of 'make-believes', it is implicit from the outset that there is a parallel between the experience of the characters within the play and our own experience as its readers/audience. It is through that parallel that Jonson involves us in the moral issues of the play.

Volpone himself is, above all, a consummate actor, whether in his continuing death-bed scenes or in his bravura performances as a seducer and a mountebank. The men he dupes into believing that he will leave them his fortune are, in this sense, an audience – one that enjoys his act all too readily and uncritically. Corbaccio's 'deafness' is symbolically appropriate here; it is typical of the inadequacies of most of the 'audiences' within the play, who do not examine the facts carefully but construe things as they *want* them to be, only becoming disturbed if they feel their wish-fulfilment is threatened:

MOSCA: His face drawn longer, than't was wont–
CORBACCIO: How? how?
    Stronger, than he was wont?
MOSCA: No, sir: his face
    Drawn longer, than't was wont.
CORBACCIO: O, good.

(I. iv. 39–41)

Naturally, Corbaccio interprets every development in Volpone's death-bed scenes in whatever way most flatters his own ego. Similarly Voltore, who as a lawyer is supposed to be concerned with the 'truth', is only capable of construing whatever 'truth' appears to be in his own interest. Even Corvino is convinced by the most transparent of charades into transforming himself from a jealous husband to a willing pimp. The 'audiences' within *Volpone* consistently distort what they see into what they want to see, and act accordingly; Jonson challenges us to do better.

The challenge is posed most forcefully at the outset of the play, in the 'entertainment' which Mosca devises for Volpone. Nano and Androgyno trace the supposed 'metempsychosis' (or transmigration of the soul) of the Greek philosopher, Pythagoras, through various unseemly residences to its latest resting place, the hermaphrodite body of Androgyno himself. It is all done in the worst possible taste; the verse is execrable doggerel and one suspects that the performance is graced with lewd embellishments. As so often in Jacobean drama, and not least the plays of Jonson, the play-within-a-play proves to be the epitome of the wider action. This mockery of the mystic philosopher, through a perverse parody of his own teachings, relegates man's divine soul and intelligence to the level of a performing freak, a perversion of nature; it is analogous to the way in which Volpone himself perverts the splendid Renaissance aspirations of Venice into a bestial circus of self-seeking. What sort of taste could find such fare entertaining? The answer, of course, is Volpone's own:

> Now very, very pretty: Mosca, this
> Was thy invention?
MOSCA: If it please my patron,
> Not else.
VOLPONE: It doth, good Mosca.
MOSCA: Then it was, sir.

(I. ii. 63–5)

The whole episode should alert the audience in a variety of ways: as a warning that our own entire entertainment in this play will be, in its way, a perversion of nature; as a clear indication of the depths to which Volpone's instincts actually sink – in contrast to the apparent splendour of his aspirations; as an object-lesson in the way that any audience (here Volpone himself) can be amused and gratified by what is implicitly an image of itself, however appalling – not suspecting the element of criticism or sheer disgust that the author may have written into it. It is significant in this regard that the show should have been written, as he hesitantly admits, by Mosca; it is the first opportunity that an alert audience has to spot that Mosca is not the loyal and unquestioning lieutenant that he prentends to be. He too is an actor, though more subdued in style than his master; Volpone only recognises when it is too late that he has failed throughout to appreciate his parasite's long-running performance – a fatal lapse of attention which begins here, with his failure to appreciate the shrewd character assessment (and contempt?) that has gone into this effort to entertain him: 'If it please my patron . . . It doth, good Mosca.' The conflation of the roles of parasite and author, patron and audience, ought to give any real audience food for thought.

Volpone's delight in this tasteless entertainment should confirm what we already suspect about his character – that, with his shameless appetites and deceits, his monstrous egotism, his blasphemous praise of gold, he is a morally outrageous character. Yet Jonson has also invested the character with wit, passion and, above all, energy, which it is difficult not to admire. Like Milton's Satan, Volpone has the makings of greatness in the true Renaissance manner; but his positive qualities have been perverted and misapplied in the service of a kind of self-worship. His besetting sin is nothing as mean as avarice or the lust for gold:

> I glory
> More in the cunning purchase of my wealth
> Than in the glad possession.
>
> (i. i. 30–2)

He has an image of his own greatness, seeing himself as a kind of god, and he is determined to live up to it; his sin is really pride. Therein, of course, lies his blindness to the threat that Mosca poses – he is too proud to acknowledge the competition from his own parasite – and also his final determination to suffer at the hands of the Court rather than allow his parasite the satisfaction of getting the better of him; he may suffer more physical punishment this way, but it will be easier on his ego. There is a kind of grandeur even in that gesture, not taking the easy and sensible way out. Jonson never allows the alert reader to forget the sheer evil which Volpone represents. It is most clearly reflected in the images of disease, death and decay which surround the roles he plays; note, for example, the mordant irony of this interchange with Mosca which, once again, Volpone himself does not appreciate:

> But, what, sir, if they ask
> After the body?
> VOLPONE: Say, it was corrupted.
> MOSCA: I'll say it stunk, sir; and was fain t'have it
> Coffin'd up instantly and sent away.
>
> (v. ii. 76–9)

Nevertheless, there is a magnificence, even generosity, about Volpone's image of himself, which cannot but compare favourably with the mean, grasping, jealous and slow-witted suitors whom he dupes. It is this which makes *Volpone* such a disconcerting play, since all the moral judgements which Jonson keeps insisting that we make seem bound to be relative, partial, less than satisfactory.

The ambivalence surrounding Volpone and his actions is perhaps best demonstrated in his attempted seduction/rape of Celia. The episode is kept within comic bounds by our knowledge that Bonario is waiting in the wings, concealed, but even so Volpone's display of charm and apparent sexual potency is not to be taken lightly. We may suspect that the man who (according to Mosca) has fathered the misbegotten brood of Nano, Castrone and Androgyno is not as potent as he would like to believe, but such doubts are driven from our mind − as so often − by his sheer command of language, which brings all his fantasies about himself to life. Therein, as with many of Jonson's most impressive characters, lies his real − if limited − power. It is a measure of this that Jonson should have given Volpone one of the most potent seduction-songs in the language with which to advance his case; 'Come, my Celia, let us prove. / While we can, the sports of love' cannot lightly be dismissed.[16] Even without the added charm of music, its graceful phrasing and plausible arguments are wickedly difficult to rebut, and we already know from the mountebank scene that Celia is sufficiently susceptible to Volpone's oratory as to have dropped her handkerchief. Here, her frosty denials are no real answer to his exultant passion, and Bonario's intervention leaves it beguilingly open to doubt which would have faltered first − Volpone's ego or Celia's virtue. The final effect of the scene is one of farcical let-down, with Volpone's grandly inflated desires rudely baulked; yet the brilliance of his virtuoso performance completely outshines the sober propriety of Celia and Bonario, who seem naive and uninteresting alongside this imaginative man of the world. In such ways, Jonson provocatively blurs the rights and wrongs of all Volpone's actions, but always making him seem so much more attractive than the opposition, even when the opposition clearly has virtue on its side. How much more so then in the cases of Corbaccio, Corvino and Voltore, who all seem far more culpable and despicable than does Volpone in duping them.

A further difficulty about judging him lies in the fact that he may be said to reveal as much corruption as he truly creates; even Celia is not *totally* innocent, and the rest of Venice proves to be a ready-made city of scavengers and parasites, as the names of the characters suggest. Volpone may be a superb confidence-trickster, but that alone cannot explain how he hits upon a formula which seems capable of subverting the fabric of society as a whole, attacking the primary bonds that hold it together. With his slightest prompting, a father disinherits and disowns his son; a husband acts as pander to his own wife; a lawyer betrays the law; a parasite even double-crosses his master – suggesting that Volpone is not totally in control of whatever power it is he wields. Even the Court of Avocatori, who seek to pass judgement on these proceedings, must (as we shall see) be suspect. Volpone seems to be the catalyst rather than the cause of this corruption, against which there seems to be little or no defence. Is anyone immune to his pernicious influence? Can the audience be certain that they would be any more immune than the characters whom, in all probability, they laugh at? Jonson includes two sets of characters – the Would-bes, and Celia and Bonario – who offer negative answers to both those questions.

Although Jonas Barish has demonstrated[17] the thematic links that the Would-bes have with the main action, they are often thought of as something of a diversion from it and are often left out of modern performances altogether. This is surely a mistake; the Would-bes are not out of place in Volpone's Venice, merely out of their depths, and in so being they offer us a usefully different perspective on it. Unlike Celia and Bonario, who do their best to opt out of the pervasive corruption, Sir Pol and his lady have come expressly to become a part of it, but with conspicuous lack of success. We never see the courtesans whom she has come to ape or the political intriguers whom he emulates, but we instinctively know that they do it with so much more style and conviction than the Would-bes. They are very much what their name proclaims them to be, anxious to achieve what they perceive to be true sophistication but incapable of doing so. They are amateurs in a world of professionals – he with his endless gullibility, whether it be about mountebanks or about 'plots', and she with her mindless 'free-thinking', about anything from philosophy to sex. This is why we see them as essentially comic characters in a comedy short on easy laughter; her 'free-thinking' appears irrelevant in a world where, morally, anything goes already, and his political intrigues are ludicrously inept in a Venice where even parasites betray their masters: he deserves to end up, pathetically, crawling about under a turtle-shell.[18] The problem with the Would-bes is that they are so *English*. Therein lies Jonson's little joke, and his challenge to the audience. The English are notorious for their contempt of foreigners – a trait which Jonson was to mock again in the use of the Spanish disguise in *The Alchemist* – and it would be only too easy to dismiss the corruption of Volpone's Venice as something typically foreign: nothing to do with *us*. The Would-bes even seem to reinforce that possibility, with their laughable failure to achieve the depths of Venetian decadence. But it is a very two-edged failure; they were trying anyway (no faulting their enthusiasm) and there is nothing greatly reassuring about the fact that it was only incompetence which stopped them from being more successfully corrupt than they were. The fact is that the Would-bes represent the thin end of the wedge that leads to the full-blown corruption of Volpone's Venice; their follies only *seem* inconsiderable by contrast with the blatant vices all around them. It is tempting simply to laugh them off, but that would be to ignore the very real threat that such characters represent, for all their incompetence. This is surely one reason why Jonson has given Sir Pol a constant companion; Peregrine is a lineal descendant of Asper, Crites and Horace, a man of real wit and judgement (though perhaps a certain arrogance) who is allowed to share his insights with the audience. Jonson eschews the use of such a character in the main action of *Volpone*, where the moral ambiguities must speak for themselves, but with Sir Pol Peregrine is able to remind the audience directly of their responsibilities as 'understanders':

> O, this knight
> (Were he well known) would be a precious
> thing
> To fit our English stage: he that should write
> But such a fellow, should be thought to feign
> Extremely, if not maliciously.
>
> (II. i. 56–60)

Such comments break directly through the dramatic illusions, reminding the audience on the one hand that this is only a play, but on the other that it has *some* kind of resemblance to real life (most obviously in the case of the Would-bes) and that it is their duty to assess it. In assessing it, we are also required to judge the moral culpability of the characters for their actions, and we should not exonerate the Would-bes simply because they are so *familiar*.

By contrast to the Would-bes, Celia and Bonario offer hope of something better than the destructive egoism that besets Venice – hope that Volpone's appeal can be resisted by positive qualities rather than incompetence. They have virtue, idealism and faith in a just providence; unfortunately, these are all qualities that the play undercuts with consistent irony. His rescue of her from the clutches of Volpone is the only selfless act in the whole play, but his derring-do oratory –

> Forbear, foul ravisher, libidinous swine,
> Free the forc'd lady, or thou diest, impostor.
>
> (III. vii. 267–8)

– is ludicrously over-alliterative, revealing the whole episode as melodramatic make-believe in the grimmer reality of Volpone's Venice. Similarly, when in Court they are asked to name their witnesses, they reply:

BONARIO: Our consciences.
CELIA: And heaven, that never fails the innocent.

> (IV. vi. 16–17)

Innocents indeed they are, and laughably out of place in this world. They bring to mind Milton's famous comment in his *Areopagitica* (1644): 'I cannot praise a fugitive and cloistered virtue, unexercised and unbreathed, that never sallies out and sees her adversary, but slinks out of the race where that immortal garland is to be run for, not without dust and heat.' There is some excuse for Celia; she has indeed been restricted to a 'cloistered virtue' by her jealous husband, but we notice just how fragile that is when she sees the mountebank Volpone from her window and lets her handkerchief fall. Bonario – whose name means 'good man' – has only youth as an excuse; for him the pursuit of virtue means being a knight in shining armour – but it is a pursuit without 'dust and heat'. Apart from carrying Celia away from a fate worse than death, he does not actually *do* anything in virtue's cause, and this is simply unrealistic in the face of the kind of deceit and corruption that Volpone represents. Such virtue cannot last long.

In the final scenes, these two praise heaven for the revelation of the villainy and their own delivery – Celia: 'O heav'n, how just thou art' (v. x. 13); Bonario: 'Heaven could not, long, let such gross crimes be hid' (v. xii. 98) – but this misses the point and only underlines their naivety: heaven had nothing to do with it. The evil characters may reveal and discredit each other, but the forces of virtue have little cause to congratulate either themselves or heaven at the end of this play. As in *Sejanus*, they are tried and found wanting; it is not enough, in this fallen world, merely to look to your private virtue and trust heaven for the rest. This surely is the truth that Jonson wishes to enforce on his audience by not allowing Celia and Bonario to marry when it is all over. No doubt many would agree with Coleridge that it would be nice if Celia were 'the ward or niece instead of wife of Corvino, and Bonario her lover',[19] but throughout the play these characters have acted as ironic foils to the audience's comfortable hopes and illusions about how things will work out well in the end, and it is no part of Jonson's plan to indulge such sentimental notions: neither they nor, perhaps, we have done enough to deserve such a positive outcome.

Wherever the audience looks in *Volpone* it will find little cause for comfort or for self-congratulation; there seems to be no answer to the power that Volpone exerts. This is most particularly so at the very end of the play, even though Volpone and Mosca are exposed and punished with exemplary severity. The problem is that, upon close examination, this stern solution proves to be no solution at all. Jonson saw fit to comment on the conclusion of the play in his Dedication of it to the twin Universities of Oxford and Cambridge; he admits that 'my catastrophe may, in the strict rigour of *comic* law, meet censure' (109–10) on the grounds that the penalties meted out are too severe for a play of this kind. He answers this objection firstly by claiming that he was responding to the more general objection that 'we never punish vice in our interludes etc.' (116) and secondly by appealing to classical precedents, where characters are often 'mulcted: and fitly, it being the office of a comic-poet, to imitate justice, and instruct to life, as well as purity of language, or stir up gentle affections' (121–4). As so often when he writes about his own practice as a dramatist, Jonson is being somewhat disingenuous. The 'justice' which he so solemnly claims to have imitated here is suspect, to say the least. For one thing, the Court of Avocatori that passes judgement is hardly above suspicion itself. At one stage, one of them sizes up Mosca as a potential son-in-law: 'A proper man! and were Volpone dead, / A fit match for my daughter' (v. xii. 50–1), while all of them are more concerned at the end of the day to preserve social distinctions rather than to mete out strict justice. So Mosca suffers the more severely of the villains, not because he was the more evil, but for having:

> abus'd the court,
> And habit of a gentleman of Venice,
> Being a fellow of no birth, or blood
> (v. xii. 110–12)

– while Volpone, by 'blood, and rank a gentleman, canst not fall / Under like censure' (117–18). It is, of course, something equally horrible and fitting that a man who has feigned death for so long should be sent to a hospital for incurables, but his own reaction to this should give us pause: 'This is called mortifying of a fox' (125). It is a sardonic line; ostensibly, Volpone acknowledges the humiliation and chastening that he is to receive. But 'to mortify' is also to hang game until it is tender and the flesh is suitably 'high'; one suspects that it will be a long time before this old fox will be fit to eat. Volpone may meet a symbolically appropriate end, but the dark forces which he represents will not be eradicated so easily.

This is comedy of a different order from the early 'humour' plays and 'comicall satyres', as Jonson himself seems to recognise from the outset; he acknowledges in the Prologue that this play will be a riposte to those who complain that 'All he writes is railing' (9), and the focus of the action upon an ambivalent anti-hero rather than a satirist-figure certainly minimises the suggestion of smug self-satis-faction in the comedy. The likes of Corbaccio and Corvino seem effortlessly to condemn themselves rather than to act as convenient butts for Jonson's superior wit. One consequence of all this, however, is that no suggestion emerges of their abandoning their vices and follies, as their counterparts do in the earlier plays; they may be 'mulcted' by the Court, but not reformed. There is no pretence in Jonson's best comedies, or his tragedies, that the problems of human nature which he depicts in them can be resolved miraculously by his art; however neatly he may orchestrate a satisfactory ending of affairs for the theatre, we are not allowed to forget that life goes on, and that mankind is as unregenerate as ever. Jonson's satire seems, in effect, to have developed a more sober estimate of its capacities. In *Volpone*, as in *Sejanus*, the eradication of a particular embodiment of evil offers no automatic hope that society will change for the better, since the circumstances which allowed that evil to flourish – the weaknesses and blindnesses of human nature, coupled with the failure of virtuous men to act positively – have only been revealed, not expunged. Jonson seems almost to comment on this change in his satire in the mountebank scene, where the disguised Volpone offers to sell 'this *unguento*, this rare extraction, that hath only power to dispense all malignant humours that proceed either of hot, cold, moist, or windy causes . . .' (II. ii. 91–3). It is a fake, of course; there is no such cure-all for the 'humours' that afflict mankind – though there are those like Sir Politic Would-be who are gullible enough to believe in it, and Celia is sufficiently impressed to drop her handker-chief.

If Jonson is now prepared to mock his earlier claims to have a remedy, an *unguento* as it were, 'to disperse all malignant humours', it may seem to some that he is abandoning altogether his pretensions to be a satirist. Harry Levin, for example, suggests that, 'As his powers of realistic depiction came into full play, he gradually relinquished his loudly proclaimed moral purpose.'[20] But what has really changed in *Volpone* and Jonson's other best plays (where, admittedly, his 'powers of realistic depiction' are at their most impressive) is not his 'loudly proclaimed moral purpose' so much as the targets on which that moral purpose concentrates and the strategies by which they are attacked. In the earlier comedies, vices were exposed and follies 'exploded', for the most part, with the tacit consent of the audience, who were scarcely called upon to do much more than admire the author's just exaction of shame and repentance from his erring creatures. That is what gives those plays their rather smug, self-satisfied air. But following on from *Sejanus*, *Volpone* casts the audience in a different, more active role; where in the tragedy they became additional members of the Senate, here they implicitly join the Court of Avocatori, charged with passing judgement on all the action and the characters of the play. As we have seen, however, this is not a play where the business of judgement is simple and clear-cut; our sympathies are often at odds with what we know to be right, and our scale of moral values is continually turned upon its head. Yet we are charged to do our best, and to do this we must recognise and overcome within ourselves the weaknesses and blindnesses that might allow a Volpone to flourish, that might prompt us to be less than just or objective in our judgements. We must, for a start, rid ourselves of the social prejudices that distort the judgement of the actual Court of Avocatori; but, more than that, we must get over the temptation simply to sneer at the likes of Corbaccio and Voltore, and to recognise what there is of a Corbaccio and a Voltore within ourselves. Jonson's satire, in other words, has turned from attacking the fictitious creatures within his plays to the real target – the elements within the audience itself which those creatures represent or mirror. There is, Jonson implies, a piece of Corvino, or Bonario, or Sir Politic Would-be in all of us, and the function of his art is to help us to deal with it. The act of understanding is thus essentially a business of seeing *through* Jonson's art, and so being able to sit in judgement upon ourselves.

When Jonson admitted in the Dedication of *Volopone* that the ending of the play might be excessively strict for a comedy, he was admitting in effect that he knew that he was flying in the face of the audience's expectations and perhaps also, in the case of Celia and Bonario's possible marriage, in the face of their hopes. But basically what he was drawing attention to was the fact that this is a play; it is a work of art, not a slice of life, though it does bear some oblique relation to life. In drawing attention to this fact (as he does repeatedly throughout the play itself) Jonson implicitly asks the audience to consider their expectations of a play and most particularly its ending: do they expect it to be more true to life, or perhaps more true to real (as opposed to poetic) justice? Do they want reality or justice at all or do they (like so many of the characters in *Volpone*) want their dreams to be fulfilled, a happy ending without work or suffering? The most important implication of all is that the audience should *think* about the ending of the play and not simply accept it. In what ways is it true, or proper, or just? These are the questions for which Jonson has been preparing the audience throughout *Volpone*. They are the questions which hallmark the endings of all his best plays.

3

Rare poems and rare friends: Jonson's *Epigrams*

'Rare poems', Jonson told the Countess of Bedford, 'ask rare friends.'[1] With the exception of a few anthologised pieces, his own poems have had difficulty finding such friends, and it is a moot point whether the fault lies primarily with the poems or with the readers. It is probably significant in this regard that Jonson left no single work of indisputably major status among his non-dramatic verse – nothing of the scale of achievement of, say, *The Faerie Queene* or *Paradise Lost*. Since Jonson's public ambitions as a poet were comparable in scale to those of Spenser and Milton, this omission is important: one major statement confers weight and dignity upon the career as a whole, and its absence may be correspondingly damning. The first thing that Drummond reports from his conversations with Jonson is 'that he had an intention to perfect an epic poem entitled *Heroologia* of the worthies of his country, roused by fame, and was to dedicate it to his country; it is all in couplets, for he detesteth all other rhymes' (1–5). Despite Drummond's hopeful use of the present tense ('it is all in couplets'), the epic was either never written or never published. This ought, perhaps, to matter less than it might in the case of other poets, since Jonson did also leave a major body of dramatic writing; but, as we have noted before and despite the lead that he himself gave in printing the poems alongside his other works in the 1616 folio, it has been rare for the poetry and the drama to be considered together. And the poetry has suffered quite badly from this compartmentalisation.

All this would probably matter less if it were not also often felt that Jonson's poetry 'lacks' something. It exhibits none of the compulsive panache of a Donne, none of the inner tensions of a Herbert, no enigmas in the manner of Marvell, and only too rarely even the lyric grace of a Herrick. It is felt that there is, in effect, nothing mysterious or untouchable about it, as Swinburne bitterly complained: 'There is nothing accidental in the works of Ben Jonson; no casual inspiration, no fortuitous impulse ever guides or misguides his genius astray or aright.'[2] It is doubtless symptomatic of these feelings that a disproportionate amount of critical attention has been lavished on those poems where something 'accidental', some small glimmer of the private man, may be seen or suspected behind the impassive public mask: 'On My First Daughter' and 'On My First Son' (*Epigrams* 22, 45), 'A Celebration of Charis in Ten Lyric Pieces' and 'My Picture Left in Scotland' (*The Underwood* 2, 9). Minor enigmas such as the identity of Elizabeth, L. H. (*Epigrams* 124) and the radical differences in tone between 'An Epigram on the Court Pucelle' (*The Underwood* 49) and the 'Epitaph of Cecilia Bulstrode' (*Ungathered Verse* 9) – both on the same lady – have also occasioned much discussion. But such exceptions serve finally to underline the lack of any apparent compelling mystery in the bulk of the poems, which are often castigated as being rather narrow in tone and range, fundamentally self-contained and self-explanatory.[3] It may be added, too, that the acknowledged charm of such lyrics as 'Queen and huntress, chaste and fair' and 'Drink to me only, with thine eyes' (*Cynthia's Revels*, V. vi. 1–8 and *The Forest* 9 respectively) has been perversely self-defeating in terms of Jonson's general reputation as a poet: rather than encouraging greater interest in what else he wrote, they have become sticks to beat him with, for not writing like that all the time.

It is not, of course, that no one has found qualities to praise in Jonson's verse; in the eloquence and assurance of poems like 'To Penshurst' (*The Forest* 2), 'Inviting a Friend to Supper' (*Epigrams* 101) and 'To the Immortal Memory, and Friendship of that Noble Pair, Sir Lucius Cary, and Sir H. Morison' (*The Underwood* 70), many have recognised Jonson's 'integrity to the experience he is trying to communicate, the honesty of the matter-and-manner relationship in his verse, and his noticeable sense of linguistic appropriateness.'[4] These are, however, qualities that it is easier to admire than to enthuse about, and relatively few of the poems have them to a degree that makes them really outstanding. Not everyone, moreover, has been content to accept that Jonson's verse lacks the kind of 'mystery' or inner-tension that we take to be characteristic of so many of his contemporaries; Jonas Barish puts it this way: 'Where other baroque writers explicitly dramatise their tensions, in Jonson the tensions remain buried. . . . But no one has ever doubted their existence. The presence of tension in Jonson reveals itself most obviously in his insistent claim to be without tension: the oftener he protests his imperturbability, the less we are inclined to believe it.'[5] This is very probably true, but it is easier to pin down in the provocative, double-edged ironies of the plays than it is in the discreet measures of the poems.

The net result of the objections and reservations I have outlined has been a kind of impasse in the appreciation of most of Jonson's poetry, a measure of complacency about it, an assumption that it is worthy, but understood. This general estimate does, however, ignore the important fact that Jonson himself presented the best of his early verse to the public not as a catch-all collection, but as two careful and deliberate selections, *Epigrams* and *The Forest*, epitomes in their selectiveness of the 1616 folio in which they both appeared. There is some evidence that Jonson intended a similar process of deliberate selection for *The Underwood* but it survives only patchily in Digby's second folio; the fact that *Epigrams* appeared in the first folio as 'Book 1' may suggest that Jonson intended a sequel, but if so it came to nothing. So *Epigrams* and *The Forest* are the only selections of Jonson's poetry published exactly as he intended them to be read – a fact that has usually been ignored or considered to be of little significance; the question of the context in which a particular piece was published is rarely raised. Nevertheless, there is clear evidence that Jonson's contemporaries were accustomed to reading poetry written in both narrative and emblematic sequences: all the major Elizabethan sonnet-sequences have some indistinct quasi-biographical narrative running through them, while George Herbert's *The Temple* is a good example of a sequence arranged emblematically around a theme, in such a way that many of the poems take on a deeper resonance when we appreciate how it fits into the larger pattern. In Jonson's case we have two sequences, indisputably as the author meant them (no Shakespearean enigmas, which may be part of the problem), yet until recently hardly anyone has bothered to enquire what their organisation implies for our reading and understanding of the poems.[6]

The arrangement of Jonson's *Epigrams* (I shall consider *The Forest* in chapter 5) is such that it is not appreciated immediately; it certainly does not fall into the narrative or emblematic categories I have described. We find poems written perhaps as early as 1595 (the putative date of the death of his first daughter) and certainly as late as 1609 (epigram 130, for example, was originally prefixed to *Airs*, by Alphonso Ferrabosco, published that year), in an apparently arbitrary mixture of praise and censure, elegy and commentary. Some local principles emerge, to be sure: a poem like 'To True Soldiers' (no. 108) clearly complements the preceding 'To Captain Hungry' (107), as 'To Learned Critic' (17) may be said to anticipate 'To My Mere English Censurer' (18). On the whole, there is a weighting of poems in praise of aristocrats and of authors towards the end of the collection, and particularly in the last third; but this is far from absolute: the three poems to the King himself (hailed as 'best of kings' and 'best of poets' in epigram 4, so setting the twin themes of society and art which clearly preoccupy the volume) are all placed well in the first half of the collection (4, 35, 51), while the later tendency towards panegyric is severely qualified by the inclusion of the scatalogical mock-heroic 'On The Famous Voyage' (133), the longest poem in the collection, at its very end. None of this gets us very far. We notice too that the censorious and satirical poems are directed anonymously (at least, names are not openly named), being either very cryptic ('On Something, that Walks Somewhere', 11) or using convenient pseudonymic labels, like 'Sir Cod' (19, 20, 50) and 'Sir Voluptuous Beast' (25, 26), which may or may not conceal a specific target; the poems of praise, on the other hand, name their subjects, indeed often seeming to treat the name itself as the most important fact about the subject, a sort of talisman which makes the poem itself almost redundant: 'I do but name thee Pembroke' ('To William, Earl of Pembroke', 102), 'a Sidney, though unnamed' ('To Mary, Lady Wroth', 103), 'Were they that named you, prophets?' ('To Susan, Countess of Montgomery', 104), and so on. But again, this only takes us so far: the 'named' figures are only in an indirect and general sense challenges to the array of vice and ignorance that surrounds them, while cryptic challenges to the apparent pattern ('One name was Elizabeth, / Th'other let it sleep with death' in 'Epitaph on Elizabeth, L.H.', 124) undermine any assumption that this is a simple 'key' to the volume.

There is, in fact, no such 'key', except possibly the recognition that, like the plays, Jonson's *Epigrams* are written with a certain kind of reader in mind: the true 'understander'. The terms of the understanding may be different in this instance, but the essential principle remains the same, and we have the advantage here that Jonson actually nominated an ideal reader for his poems and defined some of the qualities he possessed. Jonson dedicated his *Epigrams*, 'the ripest of my studies' (Dedication, line 4), to 'the Great Example of Honour and Virtue, the Most Noble William, Earl of Pembroke, L[ord] Chamberlain, etc.'. In an age when it was a matter of course to dedicate works of literature to aristocrats in the hope of attracting patronage, William Herbert, third Earl of Pembroke, stands out as a man whose taste was genuinely respected; his mansion at Wilton was known as 'an academy, as well as palace . . . an apiary, to which men that were excellent in arms, in arts, did resort, and were carress'd'.[7] He and his brother Philip, Earl of Montgomery, were both sons of Mary, Countess of Pembroke, the sister for whom Sir Philip Sidney wrote his

Arcadia, and they did their best to keep the Sidney tradition alive; they are best remembered as 'The Most Noble and Incomparable Pair of Brethren' to whom the Shakespeare First Folio was dedicated – when, of course, Shakespeare himself was beyond need of patronage, so that we may take the dedication as a real mark of respect from those of Shakespeare's fellow-actors who compiled the folio. Pembroke is one of the few male aristocrats mentioned by Jonson to Drummond who was not also calumniated in some way;[8] we hear of the regular New Year's gifts to buy books, and also this revealing anecdote: 'Pembroke and his lady discoursing the Earl said the women were men's shadows, and she maintained them; both appealing to Jonson, he affirmed it true, for which my lady gave a penance to prove it in verse; hence his epigram' (364–7).[9] This suggests a man (and a wife) of wit and some scholarship, a sense of humour, and on easy terms with Jonson. *Epigrams* was not the only work Jonson dedicated to him; he was similarly honoured in respect of *Catiline*, which Jonson bravely published in the face of its abject failure on the public stage:

> In so thick and dark an ignorance, as now almost covers the age, I crave leave to stand near your light, and by that to be read . . . you dare, in these jig-given times, to countenance a legitimate *poem*. I call it so, against all the noise of opinion; from whose crude and airy reports, I appeal to the great and singular faculty of judgement in your lordship, able to vindicate truth from error.

(Dedication, 1–10)

What Jonson respects and appeals to in Pembroke is his independent judgement, his refusal to be swayed by fashion and public opinion; he spells out in detail what this means when he goes on to address the 'Reader in Ordinary'.[10] He admonishes this reprobate creature: 'The commendation of good things may fall within a many, the approbation but in a few; for the most commend out of affection, self-tickling, an easiness or imitation: but men judge only out of knowledge. That is the trying faculty' (14–18). Knowledge in this sense is not simply an accumulation of facts or information: it is an active and prescriptive virtue, incorporating discrimination and judgement, individual discretion, based largely on a capacity to compare and contrast materials. This is the sense that gives the real edge, for example, to the closing line of 'To Mere English Censurer' (18): 'Thy faith is all the knowledge that thou hast', just as it clinches the compliment to Sir Henry Goodyere (86): 'It was a knowledge that begat that love.' Knowledge, 'the trying faculty', is what the *Epigrams* ask of those 'rare friends' Jonson speaks of (and singularly finds in Pembroke), for without it they will never really live.

This concept of knowledge, of independent discrimination, forms the underlying conceit in the epigram (102) which Jonson addressed individually to Pembroke; it is a good place to begin our consideration of the poems themselves:

> I do but name thee Pembroke, and I find
>> It is an epigram, on all mankind;
> Against the bad, but of, and to the good:
>> Both which are ask'd, to have thee understood.
> Nor could the age have miss'd thee, in this strife
>> Of vice, and virtue; wherein all great life
> Almost, is exercis'd: and scarce one knows,
>> To which, yet, of the sides himself he owes.
> They follow virtue, for reward, to day;
>> To morrow vice, if she give better pay:
> And are so good, and bad, just at a price,
>> As nothing else discerns the virtue or vice.
> But thou, whose noblesse keeps one stature still,
>> And one true posture, though besieg'd with ill
> Of what ambition, faction, pride can raise;
>> Whose life, ev'n they, that envy it, must praise;
> That art so reverenc'd, as thy coming in,
>> But in the view, doth interrupt their sin;
> Thou must draw more: and they, that hope to see
>> The common-wealth still safe, must study thee.

Where, in the various inductions and dedications, Jonson praises the concept of 'knowledge' in respect of literary judgement, this poem makes clear that it is a much more fundamental and important quality than that: it is the faculty by which the good man distinguishes vice from virtue in the private sphere, and the good citizen distinguishes them in the public. Jonson's praise of Pembroke hangs on his being a bedrock of 'knowledge' in both contexts, wittily turning the concept of understanding (in effect, the positive application of 'knowledge') on its head: the true 'understander' is, of course, 'Against the bad, but of, and to the good', but where we might expect this to lead to a compliment to his understanding, we find it simply inverted into a definition of himself: 'Both which are ask'd, to have thee understood.' The battle between virtue and vice actually defines Pembroke since he is the one fixed point in a confused and confusing world; others change sides for their own profit, or are moved by 'ambition, faction, pride', but Pembroke 'keeps one stature still, / And one true posture'. It is this singleness which makes him an object of 'study' and turns his whole being into 'an epigram, on all mankind'; he embodies all the qualities which Jonson seeks to inspire through his poetry.

A characteristic manifestation of the appeal to 'knowledge', focused here in the purpose of Pembroke, is the prominence that Jonson accords to stating *negative* principles, coupled with recurrent examples of *comparative* judgements rather than absolute ones. Two of the best examples of this occur in famous poems not among the *Epigrams*; Jonson's elegy to Shakespeare (*Ungathered Verse* 26) begins;

> To draw no envy (Shakespeare) on thy name,
>   Am I thus ample to thy book, and fame . . .

and continues unremittingly in the negative for sixteen lines before turning triumphantly ('I, therefore will begin. Soul of the age . . .') to Shakespeare's positive acheivements. Similarly, 'To Penshurst' (*The Forest* 2) opens:

> Thou art not, Penshurst, built to envious show,
>   Of touch, or marble; nor canst boast a row
> Of polish'd pillars, or a roof of gold:
>   Thou hast no lantern, whereof tales are told;
> Or stair, or courts; but stand'st an ancient pile,
>   And these grudg'd at, art reverenc'd the while.
> Thou joy'st in better marks . . .

This is partly, of course, a matter of verbal shading, darkness to emphasise the light that follows, but the bluntness and prominence of it point to the fact that it goes deeper than this; Jonson is insisting on an uncompromising principle of comparison, an assertion that there are truth and untruth, good standards and bad – and that the reader must 'know' the difference. This principle is adduced, furthermore, in such a way as to suggest that it applies not only to the subject-matter of the poems, to what they have to say, but also to the style and quality of the poems themselves: flanking the need to discriminate on the issues is a need to discriminate on their expression, the two operations of 'understanding' reinforcing each other as Jonson had suggested in the case of Pembroke. As J. G. Nichols comments on the poem to Sir Henry Goodyere (86 – a poem all about choices and 'knowing'): 'it is as though he assumes Goodyere, or anyone else reading the poem, will not allow himself to be carried away by fulsome flattery but will weigh and judge the words used and their appropriateness. It is to emphasise this care and discrimination in his praise that Jonson so often uses comparatives when others might have used superlatives.'[11] So it is that 'To Penhurst' concludes with a return to the comparative mode: 'Now, Penshurst, they that will proportion thee / With other edifices' (lines 99–100). The term 'proportion' captures perfectly the sense of balanced estimate and perspective which is necessary for the judgement equally of poetry, architecture and social values; so the poem asks us (and the Sidney family whose house it is) to weigh itself even as it speaks of weighing the building and the quality of life it contains. Jonson's praise of the household is not complete in effect (it has not established its credentials) until the reader has fully appreciated the discrimination of the poem which he has rendered in its honour. The poem is only a shadow of its full potential until it is read knowledgeably.

Clearly Nichols (and a good many other people) are uncomfortable about whether anyone will read these poems of praise in this way. Is it not likely that Pembroke, Goodyere and the Sidneys will simply lap up the flattery and ignore these sophisticated dimensions? This might be less of a worry if we could always be sure – as I think we can be in the case of Pembroke – that Jonson's praise was always sincere and unforced. But the sheer quantity of his eulogistic verse must raise doubts about the number of paragons alive in Jacobean England, while a number of comments recorded by Drummond might seem to belie the praises published in the poetry. For example, we find him saying of the dramatist, Francis Beaumont – celebrated in epigram 55 – that he 'loved too much himself and his own verses' (*Conversations*, 154). Similarly, the measured praise of 'To Sir Robert Wroth' (*The Forest* 3) sits oddly alongside the assertion that 'My Lord Lisle's daughter my Lady Wroth is unworthily married on a jealous husband' (*Conversations*, 355–6), while the three epigrams to the Earl of Salisbury (43, 63, 64) do not square very well with the sour reflection that 'Salisbury never cared for any man longer nor he could make use of him' (*Conversations*, 353–4).

I have already pointed out (p. 17) that we need to be wary of taking any opinions recorded in Drummond too seriously, and it is possible of course that Jonson's opinion of individuals changed between his writing of the poems (which is often impossible to date) and his visit to Scotland; but there were only two to three years between the *publication* of the poems in the folio and those conversations in the winter of 1618/19, which makes the charge of hypocrisy hard to rebut. Jonson has only one defence against that charge; he expounds it most fully in 'To My Muse' (*Epigrams* 65). In this poem Jonson berates his muse for betraying him to a 'worthless lord', who does not deserve the praises that he has lavished on him in his verse; the self-reproach comes to a sudden halt, however:

> But I repent me: stay. Whoe'er is rais'd
> For worth he has not, he is tax'd, not prais'd. (15–16)

This derives from the Renaissance doctrine which holds that a prime function of eulogistic verse is *laudando praecipere*, to lead or instruct by praising.[12] The poet's duty, it is held, is not to tell the literal truth about his patron so much as the ideal truth: the truth as it *should* be for a man born or raised to power and prestige, and described as attractively as possible so as to inspire the patron to achieve the ideal and become a proper model for less fortunate men to follow. This is the role of the poet as described by Sir Philip Sidney, who argued that the poet's pre-eminence lay in his ability to guide men to their better selves: 'For he doth not only show the way, but giveth so sweet a prospect into the way, as will entice any man to enter into it.'[13] In depicting the ideal, then, Jonson encourages virtue, but he is not strictly accountable for asserting that it exists in a particular instance. The onus is basically on the dedicatee of the poem to *deserve* its praises, and on all readers of the poem who are able to compare the ideal with the actual: the injunction to 'understand' is ever-present. It is a slippery doctrine, and doubtless open to abuse, but there is no evidence that Jonson did abuse it; it is inherent in his whole approach that if readers do not approach his poems 'knowledgeably', but see his poems of praise as flattery or his satires as personal lampoons, then it is their own fault and not his – due warning is given in the negatives and comparatives, the sheer discrimination with which he qualifies his comments. Behind all this lies an attitude to language itself, an assumption that it is a precision instrument, a divine gift, and to be respected as such by both parties in its interchange. Jonson has little patience for those who cannot or will not appreciate this; it is here, rather than in his supposed flattery of the aristocracy, that his real elitism lies.

There is no single poem in the *Epigrams* which so graphically demonstrates the 'comparative principle' underlying Jonson's injunction to 'understand' as does 'To Penshurst'. Nevertheless, when we examine that collection carefully, it does not take long to see that the principle *is* there, albeit manifested primarily in the arrangement – one might almost say orchestration – of the poems rather than within individual pieces.[14] We may begin to demonstrate this with a consideration of a poem which is justly famous in its own right, but which takes on further dimensions when studied in context, 'On My First Son' (45):

Farewell, thou child of my right hand, and joy;
  My sin was too much hope of thee, lov'd boy,
Seven years tho'wert lent me, and I thee pay,
  Exacted by thy fate, on the just day.
O, could I lose all father, now. For why
  Will man lament the state he should envy?
To have so soon scap'd world's, and flesh's rage,
  And, if no other misery, yet age?
Rest in soft peace, and, ask'd, say here doth lie
  Ben. Jonson his best piece of poetry.
For whose sake, hence-forth, all his vows be such,
  As what he loves may never like too much.

The apparent simplicity of the poem conveys a sense of self-restraint in the face of overwhelming emotion (see p. 7, above). Simple as the diction is, however, it is not without artifice: 'child of my right hand' is a complex pun on the child's name; he, like his father, was a Benjamin, which in Hebrew means 'fortunate' or 'dextrous' – the latter term deriving from the Latin for 'right-handed'. This in turn links up with the English associations of being on the right hand – an indispensable helper or aid, and in the position of honour. All this adds to the sense of the specialness of the child, which in turn accounts for the irrational but perfectly natural sense of guilt Jonson feels – 'my sin' – as if his own fondness had been the cause of the boy's death. He tries to counter this by picturing the brief life and premature death as a business transaction, in which he himself was a passive and unwilling agent ('lent', 'exacted'), and all his anguish is compressed into the word 'just' – ostensibly in the sense of precise or exact, and so echoing 'exacted', but inevitably invoking the question of fairness and justice. For Jonson, the day has been anything but just, and his impulse is to renounce all fatherhood; but this prompts him to recognise that the boy's death is not without its compensations – indeed, it is almost enviable, in that it has freed him from the miseries of life and old age, including the very misery of distraught fatherhood which Jonson himself now feels. This realisation frees Jonson from both guilt and sorrow, so that he is able to voice a proper valediction over the buried child, who is his 'best piece of poetry' (punning heroically on the fact that both poets and fathers are 'makers'). The poem is not complete, however, without the lesson Jonson tries to derive from the experience; he may have overcome the pain and guilt of this loss, but he makes a desperate resolution never to make such an emotional investment again. Significantly, he shifts from talking about himself in the first person to the third in this final couplet, as if the conclusion is too overwhelming to face directly, too absolute when the experience that gave rise to it still lingers. To talk, therefore, of the 'simplicity' of this poem is to risk undervaluing its subtlety; its brevity befits the boy's short life (there is a decorum even in this) but within its short measure Jonson charts a sophisticated process of thought and emotional development as psychologically accurate as it is consoling. At the same time, he is not afraid to rack the English language in order to register complex, multi-faceted responses ('child of my right hand', 'just', 'poetry'); like Donne, Jonson is aware of the exciting malleability of language, but unlike Donne he will only use it to underpin a structure which is otherwise secure. He is not in the business of erecting glittering but unsound edifices.

It may occasion some surprise that this deeply moving poem should appear, apparently at random, in the midst of a collection which is dominated on the one hand by elegant compliments to the aristocracy and to fellow artists, and on the other by satirical squibs on the foolish or vicious. Indeed, 'On My First Son' follows immediately after 'On Chuff, Banks the Usurer's Kinsman' (44) and immediately before 'To Sir Luckless Woo-All' (46). The former is a grimly ironic reflection on the pursuit of wealth and the latter a more light-hearted mockery of a man who purchases a knighthood but still fails to attract a wife. On closer examination, however, the collocation is not so inept as it may seem at first: Chuff sees 'all his race approach the blacker floods' while he himself is still obsessed with wealth and has not thought about his own death (ironically evoked in terms of its financial implications: 'ere blacks were bought for his own funeral'); Sir Luckless is perversely misguided in thinking that some bought 'honour' will win him a wife when his own personality will not – misguided, perhaps, as much in his view of what the real value of marriage is as in his estimated chances of success. All three poems thus share a concern about the quality and purpose of life, focused with greater or lesser irony on the theme of buying and payment and so evoking the fundamental questions of value and cost – not only financial, but also spiritual and human. All three discuss the idea of the family in these terms, and the kinds of commitment it entails. It seems unlikely that the three poems were initially conceived of as a unit, but that is not the point; in the arrangement in which Jonson publishes them, they take on a unity which adds additional dimensions to their individual features. They comprise a continuing dialogue, one sparking off the others or placing them in perspective. It seems important to Jonson that his 'personal' reaction to the death of his son should *not* be divorced from his 'public' satires. Ultimately they share the same concerns, if we read them 'knowledgeably'.

Even from this brief example, it should be obvious that there is no simple formula that we may apply to make sense of the arrangement of the *Epigrams*; it is rather a matter of broadening our perceptions and of being prepared to make connections where none might conventionally be expected. We can only begin to appreciate the teasing subtlety this can entail by examining a reasonably long run of the peoms, since effects are by no means confined to immediate juxtapositions. (May I hope that the reader will have a copy of *Epigrams* open at this point?) Epigrams 52 to 56 seem to offer a reasonably coherent grouping: 'To Censorious Courtling', 'To Old-End Gatherer', 'On Cheveril', 'To Francis Beaumont' and 'On Poet-Ape'. One scenario for this run of poems suggests that the point is how the unnamed or pseudonymous characters 'retreat before the great name of Francis Beaumont (55) who is contrasted, too, with Poet-Ape, the conceited poetaster'.[15] This is unexceptionable in outline, but underplays Jonson's subtlety and range. The poems are all linked in being about writing and the appreciation of writing: Courtling tries to hide his lack of judgement by praising Jonson, but only frostily; Old-End Gatherer is a pathetic plagiarist who gives himself away by dedicating his stolen work to himself, rather than actually claiming authorship; Cheveril (whose name means 'pliable leather') accuses Jonson's verses of being 'libels'; Poet-Ape is a preposterous poetaster, trying to forge a reputation by cobbling up ideas stolen from other people's works, and hoping it will not be noticed that they are not all of a piece. Clearly Beaumont, whom Jonson praises, is located here as a riposte to the spurious writing, bad judgement and false esteem all around. The fact that the poem takes the form of a reply to a flattering verse-letter from Beaumont to Jonson[16] lends weight to the latter's scorn of those who misunderstand or misinterpret his writing, and also those who look for reputation by spurious means. This small sequence is thus more than the sum of its parts: it is a continuing debate on the nature of literary fame and reputation. Let us examine the poem to Beaumont in detail and establish the precise terms of the debate:

> How I do love thee Beaumont, and thy muse,
>   That unto me dost such religion use!
> How I do fear myself that am not worth
>   The least indulgent thought thy pen drops forth!
> At once thou mak'st me happy, and unmak'st;

> And giving largely to me, more thou tak'st.
> What fate is mine, that so itself bereaves?
>   What art is thine, that so thy friend deceives?
> When even there, where most thou praisest me,
>   For writing better, I must envy thee.

How are we to take the 'religion' that Beaumont uses to Jonson, which makes him 'fear myself', or 'the least indulgent thought thy pen drops forth'? Is the tone just a little too arch for comfort? Might we compare this with the adulation of 'The Vision of Ben Jonson, on the Muses of his Friend Mr. Drayton' (*Ungathered Verse* 30), which is so heavy as to have been thought positively satirical?[17] Is the older Jonson gently accusing Beaumont of being uncritically fulsome ('thy pen drops forth'), even possibly a little condescending? When he asks, 'What art is thine, that so thy friend deceives?' are we still in the realms of witty, paradoxical compliment, or have things taken on a more critical edge? The key to the poem, as so often in Jonson, is in the closing couplet, where the crucial phrase 'For writing better' is placed with masterly ambiguity, in such a way that it refers both to Beaumont and to Jonson himself: 'thou praisest me, / For writing better'; 'For writing better, I must envy thee.' It is particularly tempting, given Jonson's jaundiced comment to Drummond about Beaumont loving 'too much himself and his own verses', to construe this as sly satire, the old master coolly putting young Beaumont in his place even while seeming to compliment him; but it does not have to be as devious as that. The mutual compliments between the two writers naturally begs the question of which of them is in fact the better poet. If Beaumont really is the 'knowing' friend that Jonson claims, he will appreciate that Ben is measuring the shrewd plain style of the epigram against Beaumont's own, more florid verse. Jonson remains within the bounds of friendship, even of compliment, but it is an adult friendship which does not scruple to mention reservations, with the kinds of doubts about styles and standards which equals, perhaps, ought to share. Jonson certainly claims (epigram 96) that he expects such rigour himself when he sends his epigrams to John Donne for comment. The great Beaumont, in short, is no more exempt from critical scrutiny than Poet-Ape, or indeed than Jonson himself; compliments must not be given lightly, even for friendship's or reputation's sake. This poem in fact confirms what has been emerging from the sequence of the *Epigrams* as a whole: that it is not simply a question of the good dispelling the bad, or of the named repudiating the unnamed, but of a need for constant scrutiny, constant standards, for what Jonson calls knowledge.

If Jonson seems to concentrate heavily in the *Epigrams* on poetry and the appreciation of poetry, it is because he is ultimately concerned to define and defend his own status as a poet – not only in this immediate collection, but in the folio as a whole, of which in this sense it is very much the heart. In his *Discoveries*, Jonson offers the traditional definition of the poet:

A poet is that, which by the Greeks is call'd . . . a maker, or a feigner: his art, an art of imitation, or feigning; expressing the life of man in fit measure, numbers and harmony. . . . Hence, he is call'd a poet, not he which writeth in measure only; but that feigneth and formeth a fable, and writes things like the truth. (2347–54)

It is in this sense that Jonson presents his plays and masques as 'poems' – even those, like *Epicoene*, written mainly in prose. When he writes in the Prologue to *Volpone*:

> In all his *poems*, still, hath been this measure,
> To mix profit, with your pleasure.   (7–8)

the claim stands for *all* his creative writing or, more precisely, for all those works fit to be preserved in the 1616 folio. For the skill of writing 'things like the truth' is neither a matter of luck nor of mere mechanical craft; it is for Jonson the art of obeying the laws of nature – that is what gives it meaning and significance. We may infer that, at least in retrospect, some of his own works did not measure up to that standard of art. The laws of nature are the eternal verities about man and the world; personalities, civilisations, styles of writing come and go, but certain essential principles of human behaviour and communication persist forever. The art of the poet – an art of discrimination, of understanding – is to identify those essential principles, and to build his writing upon them. This explains Jonson's attitude to the Greek and Roman classics, the works which have most fully demonstrated how the laws of nature may be observed; but the classics have not exhausted the observation of nature – no one could – so when Jonson borrows from them, he does so without slavish imitation and without being bound by their precedents:

I know nothing can conduce more to letters, than to examine the writings of the ancients, and not to rest in their sole authority, or take all upon trust from them. . . . For to all the observations of the ancients, we have our own experience: which, if we will use, and apply, we have better means to pronounce. It is true they open'd the gates, and made the way, that went before us; but as guides, not commanders.   (*Discoveries*, 129–39)

Perhaps some of Jonson's early works did not measure up to this image of the poet following in the footsteps of the ancients; but, he insists, all those in the 1616 folio certainly do.

Hence the repeated attacks in the *Epigrams* on the likes of Poet-Ape, Old-End Gatherer, Prowl the Plagiary (81) and most particularly on Playwright (49, 68, 100); 'playwright' is always for Jonson a term of abuse, implying a hack-dramatist rather than a true artist. All these characters – ignorant alike of art, nature and the example of the classics – represent the antithesis of the artful poet which it is Jonson's claim to be; critics like My Mere English Censurer (18) and Groom Idiot (58) similarly fail to understand the essential laws and principles upon which poetry is based. Even such satires as 'On the New Motion' (97), 'On the Town's Honest Man' (115) and 'To Mime' (129) seem ultimately to relate to Jonson's claims about his own artistic status, although on the surface they have nothing to do with poetry. It is generally agreed that they are all covert attacks on Inigo Jones,[18] Jonson's principal collaborator on the Court masques, and the emphasis of the satire seems mainly personal: Jones is characterised as proud but coarse, sociable but hypocritical, trying to be witty but actually a buffoon. This is, however, related to the artistic differences between Jones and Jonson; the former is linked with 'motions', or puppet-plays, and dismissed sarcastically as an 'architect' and 'engineer'. His art is one of a spectacular mechanised stage which reduces the actors effectively to puppets and minimises the poet's 'invention' – for Jonson, the heart of the masque; visual trickery, he implies, is a distraction from the masques' truly creative and imaginative elements – from their 'poetry'. These are all arguments which Jonson was to expound much more fully after his final altercation with Jones in 1631, in 'An Expostulation with Inigo Jones' (*Ungathered Verse* 34):

> O shows! shows! mighty shows!
> The eloquence of masques! What need of prose,
> Or verse, or sense t' express immortal you? (39–41)

On the more positive side, Jonson defends his claim to be a poet by his association with artists whom he genuinely admires – the poets Donne (*Epigrams* 22, 96) and, for all his reservations, Beaumont; the composer, Alphonso Ferrabosco (130, 131); the translators, Clement Edmonds (110, 111) and Joshua Sylvester (132) – translation being a true adjunct of understanding, and not merely a mechanical exercise. The association is not only with the artists themselves but also with those who have the discernment and generosity to patronise them – notably Pembroke and Lucy, Countess of Bedford (76, 84, 94). Not infrequently, the same names occur in the *Epigrams* as Jonson prefixes to his plays, in the dedications. Epigram 14, for example, salutes William Camden, his old master at Westminster School, to whom he dedicated the folio *Every Man In His Humour*; here Jonson acknowledges that he owes him 'All that I am in arts, all that I know.' We also find poems addressed to Esme, Lord Aubigny (128, the dedicatee of *Sejanus*), Mary, Lady Wroth (103, 105; *The Alchemist*) and, as noted before, the Earl of Pembroke (102; *Catiline*). This helps to give weight to Jonson's claim that his plays are just as much 'poems' as these epigrams, sharing the same 'rare friends' and patrons; the covert attacks on Inigo Jones may be said to imply similar claims about the masques. We also find satirical attacks on Fine Lady Would-be (62) and Captain Surly (28, 82), names that we also meet in *Volpone* and *The Alchemist*. Such cross-references between the *Epigrams* and the rest of the folio inevitably contribute to a steady sense, which Jonson clearly intends, of the poems, plays and masques all inhabiting the same world, being written for the same audience and by the same poet.

It would be easy to construe this emphasis on his own status as a poet as pretentiousness on Jonson's part – the crowing of the former bricklayer and 'playwright' who now mixes with the highest in the land. Or, if not that, the recurrent emphasis on poetry as a theme may at least seem like an inward-looking preoccupation, a mark of self-absorption. Against this, it is important to bear in mind how literally Jonson takes poetry to be a 'thing like the truth', so that an understanding of poetry amounts to an understanding of the world in all its essentials. When he chooses to compliment Pembroke by calling him an 'epigram' or his own son 'his best piece of poetry', Jonson is attesting to poetry's fitness as a metaphor for life itself: a good man is a great poem, a model for us to study and understand. A true poem, conversely, may help us to be better understanders, and so better people. It is no accident that Jonson opens the first of his epigrams to King James (4):

> How, best of kings, do'st thou a sceptre bear!
> How, best of poets, do'st thou laurel wear!

Of course this is the hyperbole of a poet who hopes to teach by praising, but it also establishes an essential principle: that ruling and writing go together, that poetry is not an ivory-tower occupation, but belongs openly at the centre of society.

So it is that, in the *Epigrams* as a whole, we cannot artificially divorce the theme of poetry from the wider concerns of the collection. If, for example, we return to the group of poems (52–6) that we isolated earlier in order to concentrate on this theme, we can quickly see how arbitrary and restrictive our selection was. We should notice, for one thing, that there is another poem (72) addressed to Courtling and another one 'On Cheveril the Lawyer' (37) besides those in our small sequence; the invitation to cross-reference the poems and their contexts seems unmistakable, though these other poems are not themselves concerned with poetry. Interesting possibilities also open up if we begin our group of poems earlier, or end it later. The poem immediately before those we considered is apparently not related to them in any way: 'To King James, Upon the Happy False Rumour of His Death, the Two and Twentieth Day of March, 1607' (51). This would seem to have nothing to do with literary judgement or reputation at all (unless we allow for echoes of the earlier 'best of poets' accolade); yet it has, since what Jonson celebrates here is not the King's survival of a real danger, but his 'scape from rumour'. Rumour, public opinion, false esteem are all heads of the same Hydra – licentious tittle-tattle – which is the very antithesis of true 'knowing' and as dangerous in the world of public affairs as it is in the world of letters. Matters of art and matters of state may thus be intimately connected: King James is, after all, head of the Court which contains Censorious Courtling, just as he is the fountain of the law which gives employment to the 'pliable' lawyer, Cheveril. It may not be coincidental that Cheveril's previous appearance in the *Epigrams* was also only one place removed from the previous address 'To King James' (35) – the poem which separated them there being 'To the Ghost of Martial' (36), in which Jonson compares himself with the progenitor of the epigram, the Roman poet, Martial: the telling trio of King, poet and misrepresentation thus occurs again.[19] If we extend our original group of poems at the other end, to include *Epigrams* 57–65, we find an even more thought-provoking collocation of false literary taste and political reputations – the literary tastes of Groom Idiot (58) and Fool, or Knave (61) alongside the reputations of William, Lord Mounteagle (60) and Robert, Earl of Salisbury (63, 64); I shall consider these poems in chapter 6, suggesting that Jonson hides behind this take-it-or-leave-it technique of allowing inferences to be drawn (or not) from the arrangement of the poems, in order to make a remarkably daring attack on these two men.

The possible range of telling juxtapositions and cross-references, both within the *Epigrams* and out from them to embrace the rest of the 1616 folio, is virtually endless – in itself, both a weakness and a strength. It encourages the reader to keep looking, but never gives him the satisfaction of feeling that he has reached a definitive conclusion. Yet this method of oblique hints and tacit questions is exactly what we should expect of a poet who appeals explicitly to the 'trying faculty' of his readers – an appeal he implicitly reiterates every time he attacks those who misread or misapply his works. There is nothing really surprising about the cryptic and cumulative nature of the *Epigrams* as I have described them, belonging as they do to an age which produced the kaleidoscopic allegory of *The Fairie Queene* or the 'dark conceit' of Chapman's *School of Night* or Donne at his most baffling ('Donne said to him he wrote that epitaph on Prince Henry, "Look to me, faith", to match Sir Ed. Herbert in obscureness', *Conversations*, 125–7) – nothing surprising except that they should have come from a poet we have become used to thinking of, rather complacently, as plain and straightforward.

4·

The masques and *Epicoene*

The whole face of the scene alter'd; scarce suff'ring the memory of any such thing.

(The Masque of Queens, 357–9)

The masque came to England in the reign of Henry VIII when, on Twelfth Night 1512,

the King with eleven other were disguised, after the manner of Italy, called a mask, a thing not seen afore in England, they were all apparelled in garments long and broad, wrought all with gold, with vizors and caps of gold, and after the banquet done, these maskers came in, with six gentlemen disguised in silk bearing staff torches, and desired the ladies to dance, some were content, and some that knew the fashion of it refused, because it was not a thing commonly seen. And after they danced and commoned together, as the fashion of the mask is, they took their leave and departed, and so did the Queen and all the ladies.[1]

After a lengthy evolution from medieval mummings, disguisings and other entertainments, the Court masque (to use the spelling standardised by Jonson) had come to England from Italy, in what was essentially the form it was to retain until the Civil War all but put an end to the tradition. Masked and disguised persons come, with at least a pretence of being unexpected, into a great hall to pay compliments to the hosts at some festive occasion, and perhaps to their principal guests; they may also bring gifts; they are accompanied by torch-bearers and musicians, who provide light and music for the essential activity of dancing; the whole performance lends itself to elaboration of a dramatic kind by singers and presenters, and to visual splendour both in the costumes and in the staging; but this tendency towards 'theatre' is kept in check both by the fact that the masquers are aristocrats who, however disguised, may not act essentially out of character (indeed they will not strictly act at all; professional entertainers will normally do the speaking and singing) and by the crucial importance of the moment when the guests/spectators will be invited to dance by the masquers: this is the revels, the climax of every masque, when spectators and performers mingle in the symbolic unity and harmony of the dance, acknowledging their social equality and the essentially amateur nature of a 'show' which is not a self-contained event, but part of a more general entertainment (the banquet, for example, remained obligatory, no matter how elaborate the spectacle of the masque).

Jonson had demonstrated in *Cynthia's Revels* that he understood the essentials of the form, but it was the advent of King James which gave him the opportunity to prove himself its master. As a young man with literary pretensions in the best Renaissance style the King himself had written a masque, while his wife, Queen Anne, was passionately devoted to revelry and theatricals; from the start they were prepared to spend quite freely (as the more prudent Queen Elizabeth had not been) and to employ professional poets, musicians, actors and stage-designers to create the most impressive events imaginable. To a later more democratic age this may seem merely extravagant self-indulgence, but most Renaissance monarchs regarded lavish Court entertainment as a necessary reflection of their dignity, magnificence and liberality. To James in particular they were a way of projecting himself to his fellow European monarchs as a sufficiently imposing King of a newly reunited Britain, after his more straitened circumstances as King of Scotland only; the diplomatic significance of the masques is attested by the endless bickerings of foreign ambassadors about their rights of precedence at these events, which more than once caused a performance to be postponed. Although the diplomatic function might encourage a spirit of self-aggrandisement in the Court, it helped to ensure that these entertainments were never purely frivolous, and Jonson brought to them the seriousness and professional concern which characterise all those writings he later wished to preserve.

This is most fully demonstrated in his Foreward to *Hymenaei* (1606):

It is a noble and just advantage, that the things subjected to understanding have of those which are objected to sense, that the one sort are but momentary, and merely taking; the other impressing, and lasting: else the glory of all these solemnities had perish'd like a blaze, and gone out, in the beholders' eyes. So short-liv'd are the bodies of all things, in comparison of their souls. And, though bodies oft-times have the ill-luck to be sensually preferr'd, they find afterwards, the good fortune (when souls live) to be utterly forgotten. This it is hath made the most royal Princes, and greatest persons (who are commonly the personators of these actions) not only studious of riches, and magnificence in the outward celebration, or show; (which rightly becomes them) but curious after the most high, and hearty *inventions*, to furnish the inward parts: (and those grounded upon antiquity, and solid learnings) which, though their voice be taught to sound to present occasions, their sense, or doth, or should always lay hold on more remov'd mysteries. And, howsoever some may squeamishly cry out, that all endeavour of learning, and sharpness in these transitory devices especially, where it steps beyond their little, or (let me not wrong'hem) no brain at all, is superfluous; I am contented, these fastidious stomachs should leave my full tables, and enjoy at home, their clean empty trenchers, fittest for such airy tastes: where perhaps a few Italian herbs, picked up, and made into a salad, may find sweeter acceptance, than all, the most nourishing, and sound meats of the world.

(Foreword, 1–28)

This is worth quoting in full not only because it demonstrates Jonson's conviction (in only his second masque for the Court) that the masque both could and should be a significant art form, but also because it shows how close his thinking on the masque was to his ideas about other forms of literature and drama: the insistence upon 'matter'; the distinction between the 'body' and the 'soul' of the work; the appeal to 'understanding' rather than mere 'sense'; the preference for 'antiquity, and solid learnings'; the idea that a work devised for a particular occasion might have a lingering universal significance (and hence warranted publication, however inadequately the text reflected the performance); the provocative conviction that it is his opponents' fault, and not his own, if they fail to appreciate his 'nourishing, and sound meats'. It might stand as a preface not only to this masque, but to Jonson's work as a whole.[2]

The essence of Jonson's argument is that masques, like all other 'poems', 'ought always to carry a mixture of profit, with them, no less than delight' (*Love's Triumph Through Callipolis*, 6–7). These splendid but evanescent entertainments were perhaps the most extreme testing of the theory of *laudando praecipere* (see p. 83, above), of teaching through praise, since what they offered to the Court was a flattering, idealised image of itself; few works of poetry have ever borne out so literally Sidney's dictum that the poet 'doth not only show the way, but giveth so sweet a prospect into the way, as will entice any man to enter into it'. It was this conviction that justified the lavish scenic and musical effects that were inseparable from the masques, since their purpose was expressly to snatch men out of the ordinary, mundane world, to put them in a state of what the age called 'admiration' or wonder, in which (the hope was) they might 'profit' from the 'remov'd mysteries' which bear so crucially on everyday human conduct. Most readers will be familiar with this idea from the experience of Ferdinand in *The Tempest*, the play of Shakespeare's which draws most heavily on the masque and its conventions; he is completely disorientated by the loss of his father and friends, and by Ariel's strange music, so that when he first sees 'admired Miranda', he takes her for 'the goddess / On whom these airs attend!' (I. ii. 422–3). He never completely understands Prospero's powers and actions, but he surrenders to them willingly and so gains Miranda's hand in marriage; the miracle inherent in that union is foreshadowed in the masque of spirits, of which Ferdinand says, 'This is a most majestic vision, and / Harmonious charmingly', praising 'So rare a wond'red father and a wise' (IV. i. 118–19; 123). In his prolonged state of 'admiration', he both learns something of the 'remov'd mysteries' of life and proves himself a worthy heir of Naples and of Milan. It is, of course, open to doubt whether the average Jacobean courtier would respond with such proper humility to these flattering spectacles.

As in the plays and poems, we may see the development of Jonson's masques in terms of continual refinements of tactics, constantly challenging the spectators and attempting to involve them in the educative process. This is most clearly seen in Jonson's most important contribution to the form of the masque, the antimasque; some comic by-play as a prelude to the solemnity of the masque proper was not unknown before Jonson's time, but he was the first to integrate the comedy with the main body of the entertainment as a 'foil, or false masque' to be repudiated by the masque proper. This is how he describes it in the foreword to *The Masque of Queens* (1609), where he gallantly credits Queen Anne with the concept. It is clear from their various spellings that other masque-writers either misunderstood or disapproved of Jonson's idea; Samuel Daniel always refers to the 'antemasque' simply as a preliminary diversion, while others call it an 'antic-' or 'antique-masque', stressing the element of grotesquery in the comedy. But Jonson consistently develops the antimasque as a significant piece of strategy, luring the spectators into an unbuttoned mood before unleashing on them the astonishments of the masque itself – which will, however, pick up themes which the antimasque has already spelled out in a different mode; such changes in context and perspective are a constant challenge to the understanding. One consequence of the increased importance of the antimasque was that the whole entertainment became something not merely spoken and sung, but in good measure acted, calling for the skills of professional actors in some roles to augment the aristocratic charms of the masquers proper. We know that the King's Men were employed for *Oberon* (1611), since they appropriate a 'dance of twelve satyrs' from it for performance in *The Winter's Tale*.[3] In the text of *Love*

Restored (1612), Jonson specifically acknowledges the assistance of 'Gentlemen, the King's Servants', something he also records of *The Irish Masque at Court* (1613/14), *The Golden Age Restored* (1615) and *Mercury Vindicated from the Alchemists at Court* (1616). Writers like Daniel objected to the fact that this breached the essential decorum of the masque's being something performed both *by* and *for* the Court – which may strictly have been true, but since the broad comedy of Jonson's antimasques pleased the principal spectator, King James, nobody paid very much attention. It has sometimes been argued that the antimasques were *simply* a sop to the King's low-brow tastes, but this is to overlook the artistry with which Jonson accommodated his great patron; the switch from one kind of play-acting to another, from bawdiness, satire or grotesquery to high seriousness (later to change again to the elegant formality and intricacy of the dance) underlines the need for alert judgement on the part of spectators – all the more so since they will themselves become participants in the 'mysteries' when the masquers descend to the revels.

The move from antimasque to masque is, metaphorically speaking, a change of perspective in an art form which came to depend increasingly on literal changes of perspective. To understand how and why this was so, we need to appreciate the contribution made to the masque by Jonson's frequent collaborator, Inigo Jones. Jones spent much of his early life in Italy, where he absorbed advanced neo-classical theories of stage-design at the same time as learning about the new Palladian style of architecture. He and Jonson first collaborated on the *Masque of Blackness* (1605) and worked together regularly and successfully thereafter, though it is clear that there were artistic and temperamental differences between the two men almost from the start (see pp. 20 and 89, above). The feature of Jones's early stagings which most struck contemporaries was his use of mechanical stage machines; these could be as simple as the pageant car which effected the floating island in *Blackness*, or more sophisticated like the moving racks which made 'waves' and 'clouds' big enough to carry masquers, or – most complex and awe-inspiring of all – the great *machina versatilis*, the turning machine, which was used to great effect, as for example in *Hymenaei*: there it turned a huge globe, to reveal the masquers sitting within it, the whole operation enhanced by artful lighting. There was no way to darken the candle-lit halls in which the masques were staged, but Jones had a number of devices to intensify the light on stage, including mirrors, magnifiers, lamps with coloured liquids (often made to look like sparkling jewels) and even light-reflecting costumes. With such resources these machines could obviously be most impressive, but they were limited in the number and range of effects they could produce, particularly in the number of 'transformations' they could achieve in one evening. Jones never abandoned their use, but from *Oberon* (1611) onwards he depended less upon them.

Before the *Masque of Blackness* it had been normal for masques to be presented with dispersed staging, scenes being enacted at various points about the hall; this allowed for a variety of scenery or properties but took up a good deal of room and cannot have made for very convenient seating arrangements. Jones changed all that; his masques were performed (with only minor exceptions) on a single stage, and the action was focused for the audience by some kind of framing at the front of the platform. In later masques this was certainly a full proscenium arch (its first use in Britain) though it is not clear how early this was introduced. On to this fixed stage, in addition to his machines, Jones brought scenery that exploited the effects of realistic perspective; and he developed this – possibly by the time of the *Masque of Queens*, certainly by that of *Oberon* – into the sophisticated *scena ductilis* or 'tractable scene'. This was essentially a series of painted flats set in grooves which could be drawn aside quickly and quietly into the wings to reveal a new setting behind them. Scenes could thus be changed as often and as quickly as the 'invention' required, the only limit being the number of grooves the stage could accommodate. This offered all the variety of dispersed staging, with none of its disadvantages. But it also offered something more; the illusion of perspective involves the spectators in a peculiar way in the action taking place on stage; their attention is drawn backwards and forwards in three-dimensional space against only the illusion of three dimensions on the flats, and so has to grapple with such arresting tricks as making the actors playing gods and goddesses seem disproportionately tall at the rear of the stage.

The whole stage, in effect, became a flexible machine capable of offering a dynamic three-dimensional interpretation of a poet's invention, and Jonson grasped the possibilities immediately. In *Oberon*, for example, the action of the masque is a movement from the 'first face of the scene' (a dark rock) to 'the frontispiece of a bright and glorious palace' and into the palace itself, where 'the nation of fays were discover'd'; then the movement is reversed as Oberon's chariot came 'as far forth as the face of the scene'; after which the masquers dance and eventually 'they danc'd their last dance, into the work . . . and the whole machine clos'd' (444–6). So the whole action flows from the mischievous antimasque world of the satyrs into the perspective and the marvellous world of the 'fays', out again for the triumphal appearance of Oberon (Prince Henry, who would first appear heroically tall) and finally in again for the conclusion, a fluid and unified piece of stage-craft. The movement from anti-masque to masque is totally integrated with the staging: the whole experience is, both literally and metaphorically, one of getting things into perspective and proportion; the spectators must come to terms with the illusions via their senses before they can comprehend their import on the higher level of understanding – just as they must adjust from bawdy and unruly satyrs (a stylised version of normal-ity) to the heroic seriousness of Oberon/Prince Henry and his fays. This is all underlined by a further consequence of the adoption of a single stage and the *sena ductilis*; perspective can only be completely true from a single vantage-point and it was absolutely necessary that this should be occupied by the King. James, unlike his Queen and children, never performed in the masques himself, but his presence as a tacit participator is always assumed by both Jonson and Jones. He occupies the crucial mid-point of judgement between the real world and the world of the masque – worlds which merge with the revels; he is both the one true observer and the one to whom lines of perspective relate, the complete focus of proceedings in a staging which is emblematically perfect.

This exploitation of sudden changes both of scene and perspective clearly has affinities with the striking *coups de théâtre* at high points in the best comedies: the revelation of Epicoene's true nature, the return of Lovewit in *The Alchemist*, the puppet's raising its garment in *Bartholomew Fair*. No scenic illusions were possible in the Jacobean public theatres, but all these moments exploit something like a scene-change – what we might call a double-take, when the audience has to assimilate new truths or re-assimilate old ones, with conse-quent changes of judgement and evaluation. A comparison between *Hymenaei* and *Epicoene* (two works essentially concerned with mar-riage) further establishes that, for all the differences of form, the masques and the plays have complementary roles in the career as Jonson preserved it in his folio. *Hymenaei* was a double masque of eight men and eight women, given to celebrate the marriage of Robert, Earl of Essex,[4] and Lady Frances Howard, second daughter of the Earl of Suffolk. It was of considerable political significance (which is why *Hymenaei* was allowed to supplant the Queen's own masque for the Christmas season), contrived to reconcile deep-seated enmities between the Devereux and Howard (and through

them Cecil) factions at Court: the bride and groom were barely
fourteen. The central theme of the masque, naturally enough, is
union; but such is the complexity of Jonson's 'invention' that the
union of man and woman, husband and wife, is seen in the widest
possible context: the union of King and country, England and Scotland, music and dancing, heaven and earth, all of which is mirrored
emblematically in Jones's use of the *machina versatilis* (this was before
the development of perspective machinery) and its 'microcosm, or
globe'.

The scene opens upon an altar which bears the inscription: 'Ioni.
Oimae. Mimae. Unioni. Sacr.' – 'mystically implying', as Jonson
glossed it, 'that both it, the place, and all the succeeding ceremonies
were sacred to marriage, or Union; over which Juno was president'
(40–2).[5] Juno, by a happy anagram, is Unio (union) the ruling spirit
of marriage, and it is appropriate that Queen Anne should play that
part. But she alone cannot represent the ideal of total union; she
must have her Jove. It is the union of James and Anne, happy and
fruitful, which is projected as a model of all the unions the masque
will celebrate. The sacred rites of marriage are scarcely begun,
however, when they are interrupted by figures representing four
humours and four affections:

as in natural bodies, so likewise in minds, there is no disease, or distem-
perature, but is caused either by some abounding humour, or perverse affection; after the same manner, in politic bodies . . . by the differences, or
predominant will of what we (metaphorically) call humours, and affections,
all things are troubled and confused. These, therefore, were tropically
brought in, before marriage, as disturbers of that mystical body, and the
rites, which were soul unto it; that afterwards, in marriage, being dutifully
tempered by her power, they might more fully celebrate the happiness of
such as live in that sweet union, to the harmonius laws of nature and reason.
(Part of note to line 112)

Humours and affections spring from the passions (see pp. 35–7,
above) which are not in themselves evil, but must be kept in check by
reason if they are not to cause discord. Thus Hymen, the god of
marriage, calls upon Reason to control her riotous subjects; she is
discovered, symbolically seated at the top of the globe ('as in the
brain, or highest part of man', 129–30) which dominates the stage, an
image of microcosmic and macrocosmic universes. Reason is not to
be confused with modern ideas of intelligence; it does not differ from
one individual to another but is the innate faculty which 'lodges in
our soul, tests and recognises all that pertains to our good'. She wears
a helmet crested with a flame because 'the flame shows that it is the

property of Reason to mount towards Heaven and seek to resemble God'.

Reason subdues the humours and affections but does not banish them; they are forced to recognise their proper places in the order which the masque invokes. Their challenge serves artistically to give strength and conviction to the order which is finally achieved. This was the principle on which Jonson was to build his more elaborate later antimasques. Union is finally celebrated in the traditional affirmation of harmony, the dance, which draws the whole society together in rhythm, order, pattern and balance. One of the dances specially devised for the masque by Master Thomas Giles ends with the participants, hands linked, arrayed in the shape of a chain; Reason draws the moral:

> Such was the golden chain let down from Heaven;
>   And not those links more even,
> Than these: so sweetly temper'd, so combin'd
>   By Union, and refin'd.
>
> (320–3)

Union thus places the marriage, and all the celebrants, in the great perspective of created Nature – God's Golden Chain, stretching down from Heaven to Earth, in which every creature has its place and must learn to know it. The masque therefore embodies as forceful an affirmation of the positive underlying principles which govern existence as it is possible to give: kings pass, but kingship is undying; weddings pass, but the ideal of union remains strong as ever. Order and the powers which enforce it are immutable, not subject to time and change:

> She that makes souls, with bodies, mix in love,
> Contracts the world in one, and therein Jove;
> Is spring, and end of all things: yet, most strange!
> Her self nor suffers spring, nor end, nor change.
>
> (141–4)

The full effect of a work like *Hymenaei* obviously depends less on the words than upon the controlled modulation of action, music and spectacle, a process which finally incorporated the spectators within its own meaning – the last perspective which the masque offers before it is summarily obliterated by 'the rage of the people, who (as a part of greatness) are privileged by custom, to deface their carcases'.[6] The triumph of such art over time and misunderstanding is necessarily short-lived, however hard Jonson tries to preserve the 'matter' in his printed text; mundane reality inevitably reasserts itself, and who can tell what real profit has been gained? It is notice-able, however, that as Jonson gained experience in conjuring up such symbolic and mythological visions for the Banqueting House at Whitehall, his plays for the public stage moved in the opposite direction, taking on a sharper realism. Jonson is often thought of, with Dickens, as the quintessential London writer;[7] it is less often appreciated how late in his career began the concentration of recog-nisable London settings, with their wealth of naturalistic detail. *Every Man In His Humour* does not count in this respect, of course, since the London version belongs after 1606 at the earliest; *Every Man Out of His Humour* is nominally set in London, but the whole style – like the characters' names – is quasi-Italian. Not until *Epicoene* did Jonson write a play which is *pointedly* set in London. We should see this not as the work of a man who is essentially a journalist by instinct, but as a tactical development in the satiric strategy which I described as beginning with *Sejanus* and *Volpone* (see pp. 72–4, above), making the audience the real target rather than the characters within the plays. In *Epicoene*, and the comedies that follow it, Jonson is able to exploit the audience's knowledge of the London setting and its typical personalities, accumulating verisimilar detail as one way of involving them in the business of understanding the 'matter' of the play. If the follies of the characters seem so much more understand-able because they are familiar, all the more reason to beware: there is no perspective so unreliable as the one which gives you a comfortably recognisable image of yourself.

It was not possible, of course, for Jonson to use the machinery and visual trickery of the masques on the public stage. Like *Cynthia's Revels* and *Poetaster*, *Epicoene* was written to be performed indoors by the Children of the Revels,[8] so that some limited use might have been made of indoor lighting effects; but none of the kind of scenic machines, devised by Inigo Jones for use at Court, was employed in a professional theatre for another thirty years. Jacobean plays were primarily verbal, rather than visual experiences. But in *Epicoene* and the later comedies Jonson plays with language, and with the audi-ence's expectations, in ways that are analogous to the disconcerting changes of perspective in the masques; and his intentions are the same – to keep the audience questioning what is real and what is illusory, what is truth and what merely a convenient fiction, and so keep them involved within the satiric process. The realistic 'back-drop' of *Epicoene* – a familiar image, but still an illusion – is one element in the playing with the audience's expectations, but what keeps them disconcertingly involved in this play is its unremitting use of *paradox*.[9] The *Oxford English Dictionary* defines paradox as 'a phenomenon that exhibits some contradiction or conflict with pre-conceived notions of what is reasonable or possible', and that des-cribes exactly the kind of cat-and-mouse game that Jonson pursues in *Epicoene*. The most obvious example of this is in the play's alternative title, *The Silent Woman*, which – as the action of the play demonstrates more than once – is a logical and proverbial impossibility; it is similarly paradoxical to make Cutbeard a *discreet* barber, when everyone knows there is no such thing, and to give Lady Haughty a woman called Trusty, whose only lines in the play (IV. iv. 116–25) are to vouch for the efficiency of two popular moral tracts as cures for sleeplessness. But the spirit of paradox goes far deeper than this, infecting virtually all of the play's characters, for example, in the matter of their sexual behaviour. So we have the 'collegiates', a group of ladies who are aggressively masculine in their habits and outlook, calling each other by their surnames in the male fashion and arguing for sexual licence with the manner (if not the wit) of a Donne: 'We are rivers, that cannot be call'd back, madam: she that now excludes her lovers, may live to lie a foresaken beldame, in a frozen bed' (IV. iii. 43–5). At the opposite extreme we find Captain Otter, 'animal amphibium' (I. iv. 26), whose manliness is always in doubt; he may attempt some pathetic bravado under the influence of drink ('Wives are nasty sluttish animals' IV. ii. 56) but is completely womanish when faced by his wife, whom he calls 'princess', 'sweet princess' and who 'commands all at home' (I. iv. 29). Their relationship is a complete inversion of that enjoined by the Bible and the (old-style) wedding service: 'Is this according to the instrument, when I mar-ried you? That I would be princess, and reign in mine own house: and you would be my subject, and obey me?' (III. i. 32–5). Ironically (for reasons I shall discuss in a moment) it is Morose who offers the clearest riposte to Mrs Otter's unwarranted dominance; tormented by the noise of her bullying the captain, 'he came down with a huge long naked weapon in both his hands, and looked so dreadfully' (IV. iii. 2–4). The unmistakable phallicism of the description makes the point graphically; the unnatural woman has been put firmly in her place by an aggressively dominant male.

That it should be Morose who offers this demonstration of the 'proper' order of things is ironic because he is at the very centre of the play's paradoxically disordered scheme of things. The action of the play hinges on the fact that he wants to repudiate his nephew and natural heir, Dauphine, and chooses to marry a young wife as the best way of cutting him out. From the start this is a perplexing situation: the folly of an old man's marrying a young wife was proverbial; as Chaucer's *The Merchant's Tale* demonstrated, it invariably led to his being cuckolded. But there is no suggestion that Morose is interested in a wife in a sexual way: she is merely a means to disinherit Dauphine; indeed, when it later appears that Daw and La Foole have actually cuckolded him such are his paradoxical requirements that he greets the news with relief, hoping that it will bring him a divorce. The fact is that, in trying to find that mythical creature, a silent wife, Morose is attempting to defy nature; it is his 'humour' that 'all discourses, but mine own, afflict me, they seem harsh, impertinent, and irksome' (II. i. 4–5). It is the concession 'but mine own' which offers the clue that what Morose suffers from is not a pathological condition, but just such a humour as Reason subdued in *Hymenaei*; where other characters in the play have adopted perverse or perverted social/sexual roles, Morose indulges in an all-consuming self-love, attempting to cut himself off from all social contact, including normal contact with either a wife or an heir. Hence his reaction, in one of the play's early reversals, when Epicoene proves to be as talkative as any woman: 'O immodesty! a manifest woman!' (III. iv. 42); he is appalled by (as it seems) natural reality, since it will shatter the egocentric world he has constructed for himself. His frantic attempts to free himself by divorce only pile additional torments and indignities upon his own head, culminating with the admission:

> I am no man, ladies.
> ALL: How!
> MOROSE: Utterly un-abled in nature, by reason of frigidity, to perform the duties, or any the least office of a husband.
> MAVIS: Now, out upon him, prodigious creature!
>
> (v. iv. 44–8)

The latter comment is, of course, a blatant case of the kettle calling the pot black, but the fact is that Morose's confession that he is 'no man' – even if it is not true that he is sexually impotent – reveals an essential truth. In the spiritual and social senses that really matter, Morose is 'no man': he is a self-created non-entity; and this is what justifies the way he is cruelly hounded by the 'wits', being dismissed at the end with a severity which is extreme even by Jonson's taxing standards: 'Now you may go in and rest, be as private as you will, sir. I'll not trouble you, till you trouble me with your funeral, which I care not how soon it come' (v. iv. 214–17).

In an earlier play, like *Every Man In His Humour*, it is probable that

Jonson would have made the young gallants at the centre of the action relatively uncomplicated characters, whose wit and high-spirits were effective antidotes to the follies around them; but nothing may be taken for granted in *Epicoene* and Truewit is perhaps the most paradoxical character in the play, his name as challenging as Epicoene itself. He tries to help Dauphine by setting about Morose (with apparent sincerity, since he suspects that Epicoene is not the silent paragon of rumour) 'thundring into him the in-commodities of a wife, and the miseries of marriage' (II. iv. 14–15) at exhaustive length. Far from disuading Morose, the harangue hastens his resolution to marry (paradox), which is apparently contrary to Dauphine's interests but (paradox) fits perfectly in fact with the scheme that young man has been hatching; so (paradox) Truewit gains the credit for what, in the long-term interests of the play, is a triumph, but does so by championing some very dubious attitudes to marriage. This is typical of his function throughout the play; for example, he argues in favour of cosmetics (IV. i. 35–46) and denies natural virtue: 'A man should not doubt to over-come any woman. Think he can vanquish 'hem, and he shall: for though they deny, their desire is to be tempted' (IV. i. 72–4). He then lists ways of going about such a temptation at great length (74–128). What he offers is a kind of mirror-image of Truewit, arguing suspect cases with great show of brilliance but to dubious ends; so he acts as a spur to the audience to make sense of the play's overall paradoxical mode. He above all should prepare us for the final resolving paradox in which Epicoene proves finally to be a boy – the reality of the plot proving to be exactly the same as that of the Jacobean theatrical experience (i.e. it was a boy in disguise all the time) and *not* its mirror-image. Jonson breaks one of the supposed cardinal rules, that the audience should be kept in the know all the time; but he does so deliberately, not merely for sensational effect, in order to overturn the whole conven-tion of suspended disbelief and throw the audience back on the first principles of literary judgement, the ability to discriminate truth from fiction.

As with earlier plays written for the private theatres, we must make some allowance for the fact the *Epicoene* was written for per-formance by the Children of the Revels rather than an adult com-pany; not only the final twist of the boy dressed as a girl actually *being* a boy dressed as a girl, but many other key moments in the play – not least Morose's 'huge long naked weapon' and his 'I am no man, ladies' – would take on additional comic infections performed by children. The whole business of children pretending to be adults pretending to be characters in a play adds an extra dimension to the dramatic artifice, an extra layer to the audience's need to discriminate and understand. *Epicoene* as a printed satire does not strictly need this dimension in that way, say, *Cynthia's Revels* does; it remains sophisticated and tactically sound even if we lose sight of the child performers. But the sheer manipulation of theatrical conventions is a joy in itself, analogous to the manipulation of the multiple perspectives of the masques, teasing, engaging and involving the audience. When the masques dissolve, the spectators find themselves back at Court implicitly charged with applying what they have experienced to the real world around them. When the final paradoxes of *Epicoene* have resolved themselves; the audience return to the fashionable district between Westminster and the City of London which has been the setting of the play, just as it is the site of the Whitefriars Theatre in which they have been watching it. The ultimate paradox is the relationship between art and nature.

On the face of it, it would be difficult to find more contrasting views of marriage than those projected in *Hymenaei* and *Epicoene* – the former an idealised celebration of Union and the latter a nightmare of the incompatibility of the sexes, in which Morose searches desperately for one of 'twelve impediments . . . all which do not . . . *take away the bond; but cause a nullity therein*' (v. iii. 78–81). Yet there is no inconsistency on Jonson's part; in each work, though in different ways, he writes against the hope or expectation of what marriage should be, trying to inspire to perfection in the one, to warn against corrosive egoism in the other. The final responsibility for what marriage *is* depends upon the understanding of his readers and audiences. In retrospect, most Jacobean masques have proved fraught with ironies, their promised perfections falling foul of time, death and human fallibility. But few proved quite so ironic as *Hymenaei*: all that art and symbolism was lavished on a union nullified seven years later on the grounds of the bridegroom's impotence. And even that was only half the squalid truth; the real reason for the divorce was so that Lady Frances could marry her lover, the King's current favourite, Robert Carr (shortly to be made Earl of Somerset, in order that his new bride should not be downgraded in the nobility).[10] Jonson provided an entertainment for the new wedding, called – from the chivalric exercise of tilting – *A Challenge at Tilt*. The new marriage proved even more disastrous than the previous one, since the couple were eventually convicted of poisoning the Countess's advisor, the physician and man of letters, Sir Thomas Overbury; they came to trial in 1616, the year of Jonson's folio. The business of revising his work for that volume must have given Jonson many occasions to reflect on events and personalities. *Epigrams* contains a respectful salute to Overbury (113), apparently written while he was still alive. The names of all the celebrants of *Hymenaei*, given in the quarto text, were now tactfully removed.

There was ample reason for the encomiast of the masques and the satirist of the plays to despair of the audience which he sought to instruct through his art; they continued to fall far short of the ideals he expressed so clearly in the one and implied so strongly in the other. But there was sufficient optimism left in Jonson to arrange an inspiring conclusion to his great work (which ended with the masques), just as he had provided a challenging opening in the prologue to *Every Man In His Humour*. He reversed the chronological order of his two most recent masques, so that the text ended with *The Golden Age Restored* (1615) rather than with *Mercury Vindicated from the Alchemists at Court* (1616); he also re-arranged the speeches of *The Golden Age Restored*, so that it – and the folio – concluded with Astraea's[11] delight at the Golden Age under King James, and her decision to remain in his kingdom:

> What change is here! I had not more
> Desire to leave the earth before,
>   Than I have now, to stay;
> My silver feet, like roots, are wreath'd
> Into the ground, my wings are sheath'd,
>   And I cannot away.
>
> Of all there seems a second birth,
> It is become a heav'n on earth,
>   And Jove is present here,
> I feel the godhead: nor will doubt
> But he can fill the place throughout,
>   Whose power is everywhere.
>
> This, this, and only such as this,
> The bright Astraea's region is,
>   Where she would pray to live,
> And in the midd'st of so much gold;
> Unbought with grace or fear unsold,
>   The law to mortals give.
>
>   (222–39)

5

The Forest, *The Alchemist*, *Catiline*: 'Manners, arms and arts': a Renaissance ideal

We do not know when Jonson first thought of compiling the short collection of poems he called *The Forest*.[1] Some of the verses go back to the beginning of the century; the 'Epistle to Elizabeth, Countess of Rutland' (12), for example, was a New Year's gift for 1600, while 'And must I sing? what subject shall I choose' (10) and 'Epode' (11) were both printed in Robert Chester's *Love's Martyr* in 1601. The first of the songs 'To Celia' (5) appeared in *Volpone* (1606); the 'Epistle. To Katherine, Lady Aubigny' (13) was written after her marriage in 1609; the 'Ode. To Sir William Sidney on His Birthday' (14) was presumably composed between his knighthood in 1610 and his death in 1612, while 'To Penshurst' (2) seems to have been written before November 1612, when Prince Henry – referred to in the poem as if alive – died. So it is most unlikely that Jonson planned these poems as a sequence when he wrote them, any more than he did with the *Epigrams*. And at first glance there seems to be even less deliberate structure about *The Forest* than there is about the earlier collection; short as it is, there is a more marked variety of poems than we find in the *Epigrams* – not only complimentary verse but love songs, an epode, a religious poem – and no real sign of the running debates and cryptic cross-references which we noticed in chapter 3.

Nevertheless, there is an organising principle, or perhaps we should say a focal issue behind *The Forest*; the collection is concerned almost exclusively with a single theme, albeit approached in a variety of ways: the virtuous life. The majority of the poems, and the weightiest, are exemplary in nature, offering images of virtue, or exhortations to it in the lives of a select band of named individuals; between them they confront a number of overlapping major issues: virtue and vice, love and life, court and country, marriage and manhood, poetry and death. Significantly, behind almost all of them, stands the figure of 'godlike Sidney', Sir Philip Sidney, the Elizabethan paragon – brother of the present lord of Penshurst, where he was born, uncle by marriage of Sir Robert Wroth (*The Forest* 3), father of the Countess of Rutland, uncle of Sir William Sidney. In Jonson's verse their lives are (or are encouraged to be) tributes to the great example that he gave; they in turn become secondary examples to us, the readers, who may – like the children of Sir Robert and Lady Sidney –

> Read, in their virtuous parents' noble parts,
> The mysteries of manners, arms and arts.
> ('To Penshurst', 97–8)

Jonson's verse takes on the daunting task of supplying for us what the living presence and family association have supplied for them.

But the complimentary poems offer the reader only one approach or perspective; to offset this Jonson has interwoven poems with radically different forms and (apparently) themes which will, however, ultimately refer us back to the same central question of the virtuous life. For example, he opens the collection not, as might be expected, with the self-evident substance of 'To Penshurst', but with a wry reflection on being too old for love poetry (he would be about forty in 1612), which becomes an implicit apology for his 'cold' moralising. Yet four poems later he offers us one of the most seductive lyrics in the language ('Come, my Celia, let us prove') and later still one of the most exquisite ('Drink to me only with thine eyes'). The turn-about is surely a rueful admission that human passions and susceptibilities are less predictable than we may think, and less tractable than moralists may like to believe; Jonson himself is not immune. These love lyrics, with their direct, sensuous apprehension of the world's delights and illusions, offer a very different perspective from the virtuous *exempla* around them. 'Come, my Celia', like all true seduction poems, places the reader in the position of the besieged lady and confronts him/her with a hymn to sensuality; in *Volpone* the force of the passionate logic is undercut, or given a comic edge, by our knowledge that Bonario lurks in the wings, waiting to save Celia if her own virtue or reason cannot. But we have no such assurance with the printed poem; we need all our wits to counter its insidiously plausible arguments. In fact Jonson has made two small but significant changes from the version that appeared in *Volpone* for its inclusion in *The Forest* (both versions, of course, appear in the first folio) and they heighten the challenge to the reader. 'Let us prove / While we can' (1–2) has become 'let us prove / While we may' and 'love's fruits' (15) has become singular, 'love's fruit'.[2] Every schoolboy is supposed to know that there is a difference between what he can do and what he may do, while the theft of a single 'fruit' inevitably evokes Eve's taking of the fruit of the tree of knowledge of good and evil in the Garden of Eden. In other words the poem surreptitiously supplies us with the idea of moral choice even while its energy appears to be directed to convincing us that there is no moral problem at all – what matters is making the most of time while we have it, sin doesn't count if you're not discovered, etc. etc. The further we look, the more we see this tension between the song's apparent message and its implied reservations: the line 'Suns that set may rise again' surely carries the stock Renaissance pun on 'sun' and 'son'[3] and so raises the whole issue of Christ's sacrifice for sinners; the very fact that Celia's name means 'heavenly one' is also not without point. As so often, Jonson rounds on us in the closing couplet:

> To be taken, to be seen,
> These have crimes accounted been.

The barest statement of the amoralist's creed is also a reminder of our responsibilities as 'knowledgeable' readers; the more *we* 'take' and 'see' ('may', 'sun', 'fruit', 'Celia') the more a whole dimension of moral accountability opens up, and the more it falls to us to distinguish between 'crimes' and innocent pleasures. The Celias among us who succumb to the poem's dubious charms do so despite Jonson's best efforts to remind us always to check the small print of life's choices. This is the essence of poetry written with avowed moral intentions, but for adult readers.

The need to 'take' and 'see' is not confined to the details of individual poems, but also to the arrangement of the sequence as a whole. It may not have the cryptic suggestiveness of the *Epigrams* but there are some pointed collocations: 'Come, my Celia' follows an intriguing antithesis, 'To the World', an unusual monologue subtitled 'A Farewell for a Gentlewoman, Virtuous and Noble', which evinces as little regret at leaving the supposed pleasures of the world as the speaker of 'Come, my Celia' does great delight at his anticipated conquest. Similarly, 'Drink to me only', that charming celebration of love's intoxicating influence, is placed in pointed juxtaposition with a far more mordant address 'To Sickness'. In such ways the reader is constantly involved and re-involved in the creation of moral perspectives in *The Forest*, a process of re-adjustment which leads inexorably 'To Heaven' (15), a contemplation of ultimate truths which, in turn, cast their shadows back over preceding doubts and apparent certainties. The sequence has a unity which would barely be suspected on a first reading.

The impression of Jonson that emerges from *The Forest* is rather different from that which we piece together in *Epigrams*, partly because there are no explicit satires, partly because in broadening his scope to include love as a theme he has ventured on an area of experience where it would be difficult to pose as more reasonable or less fallible than the next man.[4] He continues to engage us, both emotionally and intellectually, in an examination of human standards and conduct; but if he is a challenging figure, he is neither as inhuman nor as arrogant as some of his earlier works may suggest. He finds a proper humility when he confronts his Maker (which may not always be true of, say, Donne), and even before his fellow men he makes no pretence of being all-knowing: love catches even him out. It is in this context that we may appreciate Jonson's rather surprising depiction of himself as a gluttonous guest at Penshurst:

> Here no man tells my cups; nor, standing by,
>   A waiter, doth my gluttony envy.
>
> (67-8)

This is pointedly out of keeping with the decorous behaviour of everyone else associated with the Sidney estate, and is surely a joke at Jonson's own expense; where in earlier works his has been the voice of moral authority admonishing wayward humanity, here the tables are turned and this almost sacred place reveals him in a very different light – as the prime example of a self-indulgence which is all too common in the world at large, but is virtually non-existent here. In as much as this great poem is a moral lecture, it is addressed firstly to himself.

This is only a small example of the maturity that makes 'To Penshurst' a key work in Jonson's career, as well as one of the most influential poems of the seventeenth century. In it, Jonson comes as close as he ever does in a single work to spelling out the positive values by which he stands and by which he measures both the characters of his plays and their audiences. Penshurst in Jonson's poem is an organic community, in which every person, creature and thing knows and accepts its place. The fauna and flora of the estate are depicted as elements in a natural hierarchy: not the antagonism of one species over or against another, but all cooperating for the common good, anxious to be useful to their appointed master, man:

> The painted partridge lies in every field,
>   And, for thy mess, is willing to be kill'd.
>
> (29-30)

The essential sympathy of man and nature is indicated in the simplicity with which the fruit of the tree makes itself available:

> The blushing apricot, and woolly peach
> Hang on thy walls, that every child may reach.
>
> (43–4)

It is an Eden or Paradise, but not one that encourages sloth or self-indulgence; those who live within the estate may be privileged, but it is a privilege that brings with it a commensurate share of responsibility. They also follow nature's laws, performing the husbandry enjoined upon them and accepting their places in an unforced hierarchy. The keynote is hospitality, giving and receiving the things of the earth, sharing God's bounty – and doing it with liberality and goodwill. All men share a common humanity under God, even though they are not born to the same rank or fortune; some may be charged with greater power or prestige in this world, but they are also charged with greater duties, not to use their position for personal glory but for the ultimate good of all. These are the essential principles which the practice of hospitality keeps alive, and this is why Jonson places such stress on this aspect of the household. Hospitality – with all its implications of duty, selflessness and faith in the divine order of things – runs through the dealings of Lord and Lady Sidney with their humblest tenants ('the farmer and the clown'), with their self-indulgent poet guest and with the highest in the land, the King and the Prince of Wales when they rode this way.

But Penshurst is not just a recipe for social harmony (or, as some might see it, an ultra-conservative political and economic system). It is also a setting in which each individual may learn to achieve his or her highest potential; the children of the household are not only taught religion but may

> Read, in their virtuous parents' noble parts,
> The mysteries of manners, arms and arts.
>
> (97–8)

The manners of the courtier, the arms of the soldier, the arts of the scholar; the passionate, active and contemplative lives; the perfection of the soul, the body and the mind. The balance of the three, rather than an undue emphasis on any one, was a Renaissance ideal. According to Ophelia, the Hamlet we see in the play is the ruins of such a perfection, 'The courtier's, soldier's, scholar's, eye, tongue, sword' all 'o'erthrown' in the aftermath of his father's death (III. i. 150–61). In the real world, for Jonson's generation, such perfection had most nearly been achieved by Penshurst's noblest son, Sir Philip Sidney, whose memory was enshrined in

> That taller tree, which of a nut was set,
> At his great birth, where all the Muses met.
>
> (13–14)

Just as Penshurst nurtured Sidney (and the tree: both flourishing under the laws of nature observed there), so everything about the place should inspire virtue, nobility and greatness in successive generations. Penshurst is not simply an estate, it is a principle of well-being and well-doing, and that above all is what Jonson tries to enshrine in his elegant verse: it is an example to outsiders (the King, the Prince) of what a well-ordered society may be. It is a challenge to outsiders (like Jonson himself) who do instinctively share its natural values of balance and moderation. The function of this poem, as of all his encomiums, is to make the challenge and the example live on the page, for the benefit of all those who cannot know it in their daily experience – and first of all, for his own unregenerate self.

Penshurst is important not only for itself but because it points a clear moral to the world outside, a world of estates 'grudg'd at', built only for show, living by false and unnatural standards – and in some respects Jonson admits that he belongs to that world himself, even though he reverences what Penshurst has to offer. In admitting this, Jonson is not recanting his former moral earnestness, but having the confidence and maturity to confess that he is as fallible as anyone, yet all the more passionately concerned about ideals and standards because he recognises his own fallibity. It is the paradox that he was later to confront in the poem he sent to Drummond, 'My Picture Left in Scotland' (*The Underwood* 9), where the ageing poet rues the fact that his beloved is more concerned with his 'hundred of gray hairs . . . seven and forty years . . . my mountain belly, and my rocky face' than with the sweetness of his poetry, still the equal of 'the youngest he, / That sits in shadow of Apollo's tree'. He is still a poet, with all the idealism that implies, but he inhabits a graceless body, ravaged by age and self-indulgence. *The Forest* as a whole, then, is concerned with the question of how we may live virtuously, beset as we are with passions, appetites and sin, and how we may construct a civilised, just society, given the potential waywardness of all its individual members. It is these concerns which link the collection with *The Alchemist* (1610) and *Catiline* (1611), plays written, in all probability, only shortly before it was compiled.

The Alchemist is a play about the creation of a 'republic' (I. i. 110), in which Subtle is 'sovereign' (5), Doctor (of physic, astrology and alchemy) and even High Priest (of Faery); Face is 'general' (5) or Captain; and 'Royal Dol' is Queen of Faery as well as 'our castle, our

Cinque-port, / Our Dover Pier' (III. iii. 18–19). This republic in turn
spawns new commonwealths – Mammon's 'fifth monarchy' of enormous prodigality and self-indulgence, the Puritans' self-run state
where 'Casting of dollars is concluded lawful' (IV. vii. 43), and other
private fantasy worlds. Yet these strange 'states' flourish not in
Illyria or on Prospero's island, but right in the heart of fashionable
residential London; in the Prologue, Jonson announces:

> Our scene is London, 'cause we would make known,
> No Country's mirth is better than our own
>
> (5–6)

which turns out to be something of a two-edged compliment: to
laugh, or to be laughed at? This 'London' is projected with more
local detail than we find in any other Jonson play (given that
Bartholomew Fair is not actually set in the city): the precise scene is
Face's 'master's worship's house, here, in the Friars' (I. i. 17). There
is a further reference to Blackfriars and its Puritan tailors (I. i. 128),
and there are numerous allusions to other London districts: Pie
Corner, the artillery yard, St Paul's, 'the bawd of Lambeth', 'Moor-
field for lepers', 'Lethbury for the copper', 'i'the Temple church'.
Taverns also figure prominently: 'deaf John's', 'the Woolsack', 'the
Dagger' in Holborn, 'Heaven and Hell'; at the end of the play Subtle
and Dol leave 'Eastward for Ratcliffe' but 'we will turn our course /
To Brainford, westward, if thou say'st the word' or 'tickle it at The
Pigeons' (v. iv. 76–7; 89).

The cumulative effect of all this is unmistakable; the world of the
play and that of the audience are virtually identical. This must have
been particularly so if and when the play was performed in the
Blackfriars Theatre, immediately adjacent to its supposed location,
though we must assume that the King's Men also gave it at the Globe
(in a far less salubrious suburb). It is not only a matter of geogra-
phical location, but also of contemporary detail: the plague which
causes Lovewit's absence is also that which closed the theatres in
1609; Face mentions the Great Frost of 1608 (III. iii. 46) and there are
references to a number of notorious contemporary figures – Dr John
Dee (II. vi. 20) and Edward Kelly (IV. i. 90), two recently dead
alchemists; Gamaliel Ratsey, a highwayman executed in 1605; Dr
Simon Read (I. ii. 17), who had recently been prosecuted for conjuring. Perhaps most striking (though no one is actually named), the
most absurd scenes in the play, where Dapper is visited by Dol as the
Queen of Faery, are based on real and well-known incidents when
one Thomas Rodgers was swindled in just such a manner; this was

the subject of a famous Chancery suit at the time of the play's performance.[5] The implication that the world of the play is also that of the audience is finally clinched by the knowledge that Dame Pliant is 'but nineteen, at the most' (II. vi. 31), and she tells us:

> Never, sin'eighty-eight could I abide'hem,
> And that was some three year afore I was born, i'truth.
>
> (IV. iv. 29–30)

– a typical piece of Jonsonian attention to detail which fixes the play, immovably, in 1610.

But how exactly is the audience supposed to see itself mirrored in this, and what is the relationship between the 'real' world and those private 'republics' created by the characters who inhabit its mirror image? The gently understated Prologue poses the challenge in these terms: the audience

> . . . shall find things, they'd think, or wish, were done;
> They are so natural follies, but so shown,
> As even the doers may see, and yet not own.
>
> (22–4)

'Natural follies' is a wry paradox which illuminates the satiric strategies of the play as a whole; folly in Jonson's terms is by definition unnatural – an abrogation of man's reasonable self – but the implication here is that it has become so commonplace in London that it is nothing out of the ordinary, 'natural'.[6] It is so accustomed to the folly depicted here that even its perpetrators will not recognise themselves. Behind the genial tone, Jonson defies the audience not to recognise themselves afflicted by precisely the same blindness and folly that drives the dupes they have come to laugh at. There are significant similarities between the foolish fantasies which Subtle and Face propagate and the fantasy of the play itself – though, for the true understander, there are also crucial differences. It is around the need to differentiate between these similarities and differences that Jonson builds his satire of a diseased society.

The melting-pot of illusion and reality is Lovewit's house, transformed by the 'alchemy' of Subtle, Face and Dol; in their hands it is all things to all men. But before their alchemy will work on others, it must first work on themselves; the marvellously explosive opening scene demonstrates just how fragile their 'magic' is. In their quarrel Subtle and Face exposes their true natures: 'rogue', 'notorious whelp, insolent slave', 'livery-three-pound thrum', 'suburb-captain', 'doctor-dog', 'rascal', 'scarab'. The references to animals and the bodily functions indicate precisely the level of existence they represent; only their clothes disguise the reality. Face threatens to reveal all by stripping Subtle, who in turn threatens: 'I shall mar / All that the tailor has made, if you approach' (I. i. 9–10). The assumption that 'clothes maketh men' is exploited ironically throughout the play, which is why it is necessary for Surly and Lovewit to use disguise in order to assert themselves. Face in particular *is* the clothes he wears, a permanent impermanence which gives him an essential resilience throughout the play's permutations. Subtle also makes much use of disguise, but his resources are as much verbal as visual: his alchemical jargon confers enormous powers on him over the linguistic 'disguises' that his clients adopt – Mammon's sensual rhetoric, Kastril's vituperative quarrelling, the Puritans' cant etc. There may be a hint in Subtle's claim to carry a disproportionate part of the venture (I. i. 145) that he is bewitched by his own eloquence; his alchemy is all a fake, of course, but it confers an artificial dignity on him which perhaps goes to his head, in a way that distinguishes him from Face. From the beginning of the play, however, both of them are equally determined to preserve their disguises, to maintain the façades of their illusory selves; the bitterness of their quarrel grows out of a mutual determination to inflict the truth on the other – without hearing it about themselves. Face prophetically worries about being overheard from outside – 'Will you be so loud?' (I. i. 18), 'Speak lower, rogue' (14), 'You might talk softlier, rascal' (59) – while Subtle feigns deafness.

The individual truths are unpalatable, but Dol struggles to resolve the quarrel by reminding them of the attractiveness of the collective illusion – the great 'all' she is determined to preserve: 'Will you betray all?' (8), 'Will you mar all' (81), 'O, this'll o'er-throw all' (92). It is she who calls them 'sovereign', 'general', 'gentlemen', 'masters' and talks of their 'republic'. Face asks Subtle:

> Why, I pray you, have I
> Been countenanc'd by you? or you, by me?
> (21–2)

The fact is that, for the 'republic' to flourish, each must unselfishly 'countenance' the other, putting off immediate selfish gratification for long-term common benefits. Singly, they are unmanageable elements but together they can form a marvellous compound – if not exactly gold. Their 'republic' flourishes as long as they can convince themselves that common benefits outweigh private gains – but totters whenever they doubt it. The key consideration here is what the audience will make of this dubious 'social contract'. The double-edge to all the injunctions to speak lower, and pretending not to hear is that *the audience* sees and hears everything. Dol pleads:

> Shall we go make
> A sort of sober, scurvy, precise neighbours,
> (That scarce have smil'd twice, sin'the king came in)
> A feast of laughter, at our follies?
>
> (163–6)

We are in the position of those neighbours, but does not our privileged position all but ensure that our feast of laughter is *with* the 'indenture tripartite' of Subtle, Face and Dol, not against it? After all, who wants to be thought of as 'sober, scurvy, precise' (i.e. a puritan)? The fact is that there is a long tradition of sympathy for ingenious confidence-tricksters, particularly in circumstances where we can be led to feel that those they dupe somehow deserve what they get. As William Empson has remarked, 'you may decide that rogue sentiment is a rather silly self-indulgence, but that is no reason for blinding yourself to its frequent occurrence in plays'.[7] Jonson clearly exploits this 'silly self-indulgence' in both *Volpone* and *The Alchemist*, but more fully in the latter play; the familiarity of the characters and their setting, compounded by the frank insight we are allowed 'behind the scenes' is more conducive to our support than the decadent foreign splendour of Venice and its animal-type grandees (though the differences, significantly, are more apparent than real). You may object that it is only human nature to sympathise with the principal characters of a play, however immoral we may know them to be; but then, human nature is always the object of Jonson's satire.

The giddy career of Subtle, Face and Dol through the play, then, depends in important respects on *our* willingness to 'countenance' their activities, to suppress our moral judgement in the interests of comic entertainment. Just as much as Mammon, Drugger or Dapper, each member of the audience is tempted by the delights of an illusion to ignore the all-too-palpable reality; and once even a part of us has succumbed to the temptation, the farcical pace of the action gives us little respite to reconsider. We may even console ourselves with the thought that those whom our 'heroes' outwit are all in their various ways so self-important or gullible that they scarcely deserve our sympathy, much less our protection. In *Volpone* the principals often have time to gloat about their successes, and Celia and Bonario complicate our responses: they may be ineffectual but they hardly warrant the dire fates they are threatened with. But whenever Subtle or Face pause to gloat, or to contemplate a private advantage (as, for example, over Dame Pliant), their enterprise totters briefly, and it comes as something of a relief to us (having backed them thus far) that they are able to recover and further outwit their unattractive dupes. Hence the complete mastery they show in the middle part of the play, treating their 'gulls' with an ease which virtually demands the applause of the audience. Face, for example, assures Kastril, resplendent in a fortune which would today make him a millionaire:

> He made me a captain. I was a stark pimp,
> Just o'your standing, 'fore I met with him.
>
> (III. iv. 44–5)

It is no more than an embellishment of the truth; Subtle did 'make' Face a captain, and he was (rather, *is*) a 'stark pimp'. The audacity of it is irresistible. Similarly, Subtle's role as pious man *'homo frugi'*, essential in a would-be alchemist, puts him in a position where he is able to preach to 'sinners':

> (To Ananias)   Out, the varlet
> That cossen'd the Apostles! Hence, away . . .   (II. v. 72–3)

> (To Mammon)   Error?
> Guilt, guilt, my son. Give it the right name.   (IV. v. 38–9)

His outrageous pulpit oratory – 'O, the curst fruits of vice, and lust!' (IV. v. 77) – presents a curiously refracted image of the true moral picture, again irresistible in its bare-faced cheek.

The final measure of the power wielded by the 'republic' of Subtle, Face and Dol is its ability to withstand the invasions made against it by Surly. They have already absorbed the petty aspirations of Dapper and Drugger, and are about to match Mammon's enormous visions of a New World, when Surly announces himself

> somewhat costive of belief
> Toward your stone: would not be gull'd.   (II. iii. 26–7)

The question is why his scepticism is not sufficient to unmask the trickery, either initially or later with the help of disguise. It is clear that Surly is no paragon of virtue (no Crites, say), that he deals with 'the hollow die' and 'the frail card' (II. i. 9–10), and that he is not taken in by Subtle and Face simply because he is too much like them. In this respect he is not unlike Macilente in *Every Man Out of His Humour*, a foil to other humours because of his own envy. The difference is that Surly is never able to exploit that advantage as Macilente does, even though it seems within his power to do so. Subtle and Face never appear so vulnerable as at Surly's first appearance in disguise when, for the first time, the dramatic irony threatens their 'indenture' rather than supporting it:

SUBTLE: Do you mark? you shall
    Be cossened, Diego.
FACE: Cossened, do you see?
    My worthy Donzel, cossened.
SURLY: *Entiendo.*
SUBTLE: Do you intend it? So do we, dear Don.   (IV. iii. 38–41)

Yet when Surly tries to capitalise on this power, revealing himself, protesting his honour and assaulting a powerless Subtle, he gets nowhere. Face, too, is defenceless without the irony of disguise until he contrives to pit Kastril and Drugger against the triumphant vehemence; the issue is finely in the balance until the mechanistic, centripetal logic of the plot[8] re-introduces Ananias:

SURLY: Why, this is madness, sir,
    Not valour in you: I must laugh at this.
KASTRIL: It is my humour: you are a pimp, and a trig,
    And an Amadis de Gaule, or a Don Quixote.
DRUGGER: Or a knight o'the curious cox-comb. Do you see?
ANANIAS: Peace to the household.
KASTRIL: I'll keep peace, for no man.
ANANIAS: Casting of dollars is concluded lawful.
KASTRIL: Is he the constable?
SUBTLE: Peace, Ananias.
FACE: No, sir.
KASTRIL: Then you are an otter, and a shad, a whit . . .

                              (IV. vii. 37–45)

Never were peace or casting of dollars more irrelevant; but that is exactly the point. The whole scene is a chaos of self-assertion, in which none of the characters is the slightest bit interested in the objective facts of the situation; each is blindly pursuing his own passionate misapprehension of reality, which he sees threatened. Surly is beaten because he only understands the mechanisms by which trickery works; he does not appreciate the underlying insanity which makes it all possible. The republic which Subtle, Face and Dol rule exists because its inhabitants want it to exist – it is what sanctions their own private fantasy worlds. It is the failure to appreciate this which prevents Surly from ever being a true 'understander'; the same limited vision made him fail to appreciate what was really necessary for the winning of Dame Pliant and ensures that he loses out altogether through 'that same foolish vice of honesty!' (v. v. 84). We may ask ourselves what the audience makes of all this. Do we

support Surly in his attempts to expose vice? There is a fairly clear
indication of what Jonson expected most of his original audience to
make of him in the decision to give him a Spanish disguise, which
would inevitably provoke the typical xenophobic response voiced by
Dame Pliant: 'never, sin'eighty-eight could I abide 'hem'. Jonson had
clearly learned from his early 'comicall satyres' that characters who
know and seek to reveal the truth quickly and self-righteously make
themselves unpopular; and here he puts that understanding to good
effect, banking on it to create the right tone and mood at this farcical
high-spot of the play. Surly's defeat is the greatest triumph of the 'indenture tripartite' and surely marks the high-water mark of our
support for it.

The hour of triumph is also the hour of disaster, as if the energy of the
'republic' has been over-drawn; Lovewit returns unexpectedly. With
this single stroke – long before prepared for (cf. i. i. 180–8) – the most
carefully preserved of all the illusions fostered by the play is shattered.
The order of moral authority which we have 'countenanced' and
accepted as 'natural', the order in Lovewit's house, so artfully
transmuted by the 'mastery' of Subtle and Face, proves not to be
'natural' at all. The change in perspective that takes place is so absolute as to warrant the terms Jonson used of a scene change in *The
Masque of Queens* the year before: 'the whole face of the scene alter'd;
scarce suff'ring the memory of any such thing' (357–9). We move outside the house for only the second time (the first being for the entry of
Surly and Mammon, also a challenge to the trio) and find the very
neighbours that Face and Dol worried about in the first scene milling
around, perplexed and intrigued: which, in fact, would be the normal
reaction of any objective spectator to the positive riot of strange
noises, entrances and exits we have witnessed. To the extent that this
'objective view' differs from how we have responded to the previous
four acts, we may say that the return to 'normality' in the form of Lovewit poses a kind of judgement not only on what Subtle, Face and Dol
have been doing, but also on our part in sanctioning them.

The only kinds of attractions Lovewit can conceive of that might
have drawn such crowds are travelling side-shows and the sort of
freaks exhibited at fairs:

> He hung out no banners
> Of a strange calf, with five legs, to be seen?
> Or a huge lobster, with six claws?
> NEIGHBOUR 6: No, sir.
> NEIGHBOUR 3: We had gone in then, sir.

(v. i. 7–10)

But what we have watched – the gulling of a succession of fools by a charlatan alchemist and his associates – was, in a sense, just such an 'unnatural' freak; and, on the whole, with all the willing credulity of Neighbour 3, we have 'gone in'. A succession of disabused gulls returns, seeking vengeance, and Lovewit is understandably bemused:

> The world's turn'd Bet'lem.
> FACE: These are all broke loose,
> Out of S. Kather'nes, where they use to keep,
> The better sort of mad-folks.
>
>   (v. iii. 54–6)

In one sense or another, we really have spent four acts watching freaks and madmen, and we ought at least to ask ourselves what we made of them. It is not that our 'suspension of disbelief' is likely to have been so total that we have literally forgotten the reality of the 'indenture tripartite', or even what it represents in human and moral terms; what is really at issue is our capacity to ignore what we know to be true in the interests of entertainment, self-gratification, self-indulgence – call it what you will. To what extent are we who come to the theatre, looking to be entertained by a kind of fantasy or make-believe, any different from the dupes who go to the Blackfriars looking to have their dreams made reality?

This is to make of *The Alchemist* a more serious play at heart than many people like to allow, but there is no necessary incompatibility between high farce and the asking of awkward questions. A most significant feature of Jonson's best comedies is their avoidance of direct choric commentators to point the audience to a balanced judgement; the most we get in *The Alchemist* are pointed changes of perspective and the parody of a satirist-figure in Surly, but that does not mean that the critical questions no longer exist or that we are no longer responsible citizens. On the contrary, our responsibility is so much the greater because we are so much more obviously the real targets of the satire, as the final act underlines. Lovewit is practically and symbolically (note the disguise) Surly's successor, but he enjoys an authority which Surly never had, conferred on him both by his position in the plot – it is, after all, his house – and by his forthright manner. He has nothing to hide and his bluffness is a splendid anti-dote to the whining gulls, while his no-nonsense attitude makes him a credible match for Subtle and Face. The cudgel is a welcome relief after so much duplicity and chicanery, and it reveals him as a successful pragmatist, a man of the world – of the Jacobean London to which we have returned. Our doubts about Lovewit must focus partly on his dubious appropriation of the goods in the cellar, partly on his marriage to Dame Pliant but most particulary on his dependence on Face. At the end of the play he approaches the audience:

> kind spectators, if I have out-stript
> An old man's gravity, or strict canon, think
> What a young wife, and a good brain may do:
> (v. v. 153–5)

The fact is that, just as much as the earlier gulls fell for Subtle's alchemy, Lovewit has fallen for the doubtful elixir of a young wife: the rich, young widow is the epitome of the 'happy ending' in Jacobean comedy, and Dame Pliant (the name as ambiguous as ever) is all happiness to all men, the perfect sexual partner, wrapped in social and economic approval.[9] But the traditional fate of the old man with the young wife is cuckoldry, and this is surely what lies in store for Lovewit, who has already confessed 'I will be rul'd by thee in any thing, Jeremy' (v. v. 143) to the man who earlier swore ''Fore god, / She is a delicate dab-chick! I must have her' (iv. ii. 59–60). To applaud Lovewit's success, and so accept it as a satisfactory solution to the questions raised by the play about society's values, is to fall for Jonson's last trap.

The 'rich widow' solution is equivalent in many respects to the legacy in a Dickens novel – the symbol of an assured and socially respectable future, in reward for the trials and uncertainties undergone in the course of the book. In later books, like *Bleak House* and *Great Expectations*, the legacies turn sour or equivocal, and the quality of the books improves as Dickens manifests increasing dissatisfaction with this kind of bland solution. In the same way Jonson is here most equivocal about the true worth of the rich widow (is this one any less a prostitute in reality than Dol?) and about Lovewit's right to embody a final solution to the problems raised by the play. The real strength of the satire in the play lies in its refusal to accept bland, facile answers, and these include both the concept of the 'happy ending' and the suggestion that vice can be eradicated simply by punishing stage-villains. Subtle and Dol escape, albeit ignominiously by the back-window; between them they represent those commodities for which men will virtually sell their souls, and their survival underlines the fact that, while specific villains may be sent packing, temptation is always with us. Subtle and Dol are not the real problems; it is the weaknesses in human nature for which they cater. This is the significance of Face's adroit survival; he acknowledges to the audience that

> My part a little fell in this last scene,
> Yet 'twas decorum . . .
>
> (v. v. 158–9)

He recognises that this is only a play, that his 'fall' is nothing more than 'decorum' – a dramatic propriety which the audience expects and will complacently accept as true justice or judgement in the context of a theatrical entertainment. In fact it means nothing at all. Jeremy / Face remains the embodiment of wish-fulfilment; he has nothing specific to offer in himself, but he is the means for all men to find what they want – whether it be Subtle, or Dol or, as in Lovewit's case, a contented pipe of tobacco and Dame Pliant. He may no longer enjoy the vivid mastery he shared with Subtle, but his rule is far more complete, which is what add the acid touch to his sly promise in the closing line

> To feast you often, and invite new guests.
>
> (v. v. 165)

The comedy of *The Alchemist*, then, is the comedy of a society in which the principles of service, duty and affection have been abandoned in favour of self-gratification; its real hero, Face, is the embodiment of gratification, while its ostensible or would-be heroes, Surly and Lovewit, never really appreciate his power, for all their apparent 'wit'. It is this failure of insight which disqualifies them from becoming the true understanders who might combine virtue with action and so offer a proper example to a society whose leaders, like Sir Epicure Mammon, have become monsters of egoism. Mammon's dreams of gargantuan self-indulgence and extravagant acts of charity are a travesty of the principle of hospitality enshrined in 'To Penshurst', while the play's depictions of the active (Captain Face), contemplative (Doctor Subtle) and passionate (Royal Dol) dimensions of human aspiration amount to a parody of the perfection of 'manners, arms and arts' achieved by the Sidneyan 'complete' man. The urgency of the satire in *The Alchemist* lies not so much in its being a journalistically accurate depiction of Jacobean London and its vices, as in its capacity for indicting the weaknesses within the audience which may be said to allow such a society to flourish: their capacity for self-deception, their proneness to self-gratification without consideration for others. Only if that same audience will use its positive qualities – its reason and judgement, its capacity for understanding both the art of the play and the wider issues that art brings into question – will society be restored to health and sanity. It may not be given to all men to be Sidneys, but there is no excuse for not at least trying to live up to that example, trying to live by the laws of nature and to develop a truly hospitable society.

The most intriguing feature of Jonson's next play, the tragedy *Catiline*, is that while it depicts a society even farther gone in licentiousness than Jacobean London, it also depicts Cicero, the scholar–politician, as clear an example as history has produced (one might think) of the 'complete' man – able to translate real understanding into virtuous action, and so a fit leader in the state. It is, however, symptomatic of the problems that *Catiline* has faced down the years (hissed off the stage on its first performance and memorably dismissed by T. S. Eliot as 'that dreary Pyrrhic victory of tragedy'[10]) that there is no real consensus about what Jonson's depiction of Cicero actually amounts to. On one side it is claimed that he is indeed an unambiguous embodiment of the 'virtuous prince', in whom virtue is reinforced by 'vigilance, counsel, action' (v. 547); in this view, all his actions are defensible on the grounds that they are undertaken in the interests of the state, so that '*Catiline* provides a clear if unsubtle answer to the problems raised by the polluted world – the virtuous prince, working within and upon this world for the good of all.'[11] Others, however, are worried that Cicero appears to believe that the end always justifies the means: 'in attempting to deal with the corruption in his society he is after all doing no more than the Catalinarians claimed they were doing and he is reduced to embracing many of their means as well, to the extent that even his brother was capable of questioning his courses'.[12] It has even been suggested that 'his Machiavellian means of intelligency and bribery qualify his moral ends ... the preservation of the state against unlawful conspiracy is tainted by moral compromise'.[13] This marked difference of opinion about Cicero does not arise from any irreducible ambiguity about the character's psychology; as Jonson's great editors, Herford and Simpson, put it: 'In *Catiline* ... Jonson appears wholly inaccessible to the attraction of the profound "humanity" and psychology of Shakespearean tragedy'[14] – the play never focuses on a personal crisis of conscience as, say, *Julius Caesar* focuses on Brutus's dilemma. *Catiline* does offer different opinions of Cicero's character and motives, but they are all voiced by people with vested interests, so that it is never clear which – if any – is correct. Cato praises Cicero for his virtue, a judgement endorsed by the Chorus, who hail him as 'Most noble Consul' (iii. 84). His enemies, however, point to other qualities; Crassus and Caesar, for example, privately deride the studied oration with which Cicero accepts the consulship:

CRASSUS: Now the vein swells.
CAESAR: Up glory.

(III. 28)

The original spelling of 'vein' ('vaine') points up the charge of
vanity. It is open to us to dismiss this as the jealousy of a party
excluded from power by Cicero's success, but it has to be said that
one impression of Cicero which has been passed down to history (not
least by his own writings) is of a man whose great talents were
marred by self-conceit and *arriviste* vanity, the insensivity of the
self-made man. As Dryden put it: 'His action against Catiline may be
said to have ruin'd the Consul, when it sav'd the City: for it so swell'd
his soul, which was not truly great, that ever afterwards it was apt to
be over-set with vanity.'[15] The difficulty is that Jonson in his play
offers no direct answer to the question of whether Cicero really was a
'noble consul' or a vain upstart; our attention is directed more to the
rights and wrongs of what he does than why he does it. Far from
being a defect, however, I take it that the room for argument allowed
by this avoidance of 'personalities' is a key to the play's real strength.

01   *Catiline* is not a tragedy in the sense that it traces the fate of any
one, special individual; the tragedy lies in chronicling the disintegration of the Roman Republic and its associated virtues. Catiline's
career (and, curiously, Cicero's triumph) are portents of that greater
disaster, which is evoked in the exaggerated, even melodramatic
terms of the Ghost of Sylla Prologue and the play's opening acts. The
Prologue imbues Catiline with a barely credible stock of vices,
ranging fron incest to parricide, making it clear that in his own
person he represents the cancer which is eating Rome from within;
similarly his accomplices embody the qualities which foster that
cancer – rashness, vanity, duplicity, with a common thread of des-
peration. As individual characters the conspirators may be relatively
unconvincing and insignificant but (like the gulls in *The Alchemist*) in
the collective terms set by the play they have a potent identity: a
decayed and desperate nobility, physically and spiritually corrupt.
So the play makes no concessions to naturalism: its melodramatic
technique contributes to moral realism, towards a provocative
analysis of social and ethical behaviour rather than personal psychology. This is confirmed by the first Chorus, which describes the
spiritual bankruptcy overtaking Rome:

> She builds in gold; and, to the stars:
> As, if she threat'ned heav'n with wars:
> And seeks for hell, in quarries deep,

125

> Giving the fiends, that there do keep,
> A hope of day . . .
>
> (I. 551–5)

It is a vision of corporate infernal activity, not merely of a few misguided individuals.

The first two acts flesh out the suggestions of decadence and bankruptcy, not only in the actions they depict – the drinking of the slave's blood, the lovers' quarrel – but also in a precise observation of vain and misapplied language. For example, Catiline addresses the conspirators:

> *Noblest* Romans,
> If you were less, or that your *faith*, and *virtue*
> Did not hold good that title . . .
> Were we not better to fall, once, with *virtue*
> Than draw a wretched, and *dishonour'd* breath . . .
>
> (I. 326–8; 365–6)

My italics emphasise the way in which terms normally associated with honourable behaviour – nobility, faith, virtue – are here advanced in the service of what is clearly a desperate conspiracy. This process culminates in the outcry:

CETHEGUS: Free, free.
LONGINUS: 'Tis freedom.
CURIUS: Freedom we all stand for.
CATILINE: Why, these are noble voices.

> (I. 421–2)

Freedom in this bankrupt sense means licence, disintegration, a repudiation of all moral restraint; it is the savage face of the collective egoism we saw comically dealt with in *The Alchemist*. The second act introduces a different perspective, but in fact the worlds of male conspiracy and the bitchiness of the ladies' *toilette* prove to have much in common. The careers of such as Catiline and Caesar are fostered by the pique and vanity of such women as Sempronia; Curius sums up the theme in the final line of the act: 'By public ruin, private spirits must rise' (II. 362). The centre cannot hold. But, for the duration of the play, the centre *does* hold, and the crucial questions are how? and at what price?

Significantly, the conspiracy is already seriously compromised by the end of the first two acts; the quarrel between Fulvia and Curius is on the point of revealing dangerous secrets. Still, the Chorus look to the elections to provide Rome with consuls who will be

> Such, as not seek to get the start
> > In state, by power, parts, or bribes,
> > Ambition's bawds: but move the tribes
> By virtue, modesty, desert.
>
> > > (II. 379–82)

Enter Cicero, in pointed – almost technicolour – contrast to the corruption of the previous acts, apparently in fulfilment of their wishes. His name has already been linked (I. 500–1) with that of Cato, the epitome of republican virtue, but it remains to be seen how he will translate the virtue with which even Fulvia credits him (II. 121) into positive action to save the state. In fact the only public moves Cicero makes against Catiline are to gather his trusted friends around him, bar the door to the plot on his own life, enlist the aid of the Allobrogeian ambassadors and denounce the conspirators in the Senate – all passive or defensive moves which it would be difficult to construe as virtue militant. On the other hand, he takes a number of important steps in private which have a crucial bearing on the outcome; he does not scruple to take advantage of the lovers' quarrel, seizing upon this weakness in the enemy's ranks and exploiting it in ways they might have used themselves – cajoling, flattering and threatening Fulvia and Curius in ways reminiscent of nothing so much as their own quarrel. He then buys off the most serious potential opposition, that of his fellow-consul, Antonius, with some of his own consular provinces, and reflects:

> 'Tis well, if some men will do well, for price:
> So few are virtuous, when the reward's away.
> > (III. 479–80)

Both these scenes point up the paradox that virtuous actions may arise from the basest of motives, while ignoble actions (Cicero's duplicity and bribery) may arise from the most virtuous of intentions; they pose very uncomfortable questions about the relationship between means and ends, the extent to which compromise is morally or politically justifiable. Cicero himself muses on the problem, addressing Rome in soliloquy:

> Is it not strange, thou should'st be so diseas'd,
> And so secure? But more, that the first symptoms
> Of such a malady, should not rise out
> From any worthy member, but a base
> And common strumpet, worthless to be nam'd
> A hair, or part of thee?
> > (III. 447–52)

Only just before he had been protesting, of this 'common strumpet', that 'for (her) virtue, / I could almost turn lover, again' (III. 442–3). Ironically – and it is the kind of irony that breathes genuine dramatic life into this examination of political morality – the consul's remarks are echoed shortly thereafter by his arch-enemy:

> CATILINE: What ministers men must, for practice, use!
> The rash, th'ambitious, needy, desperate,
> Foolish, and wretched, ev'n the dregs of mankind,
> To whores, and women!
>
> (III. 714–17)

For all the important differences between Cicero and Catiline, there are significant and potentially compromising similarities in the tactics they pursue.

By a further irony it is one of Cicero's most dangerous and unscrupulous enemies who spells out for the audience the dangers in his policies. Compare Catiline with the spy, Latiaris, in *Sejanus* (chapter 2, p. 61), and Subtle's preaching in *The Alchemist* (chapter 5, p. 118). When Cicero denounces Catiline in the Senate, but fails to bring specific charges against him, Caesar intervenes astutely:

> What are these mischiefs, Consul? You declaim
> Against his manners, and corrupt your own:
> No wise man should, for hate of guilty men,
> Lose his own innocence.
>
> (IV. 133–6)

The devil knows his scripture well, pinpointing precisely the area of moral compromise that threatens Cicero. If it were simply a matter of unfortunate means having to be employed to the undoubtedly virtuous end of defeating Catiline, it might be possible to conclude that Cicero's actions were regrettable but effective and arguably those most likely to preserve the state at the least cost to itself; as Caesar remarks to Catiline, with a Machiavellian home-truth that might suit either side: 'Let'hem call it mischief: / When it is past, and prosper'd, 'twill be virtue' (III. 504–5). But Jonson introduces a further dimension – Caesar and Crassus – which renders this argument less than adequate. It is this which makes Cicero's lengthy oration in the Senate so much more than the pedantic translation which it is often taken for.

Cicero refuses to act against Catiline without absolute proof, or while there is the slightest public doubt of his guilt, but he is prepared to use the subtlest of weapons – words – to defeat him. Catiline himself is sceptical of the value of language; as he declares later to his troops:

I never yet knew, soldiers, that, in fight,
Words added virtue unto valiant men.

(v. 367–8)

But denouncing Catiline proves as effective for Cicero as flattering Fulvia or bribing Antonius; Catiline panics, and that is enough to destroy the conspiracy, as Caesar recognises: 'He's lost, and gone. His spirits have forsook him' (IV. 300). More than that, he has destroyed the conspiracy without forcing Caesar and Crassus to declare their support for Catiline, as direct police action might have done. Cato demands to know why nothing more positive is to be done:

> Why dare we not? What honest act is that,
> The Roman Senate should not dare, and do?
> CICERO:　Not an unprofitable, dangerous act,
> To stir too many serpents up at once.
> Caesar, and Crassus, if they be ill men,
> Are mighty ones; and, we must so provide,
> That, while we take one head, from the foul Hydra,
> There spring not twenty more.

(IV. 526–33)

While Cicero's tactics are effective, as they are against Catiline, it is arguable that the occasional moral ambiguity in his handling of affairs is excusable. But how are we to judge the political expediency of a man of virtue who judges some of his enemies to be simply too powerful and refuses to move against them at all? Cato obligingly concurs with Cicero's judgement: 'I 'prove your counsel' (IV. 533); but we need not take this to be definitive.

The closing scenes of the play – those which make its implications genuinely tragic, in spite of the triumph over Catiline – insistently raise the question of whether Cicero's refusal to move against Caesar and Crassus is proper, justifiable or even necessary. He makes it plain that he does not regard existing evidence against Caesar as sufficient to convict him, and also that he will not go looking for any more (v. 86–93); he refuses to hear what he calls 'slander' against Caesar and Crassus (v. 337–66) and intervenes with his personal authority to prevent letters incriminating Caesar from being read in the Senate (v. 572–82). It does not take a very extensive knowledge of Roman history to know that the result of these actions was that two members of the eventual First Triumvirate remained at large to plot against the Republican constitution and that one of them, Caesar, survived to become dictator, effectively destroying the Republican traditions which Cicero had sought to preserve. In other words, Cicero's triumph is a local, partial, even an illusory one; Sylla's ghost is not laid. The question is whether Cicero is to blame for this. Was the downfall of the Republic inevitable? Could or should Cicero have confronted Caesar and Crassus – given that he might either have had insufficient evidence to convict them in the courts (and so would be acting illegally) or have been convinced that in so doing he would precipitate a civil war (arguably a greater evil than that he was attempting to eradicate).

It is not in the nature of the play to offer final judgements on these issues, so much as to pose them provocatively for the audience to consider. This is most apparent in the closing scene, again in the Senate, which meets to decide on fit punishment for the surviving conspirators; as in *Sejanus*, the play's audience implicity becomes an extension of the assembled senators. Cato and Caesar offer opposing judgements, ironically each arguing on the other's more proper terri-tory. Caesar continues to show his Machiavellian guile by arguing, in favour of his former confederates, that the letter of the law (exile and not death) is the only honourable course. It has been established that Cato is a notorious stickler for the law; Gabinius Cimber had earlier taunted him with the fact that 'Cato / Do's nothing, but by law' (v. 220–1). Here, however, he insists that circumstances may necessitate the suspension of the law, *in its own interests*:

> necessity,
> Now, bids me say, let 'hem not live an hour,
> If you mean Rome should live a day.
>
> (v. 564–6)

In this instance, the Senate and Cicero both concur with Cato and overrule Caesar – asserting, in effect, that there is a higher law than the law itself (which is, to say the least, a debatable judgement). This belated resort to blunt means to deal with the small fry of the con-spiracy obviously reflects both on Cicero's earlier circumspection over Catiline and on his refusal to take action against Caesar; but it is impossible to draw absolute conclusions from these comparisons, since the safety of the state is the ultimate argument advanced in all these cases. Who is to say whether the Republic would have been preserved, or more abruptly terminated, if Cicero had acted more ruthlessly at any point? Or whether it would irreparably have tainted both his own virtue and that of the Republic he sought to defend? Who is to say that there was any path of strict integrity open to Cicero that would have secured even the defeat of Catiline?

We are left, in effect, with an irreducible ambiguity, not about Cicero's character, but about the role he played in history: there are no simple answers to the questions raised by his tactics in dealing with Catiline but not dealing with Caesar. In this respect, it is perhaps most useful to consider Cicero as belonging to that line of satirist/manipulator figures that runs through Jonson's plays, from Asper/Macilente, Crites and Horace, to Peregrine, Truewit and Surly; some might be thought more virtuous in their intentions, some might be thought more effective in their actions, but all (some more ironically than others) focus the audience's attention on the idea of applying rational and civilised standards to human behaviour. Cicero's career might seem to offer the sombre lesson that virtue is ultimately defenceless against astute, pre-meditated evil, whatever inroads it may make against those like Catiline, foolish or desperate enough to destroy themselves. But it is useful to remember that this also *seemed* to be the lesson offered by the Germanicans in *Sejanus*, yet proved not to be (see pp. 59–61, above). And the analogy between Cicero and Surly may also be instructive. He was unable to overthrow Subtle, Face and Dol, who in all important respects are still dangers to society at the end of *The Alchemist*: yet the final emphasis of that play is not negative or pessimistic: the audience has been warned, and invited to profit from its warning.

It is implicit in Jonson's whole approach that true understanding can lead to a better life and a better society, if we will make the effort. When Jonson defiantly published *Catiline* and dedicated it to his ideal 'understander', the Earl of Pembroke (see pp. 78–81, above), he placed confidence in 'that great and singular faculty of judgement in your Lordship, able to vindicate truth from error' (Dedication, 8–10). The true understander will not make the partial judgement (in every sense) that befell the play on its first performance, about which Jonson was ironically condescending in the quarto text: 'Though you commend the first two acts, with the people, because they are worst; and dislike the oration of Cicero, in regard you read some pieces of it, at school, and, understand them not yet; I shall find the way to forgive you' (To the Reader in Ordinary, 7–10). It is often assumed that the audience rebelled against Jonson's tedious 'classicism' and wholesale translation of Cicero, but what he accuses the audience of is less poor taste than simple laziness: the people obviously enjoyed the lurid details of the opening scenes, but found Cicero's oration difficult to swallow, perhaps half-remembering it and thinking that they understood it. This is what rankles with Jonson: they had judged without hearing the whole story, given up when the going got too difficult or, apparently, familiar. They had self-evidently fallen at the first hurdle of understanding.

Will those of us who follow the play though to the end fare any better? The Allobrogeian embassadors – outsiders, seeing Rome for the first time – offer an interesting perspective on Cicero and his methods. They make the wish:

> May we find good, and great men: that know how
> To stoop to wants, and meet necessities,
> And will not turn from any equal suits.

(IV. 53–5)

Their words are curiously ambiguous. On the one hand, they may simply be hoping for someone who will hear their case sympathetically; on the other, they may be looking for precisely the kind of politician Cicero proves to be: continually stooping to wants and meeting necessities, a shrewd – or over-shrewd – reader of 'equal' suits. The collocation of the accolades 'good, and great' is intriguing here. Might Jonson be implying that Cicero was virtuous, but not virtuous enough, and astute, but not astute enough? Good, but not great? As Horace in *Poetaster* was equal to the challenge of Crispinus but not of Ovid, is Cicero equal to Catiline but not to Caesar? The situation at the end of the play, with Catiline defeated but Caesar ominously waiting, is strangely reminiscent of St Augustine's words about the thieves who died with Christ: 'Do not despair; one of the thieves was saved. Do not presume; one of the thieves was damned.' Cicero's flawed triumph is surely Jonson's warning to his audience neither to despair nor to presume, but to understand: neither to be complacent that one evil was overcome, nor despondent that another was not. In *Catiline* as in his best comedies, Jonson is appealing for an alliance of virtue, judgement and action in order to preserve society; the partial failure, partial success of Cicero simply underlines the difficulty of achieving that alliance.

Catiline is not the great aberration in Jonson's career it is often dismissed as being; it is the logical counterpart of *The Forest* and *The Alchemist*, which have enjoyed a much better press, if not always for the right reasons. We should perhaps remember, not that the play failed on its first performance, but that it became the most respected of English tragedies in the period from the Restoration to the middle of the eighteenth century; this may not only have been predictable approval of its neo-classical form but genuine admiration for its handling of living questions of history, politics and ethics.

6

Covert allusions: state decipherers and politic picklocks[1]

With the three works considered in the last chapter, we come to the end of the 1616 folio; the volume concludes, as we saw in chapter 4, with the masques, but *The Forest* is the last selection of poems, *The Alchemist* is the last comedy and *Catiline* is the last tragedy, indeed the last play, included in that volume. We should by now have a clear view of Jonson and his works; throughout his career, he remained true to certain principles and beliefs – essentially those of a Renaissance humanist and classicist, his enthusiasm for man's potential balanced only by an acute sense of his shortcomings. He was conservative by instinct, but in an age much obsessed by death and decay, he refused to accept that men could not live honourably or erect a worthwhile civilisation if only they would apply themselves to it; 'I cannot think nature is so spent, and decay'd, that she can bring forth nothing worth her former years. She is always the same, like herself: and when she collects her strength, is abler still. Men are decay'd, and studies: she is not' (*Discoveries*, 124–8). The *possibility*, not so much of progress as of a renewal of the higher achievements of the past, is always implicit in his writing. These beliefs and attitudes are not original in Jonson, and they remain virtually constant throughout his career. What is original, and does develop, is Jonson's skill in propagating his beliefs, his strategic skill as a satirist in his plays, as an encomiast in his masques and in a mixture of the two roles in his non-dramatic verse. Whatever strategy he employs, he is always looking essentially for the same thing: understanding, the trying faculty, the ability to judge both men and literature by true standards. There is an element of spurious democracy about all this, to be sure. Jonson always implies that we should judge things for ourselves, while making it equally plain that the only true standards of judgement are his own; at best, you might say that he dares us to disagree. But the art of any writer is to seduce us into looking at the world, and so at ourselves, with new eyes. We may not always like or agree with what we see, but the great writers engage us so compellingly that we cannot simply ignore the vision they offer us: it is too disturbing, too truthful. So it is with Jonson; his best works engage us both imaginatively and intellectually in a reappraisal of our ideas of ourself. This may not always make him a very popular writer, but it makes him one we should not lightly ignore.

It is legitimate to ask how Jonson's vision of the world can still be relevant, even disturbing, today, when so much of it is tied to the particularities of his own time and place. It is a question that can only be answered in terms of the *way* that he looked at his own life and times. It used to be assumed that the references to contemporary people, places and events in his comedies reflected an artless realism, that it was simply Jonson's *forte* to offer literal, quasi-photographic images of the world around him, and particularly of its seedier reaches. So, for example, J. A. Symonds praised the opening of *The Alchemist*, with its 'realistically coarse abuse', as the basis for a 'faithful transcript from low-life'.[2] At about the same time, Swinburne was condemning what he called this 'tedious and intolerable realism'[3] in Jonson's writing, but both men agree that it reflects a temperamental characteristic in the writer.

We are now better placed to appreciate that Jonson's realism is far from artless, and that it derives from the same 'strategic' impulses as the historical authenticity of the tragedies and even the idealism of the panegyric verse. It is, in fact, a facet of his classicism; he attempts to place contemporary manners and behaviour against a wider perspective of human nature and history. His art, in this respect, belongs to the tradition that also includes Spenser, Milton, Dryden and Pope, who all in their various ways address the events and personalities of their own time in the light of what a classical humanist education teaches them to be both permanent and valuable in life and literature. Jonson's art is always concerned with looking through the particular manifestation – of folly or wisdom, virtue or vice – to the general truth that underlies it; his continual attempts to make his audiences 'understand' all relate to that concern.

There remains, however, one dimension of this whole approach to art and literature which we have so far scarcely touched upon; it is important because it explains how it was that such a man – scholarly and conservative by nature, virtual Poet Laureate and apparent pillar of the establishment – managed so frequently to find himself in trouble with the authorities. I refer to the possibility that, in some of his works, Jonson's 'realism' went beyond a generalised reflection of his life and times and made covert allusions to specific contemporary issues and personalities – what the Jacobeans would call 'glancings'. The significance of this possibility is only intelligible today if we bear in mind that neither comment nor publication was free in Jacobean England. The King and his Privy Council were extremely jealous of their authority and permitted no public debate on matters pertaining to their prerogative – which effectively meant all government activity and most aspects of the exercise of religion, which inevitably had political and constitutional implications at that time. Even Parliament was severely circumscribed in terms of what it could discuss; King James, for example, repeatedly insisted that foreign affairs were entirely his own concern, and not those of Parliament. All books were censored by the Church, which was effectively an arm of the government. And all plays had to be 'allowed' by the Master of the Revels, a royal official in the Lord Chamberlain's office,[4] before they could be either performed or printed. There were no newspapers as we know them, though the earliest prototypes emerged in the 1620s, giving Jonson the central topic of *The Staple of News*.

In the circumstances, it was perhaps inevitable that the drama, the most popular professional entertainment of the day, should attempt to make capital out of this proscribed area; there are obvious analogies to be drawn with recent theatre and cinema in Eastern Europe. That Jonson and his fellow dramatists did contrive to 'glance' at forbidden topics, despite all the censorship, is beyond dispute. To take only two clear-cut cases: early in 1601, when the Earl of Essex and his supporters were plotting to overthrow Queen Elizabeth and her ministers, they persuaded Shakespeare's company, the Lord Chamberlain's Men, to revive his old play, *Richard II*. The play had clearly caused the authorities disquiet before since, on its first printing, the scene of Richard's deposition was left out. Now the play was obviously intended to promote sympathy for the Earl's cause by drawing the analogy between Richard and Elizabeth (two self-centred monarchs, surrounded by flatterers) and between Bolingbroke and Essex (two men wronged by these monarchs, claiming their just dues). The performance was on 7 February 1601, the day before the abortive coup; afterwards, the actors were questioned very closely about the whole affair by the Privy Council, but finally suffered no penalty – perhaps because they could point convincingly to the 'innocence' of the play, an old work which could scarcely contain contemporary 'glancings'. It is ironic, though it may well not be accidental, that *Hamlet* (written about this time) demonstrates very clearly how an 'innocent' old play, *The Murder of Gonzago*, may suddenly be given great contemporary relevance by the turn of events.

It was, however, clearly no turn of events that made Thomas Middleton's *A Game at Chess* such a transparent allegory of current politics in 1624.[5] Its satire patently focuses on the fiercely unpopular figure of the Count of Gondomar, who had been the influential Spanish Ambassador in London until 1622, while a good deal of the action symbolically re-enacts the ill-conceived journey by Prince Charles and the Duke of Buckingham to Madrid in 1623 to find a Spanish bride for the former. The new Spanish Ambassador was outraged by it all and the London public loved it; the play ran at the Globe for nine successive days, excluding Sundays, making it by far the greatest popular success of the whole period. It would un-doubtedly have run for longer, had the authorities not finally inter-vened to suppress it. The only real questions are why the Master of the Revels did not spot so transparent an allegory of events in the first place and why the authorities did not intervene sooner. The only reasonable explanation is that powerful people must, for their own purposes, have interceded, perhaps wanting to whip up anti-Spanish and anti-Catholic feeling. Middleton's success was certainly unusual, but it proves that 'glancings' were not merely figments of the authorities' imagination and gives us some idea of why the actors and dramatists might have risked them, in spite of all the dangers: they could be very good box office.

What these two examples do not establish, however, is how wide-spread the practice of covert allusion was, or how important a role it played in Jacobean drama as a whole. There can be no simple answers to these questions. In the very nature of things, most allu-sions had to be covert at the time, to escape the scrutiny of the Masters of the Revels; they must inevitably now be even more difficult to construe. It is likely, moreover, that the actors were quite capable of injecting 'business' and innuendo into the most in-nocuous-seeming scenes. Nor can we always be certain that the printed texts we have reflect the plays as they were written, much less as they were performed. Given these difficulties, it is understandable that most modern criticism steers clear of the whole issue; but to do so is to ignore a dimension of the dramatists' writing which was daring, inventive, witty and – at least in Jonson's case – intellec-tually important.

As we have already seen, Jonson found himself in trouble with the authorities over his plays on at least four occasions: over the lost *Isle of Dogs*, for which he was imprisoned; over *Sejanus*, for which 'he was called before the Council' (and perhaps 'accused both of popery and treason'); over *Eastward Ho*, when he and Chapman 'voluntarily' imprisoned themselves and 'the report was, that they should then have their ears cut and noses'; and over *The Devil is an Ass*, 'upon which he was accused'. There was also apparently trouble of a slightly different kind about *Epicoene*. The Venetian Ambassador reported how the King's cousin, Lady Arbella Stuart, complained 'that in a certain comedy the playwright introduced an allusion to her person and the part played by the Prince of Moldavia. The play was suppressed.'[6] This is almost certainly a reference to the lines in *Epicoene* relating to Sir John Daw's map-making:

CLERIMONT: How, maps of persons!
LA FOOLE: Yes, sir, of Nomentack, when he was here, and of the Prince of Moldavia, and of his mistress, Mistress Epicoene.

(v. i. 22–5)

The lines are highly ambiguous – Sir John Daw's mistress or the Prince of Moldavia's? The so-called Prince of Moldavia was one Stephano Janiculo, who had once escaped from a Turkish prison disguised as a woman, and was now pretending to be engaged to the Lady Arbella. This was all the more embarrassing for the poor lady because she was actually conspiring at the time to marry William Seymour, without the King's knowledge and against his wishes.[7] It is not surprising that she should use her influence to put a stop to Jonson's pointed allusion. What is perhaps more surprising is that the allusion should have survived the play's being 'suppressed' (whatever that means) and appeared in print. This may be explained by the fact that the play was not printed before the 1616 folio, and by that time Lady Arbella was dead, so the allusion may no longer have been pointed enough to cause offence.

Another question which cannot now be resolved is whether this single, identifiable allusion is all that caused offence in the first place. At this remove, there is nothing else in the play that necessarily or even probably refers to Lady Arbella and her problems. But would a single ambiguous line be sufficient to cause the lady to intervene and to have the Venetian Ambassador mention it in his despatches home? Should we put it down to the extreme sensitivity of the particular case, or perhaps assume that there was something in the acting – costume, accents, incidental business, for instance – that gave more weight to the whole 'glancing'? A comparison with *Eastward Ho* is instructive here. It is generally assumed that it was a questionable passage about 'a few industrious Scots' in Virginia (III. iii. 40–7) that really caused offence at Court, but the play contains a number of references to things Scottish which might have been 'misconstrued'. For example, the tailor brings a Scotch farthingale, a type of gown, with him: 'Tailor, Poldavis, prithee fit it, fit it: is this a right Scot? Does it clip close? and bear up round?' (I. ii. 48–50). There is nothing in the words *per se* to cause offence, but this seems fairly obviously to be a cue for some bawdy by-play; moreover, the comedy on stage may have been given a further dimension by the presence of a performing ape. We have Jonson's own testimony for the tricks such apes might perform; in the Induction to *Bartholomew Fair* he tells of a 'well-educated ape' able 'to come over the chain, for the King of England, and back again for the Prince, and sit still on his arse for the Pope, and the King of Spain!' (17–20). Heaven only knows what such an ape might have been trained to do, say, at the word 'Scot'. The play is shot through, in other words, with possible satiric gibes aimed at the Scots who had come south with the King, and also at the proliferating knighthoods bestowed by him, which were widely thought to demean that honour; the one genuinely undiplomatic line in the play only distils and points up something with must have given it a general piquancy for its original audiences. Perhaps this is also true of *Epicoene*, though in ways we can no longer discover.

All the evidence suggests that this *was* essentially the case with *Sejanus*. Modern critics have often voiced their bafflement that a play so notable for its historical accuracy could even have been suspected of 'glancing' at contemporary events:

> The prosecution of Jonson before the Privy Council is but another instance of the incomprehensible vagaries of censorship. *Sejanus* would seem incapable of local or contemporary application. It is a transcript from Tacitus and Suetonius done after the high Roman fashion. There is never a hint of English manners or mentality. It is a record of marble tyrannies, alabaster oppressions, liberties and rebellions in stone. There is no suggestion that the freedoms for which the victims of Sejanus died or the sinister divinity of Tiberius have the faintest analogy with anything to be observed in contemporary laws, liberties or persons.[8]

It should already be clear that this is a naive view of the context of Jacobean drama; no play was so innocent as not to be capable of 'application', and the Privy Council were not fools. But there is something doubly worrying about this kind of naivety; in denying the possibility of contemporary 'glancings', the author is also effectively arguing that this is a *dead* play ('marble tyrannies, alabaster oppressions'). If this is true of the historical realism of the tragedies, is it not equally true – nearly four hundred years later – of the contemporary realism of Jonson's comedies? I do not wish to argue that Jonson's 'glancings' are what make his plays – either tragedies or comedies – a living force; but they are indicative of the approach, both to art and to life, which keeps Jonson as a living and challenging figure in our literary traditions, and it is to ignore an essential part of the man to deny even the possibility of their existence. Jonson's works are never merely 'transcripts', whether of the past or of the present, but intellectually passionate attempts to understand the world in which he lived, and the 'glancings' form a part of those attempts.

In the case of *Sejanus*, we can never really be sure what caused offence in the original production, because we know for a fact that the printed text 'in all numbers, is not the same with that which was acted on the public stage; wherein a second pen had good share' (To the Reader, 43–5). But the best clue to where the problem arose probably lies in that feature which Jonson remembered and boasted about years later to Drummond: 'In his *Sejanus* he hath translated a whole oration of Tacitus.' This translation (III. 407–60) is often cited as an example of Jonson's pedantic scholarship, but nothing could be farther from the truth; this long speech by Cremutius Cordus is a spirited defence of the impartiality of history, and a refutation of those who read into histories analogies with their own times never intended by their authors. We may almost imagine Jonson quoting this very speech in his own defence before the Privy Council – but thereby paradoxically contradicting himself, since that very speech of Cordus would become a piece of history with modern implications that Tacitus never dreamed of. The fact is that, through Cordus, Jonson doth protest too much: 'The weakness in Cordus's defence lies in its element of disingenuousness, in Jonson's reluctance to admit that historical writing does, sometimes, allude to current events and is designed to illuminate them. We have, then, the odd spectacle of a manifesto of the disinterestedness of historical writing that is itself anything but disinterested.'[9] This particular kind of 'odd spectacle' is one we repeatedly find in relation to Jonson and covert allusions.

There is every possibility, in short, that Jonson had deliberately done in *Sejanus* what Shakespeare found himself inadvertently having done in *Richard II*: constructed an allegory of contemporary events. Indeed, the likelihood is that the same events were involved, albeit seen from a very different perspective. The fact that Jonson had chosen to write about the fall and death of a royal favourite only two years after the traumatic eclipse of the Earl of Essex must be suspicious in itself; the fall (though not death) of Raleigh and the rise of the Salisbury/Northampton faction at Court in July 1603 may also have been too similar in essence to ancient Rome for some people's comfort. It was Northampton, of course, who accused Jonson of 'popery and treason', apparently in connection with the play. Moreover, the use of spies and informers to trap the Germanicans was suspiciously similar to the tactics used by contemporary authorities to deal with the Roman Catholic question: it remains a moot point whether they were dealing with a real threat of fabricating evidence for their own purposes. Jonson, of course, was involved in this question from both sides (see pp. 6–10, above). The Privy Council probably had every reason for finding *Sejanus* a slyly provocative play, posing uncomfortable questions about the nature of liberty and political virtue, the use of spies, the careers of royal favourites and ministers, even the scope of royal power itself. And all, it would seem, in the form of a scrupulously authentic history.

Jonson, of course, vehemently and repeatedly denies that any such 'applications' are intended in his plays; in the dedicatory Epistle to *Volpone*, he directly addresses the question of 'glancings':

And, howsoever I cannot escape, from some, the imputation of sharpness, but that they will say, I have taken a pride, or lust, to be bitter, and not my youngest infant (i.e. *Sejanus*) but hath come into the world with all his teeth; I would ask of these supercilious politics, what nation, society, or general order, or state I have provok'd? what public person? whether I have not (in all these) preserv'd their dignity, as mine own person, safe? (47–54)

Jonson writes from the security of the allegorical method, drawing on the age-old defence of the satirist: he depicts only historical figures and generalised embodiments of vice – it is not his fault if malicious or ill-informed people decide that the cap fits some particular modern figure. 'What broad reproofs have I us'd? Where have I been particular? Where personal? except to a mimic, cheater, bawd, or buffon, creatures (for their insolencies) worthy to be tax'd?' (55–8).

He proceeds to warn against over-ingenious interpretations, in a way that any modern reader must take to heart:

I know, that nothing can be so innocently writ, or carried, but may be made obnoxious to construction; marry, whil'st I bear mine own innocence about me, I fear it not. Application, is now, grown a trade with many; and there are, that profess to have a key for the deciphering of everything: but let wise and noble persons take heed how they be too credulous, or give leave to these invading interpreters, to be over-familiar with their fames, who cunningly, and often, utter their own virulent malice, under other men's simplest meanings. (62–70)

He returns to the theme, in rather more jocular tone, in the Induction to *Bartholomew Fair*, where he makes it one of the Articles of Agreement between himself and the

hearers and spectators that they neither in themselves conceal, nor suffer by them to be concealed, any state-decipherer, or politic picklock of the scene, so solemnly ridiculous as to search out who was meant by the gingerbread woman, who by the hobby-horse-man, who by the costermonger, nay, who by their wares. Or that will pretend to affirm, on his own inspired ignorance, what Mirror of Magistrates is meant by the Justice, what great lady by the pig-woman, what concealed statesman by the seller of mousetraps, and so of the rest. (136–45)

It is possible, of course, that Jonson is perfectly sincere; certainly, it would be difficult to *prove* that he is not. In the end, we can only weigh the balance of probabilities. The fact that the authorities repeatedly accused Jonson of doing what he denies is not proof, but it must promote suspicion. The fact that Jonson so consistently denies it proves nothing either; obviously he was not going to *admit* it. It is, however, possible to construe the denials in the end as protesting too much: in effect (as in Cordus's speech) drawing attention to something in the writing by publicly insisting that it is not there. That is the assumption I make throughout this chapter. It must certainly be the case in those instances of allusions to contemporary figures where politics and the aristocracy are not involved, and where Jonson felt correspondingly less need to cover his tracks – there was no law of libel, as such. All the evidence, for example, suggests that the figure of Crispinus in *Poetaster* is a satirical portrait of the poet and playwright, John Marston; not only does Crispinus use inflated language and neologisms associated with Marston, but we even have Jonson's own admission to Drummond that he 'wrote his *Poetaster* on him'. It simply will not do in this case for Jonson to claim that he depicted the vice and that it is Marston's hard luck if the cap fits. Similarly, we know that in *The Alchemist* the ludicrous scenes where Dapper is swindled out of his money by Dol in the guise of the Queen of Faery are a close reproduction of what actually happened to one Thomas Rodgers – events which were common knowledge when the play was first performed (see p. 114, above). It would be stretching naivety too far to suggest that Jonson happened accidentally to dream up such a similar situation, or that he did not expect his audience to recognise the similarities. In such contexts, Jonson's protestations of innocence look suspiciously like intriguing advertisements: come and see what this play is *not* about . . .

These two very different examples do indicate how difficult it may be to generalise about the significance we should attach to such 'glancings'. There is every reason to suppose that there was a degree of personal animosity behind Jonson's attack on Marston, but no reason to suppose that he even knew Thomas Rodgers. Rather than speculate about Jonson's personal motivation in such cases, it is more fruitful to consider what, if anything, they add to the plays and how they contribute to the works as a whole. In the cases of both Crispinus in *Poetaster* and Dapper in *The Alchemist*, these are relatively minor characters, though both enjoy (if that is the word) set-piece moments of extreme discomfiture. There is no way that we can say that, having spotted the real-life characters to whom they allude, we now have a 'key' which opens up those plays and all their enigmas. On the contrary, we see in Crispinus just one example of a bad poet among many such, in Dapper one dupe among a multitude. We may be able to extend the net of allusions a little – Demetrius in *Poetaster* may represent Dekker, for example – but never to the point where such allusions take over, as it were, the imaginative centre of the plays. No one has suggested (or, I suspect, is likely to suggest) that Ovid in *Poetaster* or Sir Epicure Mammon in *The Alchemist* 'shadow' any specific contemporary figures. The covert allusions in these plays are not the most important things about them; they are not the 'point' of Jonson's writing them. What they do offer is an additional dimension or perspective to the main action; the audience is confronted, through them, with the suggestion that the themes and issues of the play do not exist purely in the realms of imagination and fiction – they have a tangible existence in the world the audience inhabits.

Such allusions therefore constitute a challenge to the audience – not merely to spot them in the first instance, but to 'appply' them when spotted, to ask how the play relates in general terms to their own world. The allusions offer, in effect, windows between the world of the play and the real world, and so act as spurs to understanding. They are a hallmark of Jonson's classicism, of that capacity for seeing through a particular event to a general truth which allowed Milton to create *Lycidas* out of the death of Edward King, Dryden to create *Absalom and Achitophel* out of the 1681 exclusion crisis or Pope to create *The Rape of the Lock* out of an assault on Miss Arabella Fermor's hair. It is, as we have seen, Jonson's capacity for teasing the general significance out of a particular event, place or person which makes him the master of the masque and gives such weight to the best of his poetry. We should not, therefore, be surprised to find it in his plays even if, for diplomatic reasons, his allusions to persons and events there had to be more ambiguous and indirect; they tend, on the whole, to be less complimentary. I do not intend here to pursue all the covert allusions there might be in Jonson's works – a monumental task. But I think it is appropriate to try to convey something of the flavour of the daring and wit with which he pursued his art; it must have contributed to his contemporaries' esteem of him, and may do something to dispel our modern complacency about him. I shall, therefore, conclude this chapter by tracing the forbidden topic to which Jonson alluded most persistently, presumably because of his first-hand involvement in it – the Gunpowder Plot. I cannot claim that these are 'typical' of Jonson's covert allusions; each of these allusions is its own animal, each a different kind of spur to our understanding. But the sheer range of Jonson's allusions to the Gunpowder Plot does reflect his inventiveness and persistence, and indicates how integral the allusive method was to his art. It is also convenient that the Gunpowder Plot is an unusually familiar episode in our history, part of our folklore, no less.

There are, I believe, significant references to the Gunpowder Plot in the *Epigrams*, *Volpone* and *Catiline*. Before assessing what they add up to, it will be useful to remind ourselves of the historical events to which they allude. This is not as easy as it might be, for the simple reason that historians are divided on the question of exactly what happened. There was apparently a conspiracy by a number of fanatical Roman Catholics to blow up the Houses of Parliament while the King, peers and MPs were all assembled there for the state opening of Parliament on 5 November 1605; their leaders were Robert Catesby, Thomas Winter and John Wright, while other notable conspirators included Guy Fawkes and Sir Everard Digby – father of the Sir Kenelm Digby who was later to edit the Jonson second folio. They were supposedly driven to this desperate measure by the revival of repressive measures against the Catholics, after early promises by the new King that loyal Catholics had nothing to fear. In March 1605 they gained access to a vault under the House of Lords and stored thirty-six barrels of gunpowder in it. The Plot was discovered when an anonymous letter was sent to Lord Monteagle (Jonson spells his name Mounteagle), a Catholic peer, warning him in mysterious terms to avoid the state opening of Parliament. He took the letter to the Privy Council; they showed it to the King, who was later given credit for having deciphered within it a threat of violence against himself and Parliament. The cellars under the Parliament buildings were consequently searched, and Guy Fawkes was found in position, waiting to light the fuse. He was arrested, tortured and subsequently executed, as were those other conspirators who were captured alive after an abortive rising in the Midlands, timed to coincide with the explosion. Among those executed were two Jesuit priests, Fathers Greenway and Garnet, who probably had little or nothing to do with the conspiracy, though they may have known about it in advance; among those who died during the rising was very probably the one man who knew the whole truth of the affair, Robert Catesby.

The main controversy about this version of events centres on the role played in it by the Privy Council or, more specifically, by its effective head, Robert Cecil, Earl of Salisbury. That there was a conspiracy of some sort seems certain; that it was discovered in this dramatic manner at the eleventh hour, and that the Jesuits were involved, is far more open to doubt. We have already seen that Jonson himself was seen in the company of the plotters barely a month before the appointed date of the coup, and that he was used by Salisbury in the investigations immediately after its discovery. The possibility that he was all along Salisbury's agent, using his known Catholic sympathies to gain access to the Plotters' counsels, cannot easily be dismissed. Nor, in all probability, would he have been alone in this; Lord Monteagle must be suspect. For one thing, Thomas Winter was in his service; for another, he was related by marriage to one of the Plotters (Francis Tresham). There is also the fact that he, like some of the Plotters, had been involved in the Essex rebellion of 1601, for which he was heavily fined, and was still deeply in debt. There is every likelihood that he, like Jonson, was an agent of Salisbury and that, if the conspiracy was not actually concocted by Salisbury, it was carefully watched, nurtured and finally 'discovered' by him, via his double-agents, in such a way as to gain him the maximum possible political advantage. It was argued at the time, and repeatedly since, that such a Machiavellian course of action might benefit Salisbury in two ways: firstly it would give him – an apparently zealous Protestant – an opportunity to discredit Roman Catholics in general and Jesuits in particular, enabling him to bring in even stiffer measures against them and to intensify the use of his extensive spy network; secondly, his success against the conspiracy would serve to make him even more indispensable in the eyes of the King, who was pathologically afraid of plots against his life. These 'benefits' certainly accrued to Salisbury in the wake of the Plot, but whether through his policy or not it is impossible finally to determine.

Jonson refers most openly to the figures involved in the Gunpowder Plot in the *Epigrams*, which contains a poem 'To William, Lord Mounteagle' (60) and three 'To Robert, Earl of Salisbury' (43, 63, 64). If we read these poems independently of each other and of their context in the sequence of epigrams, we will find little that is exceptionable. Mounteagle is hailed as 'saver of my country' (line 10) for his part in the discovery of the Plot; Jonson asks of Salisbury 'What need hast though of me, or my muse?' (43, line 1), but insists on praising him despite his modesty (63), and comes to a climax with the conclusion:

> That whilst I meant but thine to gratulate,
> I have sung the greater fortunes of our state.
>
> (64, lines 17–18)

Jonson would seem, in fact, to be endorsing the public reputations of these men as great servants of the state. It is only when we look, as we learned in chapter 3, at the context of these praises that doubts begin to arise. 'To William, Lord Mounteagle', for example, is placed immediately after that epigram 'On Spies' (59), which Jonson mentioned to Drummond:

> Spies, you are lights in state, but of base stuff,
> Who, when you'have burnt yourselves down to the snuff,
> Stink, and are thrown away. End fair enough.

And the two poems 'To Robert, Earl of Salisbury' placed close after, as epigrams 63 and 64, are immediately followed by 'To My Muse' (65), which begins:

> Away, and leave me, thou thing most abhor'd,
> That hast betray'd me to a worthless lord.
>
> (1–2)

There is nothing, of course, to prove that this 'worthless lord' is Salisbury, but it is uncommonly careless of Jonson to have encouraged the inference if he did not mean it. Similarly, it was most unfortunate that he should make Mounteagle rub shoulders with spies, unless he intended the implication to stick.

What emerge from a careful reading of the *sequence* of poems are accusations, by implication and inference, of guilt and unworthiness. Consider *Epigrams* 58–65 as a sequence: 'To Groom Idiot', 'On Spies', 'To William, Lord Mounteagle', 'To Fool, or Knave', 'To Fine Lady Would-be', 'To Robert, Earl of Salisbury', 'To the Same', and 'To My Muse'. Some of these seem completely out of place – Groom Idiot and Fool, or Knave are unlikely associates for peers of the realm. They seem rather to belong to the sequence just before this, which we considered in chapter 3, containing such figures as Censorious Courtling, Cheveril and Poet-Ape; like them, they are involved with poetry, and specifically Jonson's own verse. Groom Idiot is mocked for completely misreading Jonson's poems, 'losing my points' – that is, both the punctuation and the sense. The opinions of Fool, or Knave are simply scorned; Jonson expresses indifference as to whether misvaluations of his verse arise from foolish ignorance or malicious knavery. The question of misreading or misvaluing Jonson's poetry may not, however, seem so unrelated to his praise of Mounteagle and Salisbury if it is linked with 'To My Muse', where Jonson confronts the issue of the 'truth' of his own panegyric verse. He concludes that poem, as we noted before, with what in effect is the escape clause for all Renaissance writers of panegyrics:

> But I repent me: stay. Whoe'er is rais'd,
> For worth he has not, he is tax'd, not prais'd.
> (15–16)

His poems describe men as they ought to be, not necessarily as they are; if they do not live up to Jonson's praise, so much the more they condemn themselves. It is a doctrine which echoes back over all these poems. The sequence as a whole, then, poses a challenge to any reader not to 'lose [its] points', not to misconstrue it either maliciously or foolishly, but to be an understander, to weigh the truth of what Jonson offers in all particulars. It is difficult to ignore the implication that, even as Jonson salutes these two peers, he is seriously questioning their reputations.

Even if we accept that the collocation of these poems implies criticism of Mounteagle and Salisbury, can we be sure that it relates to the Gunpowder Plot? The poems that comprise the sequence were not all written at the same time, or with the final printed context in mind. 'On Spies' seems to date back to Jonson's 1598 imprisonment, while the last of his poems to Salisbury was written 'Upon the Accession of the Treasurership to Him' – that is, in 1608. It was probably only when the *Epigrams* were assembled for publication in the 1616 folio that the pieces came together to form a larger whole; this was ten years after the Gunpowder Plot (when, incidentally, Salisbury was dead – which may have made criticism of him, albeit oblique, somewhat easier). The strongest evidence has to be the juxtaposing of the names of Mounteagle and Salisbury; the latter had a long and distinguished political career, in which the handling of the Gunpowder Plot and its aftermath was only one significant item, but the former achieved prominence in no other context. To cast doubts on the reputations of both men, and to place them side by side, surely points to the one major event in which they both participated. There is, moreover, one further clue which refers us back to the events of 1605/6 and seems to suggest that Jonson's doubts about Mounteagle and Salisbury are not belated reflections but date from the Gunpowder Plot itself. This is the one poem in the sequence we have not discussed at all and which seems completely out of place: 'To Fine Lady Would-be' (62). She is a lady of the Court, dedicated to its pleasures rather than to the duties and responsibilities of motherhood, which she wards off with abortion-inducing drugs; she seems irrelevant in this world of bad reading, spies and political reputations, except as a very indirect comment on the unnatural moral climate. A Lady Would-be does occur elsewhere in the 1616 folio, however, and we should not ignore the possibility that Jonson is here suggesting a link between these poems and that other context, *Volpone*.

Volpone was the first play that Jonson wrote after the Gunpowder Plot; indeed, he must have written it in the months immediately after his employment in the affair by the Privy Council. The title-page of the folio text assures us that it was first acted in 1605; given that Old Style dating was still in use in England at the time, that could mean any time up to what we should call 1 March 1606. To judge from internal evidence, the play cannot have been completed before January 1606, when a porpoise and a whale such as Sir Politic and Peregrine discuss (II. i. 40, 60) were actually seen in England. So a first performance in late January or February 1606 seems likely. Jonson claims that 'this his creature . . . was, two months since, no feature' and that 'five weeks fully penn'd it' (Prologue, 13–14, 16). In other words, the writing of *Volpone* could not have begun more than two months after Jonson's part in the discovery of the Plot. The lines in the prologue were clearly a riposte to those who mocked Jonson's normally slow writing (artful rather than popular), but they also announce to anyone interested that the play has been wholly devised *since* the Plot, which was still the biggest news of the day. Most of the captured Plotters were executed on 30 and 31 January 1606 and, by coincidence, the last major figure to be implicated in the Plot, the Jesuit Henry Garnet, was finally captured on 30 January. Whatever the precise date of *Volpone*'s first performance, the whole affair must have been very much in the minds of Jonson and his audience. It should not be surprising, therefore to find *Volpone* 'glancing' at the Plot. Bearing in mind, however, the official reactions to *Sejanus* and *Eastward Ho*, it would have to be done with extreme discretion, the more so since the Plot was already a source of deep controversy. Early in 1606, the Privy Council was anxious to establish an 'official' view of what had happened; an account was published, known as the *King's Book*, purporting to give James's own view of events, and this was shortly followed by Salisbury's own *An Answer to Certain Scandalous Papers*, which attempted to scotch rumours doubting the authenticity of the Plot. It clearly would not do for Jonson to be associated with indiscretions on this extremely sensitive topic.

For all this, there is a fairly obvious link between *Volpone* and Salisbury even in the title. Volpone, of course, means the Fox, and Jonson's contemporaries used the Italian and English versions of the title interchangeably. The Fox, as it happens, had been widely used as a nickname for Salisbury's father, the first Lord Burghley; Burghley, like his younger son, was often characterised as crafty and devious (he has been suggested as the original of Polonius in *Hamlet*) and we find, for example, Francis Bacon sneering at one of his political manoeuvres: 'The old fox crouches and whines.'[10] But Burghley had died in 1598; there is considerable evidence, however, that the nickname attached itself to his younger son and political successor.[11] One of the most tantalising pieces of evidence is an epitaph penned by Samuel Rowlandson and entitled 'In Vulponem':

> The Fox is earth'd now in the ground,
> Who living, fear'd not horn nor hound,
> That kept the huntsmen at a bay,
> Before their faces seiz'd their prey.
> Of whose successful thriving wit,
> Books have been made, and plays been writ.[12]

The hunting references allude to King James's passion for the sport, which ambitious courtiers naturally made the most of; Salisbury was physically disabled and so did not join in, but nevertheless outwitted his competitors until his death. It is tempting and, I hope to show, reasonable to suppose that one of the plays that had 'been writ' about him is *Volpone*.

Jonson's audience would, then, have been alerted to possible 'glancings' at Salisbury by the mere title of the play, though its traditional beast–fable format makes the allusion less than immediately incriminating. In the play itself we find no simple allegory of contemporary events, or any single character 'shadowing' Salisbury and his policies; given the dangers, this was unthinkable. But there are two characters who do, in their own ways, seem to 'glance' at him: Nano and Sir Politic Would-be. First, and on stage most visually effective, is the zany dwarf, Nano; he is the most prominent of the three unnatural 'bastards' of Volpone, taking the main role in the burlesque descent of Pythagoras's soul (I. ii. 1–62), helping Volpone in the mountebank scene (II. ii.), claiming 'precedency' over his two fellows in the second recitation (III. iii. 2–20) and being generally involved in the scenes with Lady Would-be. The significant link between Nano and Salisbury is that the latter was abnormally small, as well as being hunch-backed. Queen Elizabeth, an inveterate nicknamer, called him her elf and her pigmy, to his great distress.[13] King James more notoriously used to call him his 'little beagle'. The dwarf who acts as zany to the Venetian magnifico is an obvious parallel to the little, deformed politician:

> First, for your dwarf, he's little, and witty,
>   And everything, as it is little, is pretty;
> Else, why do men say to a creature of my shape,
>   So soon as they see him, it's a pretty little ape.
> And why a pretty ape? but for pleasing imitation,
> Of greater men's action, in a ridiculous fashion.
>
> (III. iii. 9–14)

This may simply mean that the dwarf amuses people by imitating fully grown-up men, but it could equally mean that Nano's role in the play was to parody some 'greater' man who, all the circumstantial evidence suggests, would have to be Salisbury. He is certainly called on to be present on a number of occasions which might well give scope for inventive parody, and when indeed it is difficult to see why he is at all if not for some such purpose. If a 'well-educated ape' could point the satire in *Eastward Ho*, there is no knowing what the actor who first created Nano might get away with; the part was almost certainly played by the King's Men's usual player of witty fools (Touchstone, Feste and Lear's Fool among them), Robert Armin. He was certainly capable of 'pointing' such a role with all the necessary embellishments.

Clearly we cannot expect to tell from the printed text what form such embellishments might take, but we can identify passages where they might turn 'innocent' text into something far more satirical – for example, the 'transmigration' entertainment and the mountebank scene. We noticed in chapter 2, p. 65, how significant the former scene was as an epitome of the play as a whole, an image of the degeneration which Volpone's baleful influence promotes. Given that *Volpone* is a play about inheritance, about the passing on of wealth and power, parallels with the Cecil 'dynasty' are only too likely: the hunch-backed Salisbury's body receiving his father's transmigrant soul. The idea would seem even more cruelly apt to anyone who knew that Salisbury's daughter, Frances, was also physically deformed. We should also notice that, in the last three transmigrations of Pythagoras's soul before it reaches Androgyno, Nano's recitation suddenly focuses – for no apparent reason – on the religious dissensions of 'these days of reformation' (I. ii. 30). Firstly the soul was a Protestant, 'one of the reformed' (31); then a Catholic monk, a 'Carthusian' (34); and latterly a Puritan, 'a precise, pure, illuminate brother' (43). It seemed to some of Jonson's contemporaries that Salisbury had similarly 'shifted [his] coat' in the years leading up to his militant anti-Catholicism in the wake of the Gunpowder Plot – once a conventional upholder of the Protestant settlement in England, then encouraging James's toleration of the Catholics at the outset of the reign and now turning on them with Puritan zeal.

This should alert us to the specific contemporary relevance of choosing Venice as the setting for this play. Discussions of the play have emphasised its fame as a cosmopolitan commercial centre (the Venice of *The Merchant of Venice*, though its wealth is viewed with a more jaundiced eye), and this is obviously relevant. But its status as, in effect, middle ground in the struggle between the Protestants and the Catholics in the Counter-Reformation is also undoubtedly significant. The city was Catholic but maintained its independence of the Papacy and of other Catholic powers to such an extent that Sir Henry Wotton, an English ambassador at this time, even entertained hopes of its turning Protestant. It is indicative of its equivocal position that, when Jonson wanted to find the Catholic priest for the Privy Council, he first approached the chaplain of the Venetian ambassador, presumably expecting a sympathetic response; no one seems to have connected this fact with the choice of Venice as the setting of the play he had finished writing two to three months later. It is the city's role as a centre of Counter-Reformation politics that makes it so attractive to Sir Politic Would-be. And there can be no doubt that the most significant figure directing England's role in the Counter-Reformation was the Earl of Salisbury.

The mountebank scene also offers considerable scope for extempore parodic pointing; Nano is certainly there – Volpone's first words, 'Mount, zany' (II. ii. 28) draw attention to him, and he later addresses him as 'Zan Fritada' (114–15) – but he says nothing. His only given function is to sing the two songs – but it would be unlike a true zany to stand quietly by while other characters perform. One significant feature of this scene is that it is the only occasion on which Volpone and Sir Politic Would-be are on stage together – the latter a credulous believer in everything Volpone says; we may suspect that Nano directs his attentions to him. The evidence for this comes in a later scene, when Mosca 'rescues' Volpone from the clutches of Lady

Would-be by telling her (falsely, as it happens) that her husband is consorting with 'the most cunning courtesan, of Venice' (III. v. 20). She rushes out in a fit of jealousy, only to return immediately, to ask which way they were heading and to add, rather mysteriously: 'I pray you lend me your dwarf' (29). Thus Nano is present when she confronts her husband and the supposed courtesan (IV. ii; iii), but in fact he does nothing; he has only one more or less superfluous line (IV. ii. 2) and then appears to take no further part in the proceedings, despite the care which Jonson has taken to have him there. As in the mountebank scene, the likeliest explanation is that Jonson wants him there to 'ape' Sir Pol.

If Nano is in some way a physical reminder of Salisbury, Sir Pol seems to be a comic version of the arch-politician. There may even be a particular significance in his name; Salisbury complains in one of his letters about the endless succession of titles and nicknames that the King was pouring on him: 'From Essendon to Cranborne, from Cranborne to Salisbury, from Salisbury to Beagle, from Beagle to Thom Derry, from Thom Derry to Parrot, which I hate most . . .'[14] No doubt to be known as Pol-Parrot was the common fate of politicians (see *Epigrams* 71, 'On Court Parrot'), but if the King applied it to his hunchbacked Principal Secretary, it was surely likely to stick. For all that, the most convincing parallel between Sir Pol and Salisbury lies in their both being pedlars and discoverers of plots. From the outset, Sir Pol's talk is full of schemes and espionage:

> it is no salt desire
> Of seeing countries, shifting a religion,
> Nor any disaffection to the state
> Where I was bred (and, unto which I owe
> My dearest plots,) hath brought me out . . .
> (II. i. 4–8)

He receives the news of Stone the fool's death:

> I knew him one of the most dangerous heads
> Living within the state . . .
> He has receiv'd weekly intelligence,
> Upon my knowledge, out of the Low Countries
> (For all parts of the world) in cabbages;
> And those dispens'd, again, to'ambassadors,
> In oranges, musk-melons . . .
> (II. i. 65–6; 68–72)

There was, as everyone knew, only one man in England receiving

'weekly intelligence' and communicating it to ambassadors, and that
was the Earl of Salisbury. Peregrine, in one of the most pointed
asides of the play (which we noted in another context: chapter 2, p.
69), virtually challenges the audience not to recognise the allusion:

> O this knight
> (Were he well known) would be a precious thing
> To fit our English stage: he that should write
> But such a fellow, should be thought to feign
> Extremely, if not maliciously.
>
> (II. i. 56–60)

Sir Pol's whole part, in fact, is a marvellous parodic commentary on
the world of spies and 'conceal'd statesmen' of which Salisbury was
the centre and which we have some reason for supposing that Jonson
knew at first hand. He confidently claims to 'Know the ebbs / And
flows of state' (II. i. 104–5), but it is his own vacuous 'plot, / To sell
the state of Venice, to the Turk' (v. iv. 37–8) which gives Peregrine
the inspiration for the counter-plot which undoes him. It is difficult
to believe that it is entirely coincidental that this plot for betraying
Christian Venice to the Infidels parallels the Gunpowder Plot's aim
of replacing Protestantism in England with Catholicism.

Paradoxically, it may well be that Sir Pol's real significance in
Volpone lies in his irrelevance, the fact that all his talk of plots and
cyphers obfuscates the simple truth that the state of Venice is in far
more danger from the cancer within itself than it is from his 'politic'
scheming. Is this Jonson's real reflection on the Gunpowder Plot –
that the fabric of society is being undermined insidiously by the Fox
within, while so much attention is diverted on to the pathetic Plotters? Sir Pol's fate in the play is not without its ironies; hiding under
the tortoise shell, he succumbs to a form of poetic justice such as
occurs only in literature, having desperately admitted that his plots
were not real but 'Drawn out of play-books' (v. iv. 42). This is the
exact inverse of the fate of Volpone, who suffers a fate appropriate for
real life rather than for comic art. These two versions of justice,
mirror-images of each other, perfectly define that distinction
between 'real' world and 'play' world which is so often central to
Jonson's testing of the 'understanding' of his audience. We are left to
wonder, from *Volpone*, what real justice awaits the politicians and
plotters of Jacobean London, and how many of their own plots were
only 'drawn out of play-books'.

There is room for a good deal of debate about some of what I have
claimed here as 'glancings' and what they add up to. It seems to me

incontrovertible that there is something 'covert' about Nano's role in the play and that Sir Pol's inanities reflect directly on the current political scene; it is particularly significant that Jonson went out of his way to have both characters on stage at the same time. But it may be asking too much to try to translate all these nuances and possibilities into a cryptic but coherent statement about Salisbury, or the Gunpowder Plot, or anything; the Master of the Revels apparently could not do so then, so it is asking a good deal to try to do it now. Yet it seems certain that some such dimension exists in the play and would have added a particular piquancy for its original audiences. It is worth repeating, however, that this 'dimension' would not have constituted the real 'meaning' or even the primary 'significance' of the play for Jonson. In the figure of Volpone, he has created a universal symbol of the greed, gullibility and corruptibility of mankind; the implicit suggestion that, in some respects, such a figure lives and flourishes in Jacobean London, and will take a good deal of 'mortifying', only adds a particular urgency to the general truth. This is worth bearing in mind when considering the question of the extent to which *Catiline* may also have something to say about the Gunpowder Plot. I shall say less in this regard about *Catiline* than I have about the *Epigrams* and *Volpone*, for two reasons. Firstly, the topic has been dealt with at exhaustive length by B. N. de Luna in her *Jonson's Romish Plot*. And secondly because my own 'understanding' readers should by now be in a position themselves to assess the nature and likelihood of any such 'glancings' in this play.

Dr de Luna makes a very good case for the general similarities to be drawn between the Catiline conspiracy and the Gunpowder Plot – desperate men of the 'old order' determined to overthrow the new, the use of spies and informers, even some uncanny parallels in the names – Catiline/Catesby, Cicero/Cecil etc.; she also draws attention to some pointedly anachronistic allusions to violent explosions in the imagery of the play. But whether she establishes that *Catiline* is a 'self-justifying parallelograph on the Powder Plot' (p. 143) as she claims – virtually every detail of the historical record tailored to shadow contemporary events and justify Jonson's own part in the proceedings – must be much more open to question. It is always possible that Jonson was trying to do something exceptional, aiming for a 'parallelograph' rather than the diffuse and discreet allusions apparent elsewhere in his works, but I would need more convincing. Such a 'parallelograph' would not just be a feature or dimension of the play; it would be its whole *raison d'etre*, and that is contrary to Jonson's usual practice. It is more reasonable to assume that the play is similar in essence to the other works we have considered: no doubt it capitalises on the remarkable parallels between Roman and Jacobean history, but this remains a provocative additional dimension to the work and not its whole purpose or meaning. The similarities between the past and the more familiar present open windows on to the general and recurrent truths of human nature and behaviour.

It seems indisputable that such covert allusions gave Jonson's works an edge or a piquancy for contemporaries which, on the whole, they cannot have for us today. The 1616 folio, with its recurrent 'glancings' at the Essex rebellion, at the Gunpowder Plot, at Salisbury, at Lady Arbella Stuart, at Marston, at the Thomas Rodgers swindle, and doubtless many other persons and events – besides the above-board salutations to the King, Jonson's noble patrons and his fellow artists – must have been a very pointed record of recent history for its original readers; this aspect of it must have contributed to the challenging reputation Jonson enjoyed in his day, and even in the century after his death, while some of those events and personalities were more vividly recalled than has since been the case. But we must not get such things out of proportion or assume that they make Jonson's works a closed book for most readers today. In many ways the fact that most of the allusions are covert is their saving grace; the poems, plays and masques were designed to be perfectly intelligible even if the reader – then or now – is not aware of a particular 'glancing'. This is in perfect accord with Jonson's artistic principles. As a writer in the classical tradition, he is anxious to confront what is permanent and recurrent in the human condition, following models and styles of writing which have best stood the test of time. So there must always be an ambivalence about his contemporary 'glancings'; their journalistic or scandal value must not obscure the representative truth, or universal principle, that they embody. So if we see Sir Politic Would-be as the type of the over-devious politician, or Crispinus as the model of a poetaster, or Dapper as gullibility incarnate, we are not missing anything crucial if we do not catch the allusions to Salisbury, Marston or Thomas Rodgers. We have seen through to their representative significance, as valid now as it was in Jonson's day.

What we might miss, however, is the flavour of Jonson as a satiric tactician. Modern readers often find this concentration on 'models' or 'types' of human behaviour off-putting in literature (though the same readers may find it quite acceptable when it is wrapped in the jargon of modern sociology or psychology); it is, they object, all too abstract and not part of the real experience of people. The pressure in

Jonson's art, however, is always to bridge the gulf between 'real experience' and the general truths which underlie it. Volpone is not merely an artistic symbol; his counterparts really live among us – then, now and always; paradoxically, the more closely Jonson identifies the foibles of his own age, the more accurately he delineates those of all ages. The art of 'glancing', in other words, is an epitome of Jonson's art as a whole, something which draws the reader into the complex business of judging art and life; covert allusions are calls to our 'understanding', to our appreciation of the significant ways in which art meets life.

7

Bartholomew Fair

In *Bartholomew-Fair*, or the lowest kind of comedy . . . he does so raise his matter . . . as to render it delightful; which he could never have performed, had he only said or done those very things that are daily spoken or practised in the Fair: for then the Fair itself would be as full of pleasure to an ingenious person as the play; which we manifestly see it is not. But he hath made an excellent lazar of it; the copy is of price, though the original be vile.[1]

Bartholomew Fair is one of the most ambitious plays of the Renaissance period. It runs to over 4000 lines of text, when most of its contemporaries have around 2500. There are well over thirty speaking parts, if we include the puppets and the characters from the Induction; the closing scene alone requires eighteen characters with speaking parts besides any 'passengers' and incidental fair-folk who might be assumed to be there. Most Jacobean plays were written to be performed by a company of twelve adult actors and up to four boys, who took junior and female roles, so we can only assume that the newly formed Lady Elizabeth's Men who gave the first performances of this play were specially augmented for the production. Two other factors also single out this play as special. Its first performance was on 31 October 1614, 'at the Hope [Theatre] on the Bankside, in the county of Surrey' (Induction, 65–6); its second performance was the following night, at Court – the only occasion we know of when a play was transferred so quickly from the public stage to Court, which has suggested to some people that it was really written with the Court performance in mind, the public showing being something of a dress rehearsal. This hypothesis is given more plausibility by the play's other unique feature: it is the only such work that Jonson dedicated to his greatest patron, King James.

The play also occupies a special place in Jonson's canon. It was completed two years before the first folio was published, but was not included there for lack of space; there is good reason, however, for supposing that Jonson was well advanced with the business of revising and editing his works for the folio at the time he wrote the play (*c*. 1613–14), since publication of that volume was delayed for a time by the printer's complete preoccupation with Sir Walter

Raleigh's monumental *The History of the World*. Perhaps this is one reason why there is so much about *Bartholomew Fair* that reminds us of Jonson's earlier work, almost as if it was designed to stand as the keystone of his writing to that point. To mention only some of the more obvious examples: Quarlous and Winwife, two witty young gallants, remind us of Kno'well Jr and Wellbred in *Every Man In His Humour*; Grace Wellborn reminds us of Bridget Kitely in the same play, and also of Dame Pliant in *The Alchemist*; the anti-Puritan satire aimed at Zeal-of-the-Land Busy and Dame Purecraft carries on from the exposure of Tribulation and Ananias in *The Alchemist*; the accusation that the 'male' puppets wear female clothing echoes the key deception in *Epicoene*; the game of vapours is only a more extreme version of the games of 'substantives and adjectives' and 'a thing done and who did it' in *Cynthia's Revels*; Littlewit as the proud author of a puppet-play might come out of *Poetaster*; the stage-Irish of Whit is a clear sequel to that in *The Irish Masque at Court*, performed twice in the Christmas festivities of 1613–14.

Perhaps the most telling of all Jonson's backward glances in the play is Adam Overdo, an orator/magistrate who is a lively parody of Cicero in *Catiline*; he discovers 'enormities' where Cicero discovered plots and even begins one of his tirades with Cicero's famous lament, 'O tempora! O mores!' (II. ii. 113), which had been used in its original context ('O age, and manners!' IV. 190) in *Catiline*. This implicit self-parody is all the more pointed if we link it with the worldly wise observation of the puppeteer Lantern Leatherhead: '*The Gunpowder Plot*, there was a get-penny! I have presented that to an eighteen- or twenty-pence audience, nine times in an afternoon. Your home-born projects prove ever the best, they are so easy, and familiar, they put too much learning i'their things now o'days' (v. i. 12–16). Is this a wry reflection on his own 'learned tragedy' about the Gunpowder Plot and its failure with an audience which would, nevertheless, lap up some crude puppet-play on the same subject? Is it possible that *Bartholomew Fair* is in some respects an 'answer' to the failure of *Catiline* with the public? Both plays point to the extreme difficulty of achieving the blend of true judgement and action upon which the defence of virtue depends; both plays explore the dangers of allowing ends to justify means – Caesar's ironic warning to Cicero, for example, that 'No man should, for hate of guilty men, / Lose his own innocence' (IV. 135–6) is paralleled by Quarlous's learning that 'Facinus quos inquinat, aequat' (IV. vi. 29–30) – crime levels those it pollutes. Both plays, in short, display a concern for the severe limitations of reason, virtue and authority in the face of passion, unreason, ignorance and 'licence'. It is because *Bartholomew Fair* is so self-consciously an extension of the themes and concerns of the works in the 1616 folio that it seems proper to consider it here, even though it does not appear in that volume.

It would not be difficult to construe the 'easy' and 'familiar' manner of *Bartholomew Fair* as, in effect, a recantation on Jonson's part of his former 'high seriousness' – to see this play as a celebration of human nature, inadequacies and all, rather than a censure of it. For example, all of the characters in the play who set themselves up as figures of authority – Overdo, Busy and Waspe – undergo moments of extreme discomfiture, when their self-importance is publicly deflated. But we should have learned from *Volpone, Epicoene* and *The Alchemist* that in the best of Jonson's comedies there is an ironic, challenging relationship between the manner of his writing and its matter; the attractiveness of the entertainment is provocatively at odds with what Jonson implies about the audience's capacity to 'understand' and profit from his art. Earlier figures of judgement and authority – the Court of Avocatori, Truewit, Surly – were shown to be inadequate, without Jonson repudiating his satiric and moral seriousness. So it is here. If Jonson recants at all, it is for offering a 'learned tragedy' like *Catiline* to an audience he should have known was incapable of appreciating it; the 'easy' and 'familiar' manner of *Bartholomew Fair* is mock-deference to a public which has shown itself unfit for anything more taxing – a mock-deference which becomes all the more ironic if we assume that the specific audience in mind for the comedy was the Court rather than the groundlings in that bear-pit of a theatre used for the first performance.

All this is spelled out, in fact, in the effortless paradoxes of the Induction,[2] which points out for any truly 'understanding gentlemen' (line 49) the qualities of art, wit and judgement that make this play so much more than the broad slice of low-life it seems at first to be (see the quotation from Dryden at the head of this chapter). The Stage-Keeper who appears first is displeased with the play because it does not contain real 'Bartholomew-birds' like 'little Davy', the bully, or 'Kindheart', the tooth-drawer. In his garrulous naivety he explains that he 'kept the stage in Master Tarleton's time, I thank my stars' (Induction, 36–7); Tarleton, a great comic actor, died in 1588, so the old man is really living in the past and longs for simple realism, combined with the crudest of entertainment: 'a juggler with a well-educated ape to come over the chain, for the King of England, and back again for the Prince, and sit still on his arse for the Pope, and the King of Spain' (17–20); he is doubtless one of those whom the Scrivener will commend for their 'virtuous and stay'd ignorance', 'that will swear, *Ieronimo*, or *Andronicus* are the best plays, yet' (110, 106–7).³ By appearing *in propria persona* the Stage-Keeper becomes a piece of that very simple realism which he himself recommends, but the implication is clear that only a 'well-educated ape' would really appreciate the things he approves of. His appearance is thus an attempt to forestall any expectation of simple realism in the play proper by pointing out its severe limitations; as so often, Jonson begins the process of buiding a positive case by demolishing the negative alternatives.

He develops this in the mock-serious 'Articles of Agreement' between the audience and the author outlined by the Scrivener, which are a distillation of all the inductions, prefaces and prologues Jonson had employed before. In essence the 'articles' spell out what for Jonson is the essence of the theatrical experience: that his responsibility is to provide a work of art (not a slice of life) which will both entertain and instruct an audience, while the audience's responsibility is to pass a reasoned judgement upon it in as far as they are able. The articles are, of course, peppered with provocative examples of what this contract entails, which keep them entertaining even while the serious points are made: these include the point that the audience shall be free 'to like or dislike at their own charge' (86–7), drawing attention to different rates charged for entrance to different parts of the theatre and implicitly to different qualities of judgement to be found there; we are solemnly warned against asking 'what Mirror of Magistrates is meant by the Justice, what great lady by the pig-woman, what conceal'd statesman, by the seller of mouse-traps' (142–5) but as in the past we may wonder to what extent this is disingenuous;⁴ Jonson even draws attention to the physical nature of the play-house itself in pleading, 'though the Fair be not kept in the same region, that some here, perhaps, would have it, yet think, that therein the Author hath observ'd a special decorum, the place being as dirty as Smithfield, and as stinking every whit' (156–60). *Like* the Fair, but *not* the Fair: we are constantly reminded that this is a work of art, which should be judged as such, deliberately constructed and not merely copied.

This insistence also lies behind the most notorious passage in the Induction: 'If there be never a servant-monster i'the Fair; who can help it? he says; nor a nest of antiques? He is loth to make Nature afraid in his plays, like those that beget Tales, Tempests, and such like drolleries, to mix his head with other men's heels' (127–31). This is clearly a disparaging allusion to Shakespeare's late romances: the servant-monster must be Caliban, who is so called three times in *The Tempest* (III. ii. 1–8); the 'nest of antiques' is almost as certainly a reference to the dance of twelve satyrs in *The Winter's Tale* (after IV. iv. 335). Tales and Tempests speak for themselves, while 'drolleries' probably refers to such items as the dumb-show of 'several strange shapes' in *The Tempest* which is there called 'a living drollery' (III. iii. 21). It is very easy to read this as sour grapes, envy on Jonson's part at the old master's continuing success, which would be all the more galling in the wake of *Catiline*'s failure. Both *The Winter's Tale* and *The Tempest* were performed at Court in November 1611 and both were among the five or six plays of Shakespeare chosen to celebrate the marriage of Princess Elizabeth to the Elector Palatine in February 1613; only one of Jonson's, *The Alchemist*, was chosen. We cannot ever really be sure of the level of personal animosity here,[5] but we should recognise that these comments do have a legitimate purpose in championing Jonson's dramatic style, which we may call artful realism, against the masque-like fantasies of Shakespeare's late romances. Sixteen years after *Every Man In His Humour* Jonson is still arguing for the validity and integrity of his own style, and Shakespeare is still the principal opposition. As we shall see later, the jibes in the Induction are only the opening shots in a far more detailed response to Shakespeare's latest plays, contained within *Bartholomew Fair* itself.

The Induction is, then, Jonson's typically bantering and provocative way of beginning the process of sorting the sheep from the goats in his audience; the play, he promises, is 'made to delight all, and to offend none. Provided they have either, the wit, or the honesty to think well of themselves' (82–4). In other words, it will offend no one who assesses it honestly and independently – or it will offend no one with a sufficiently high opinion of himself, since he implicitly is the play's subject but will hardly recognise himself. In paying their money to come in, the audience have contracted to sit in judgement upon themselves. The relationship of the audience to the play is mirrored in that of the characters who assemble at Littlewit's house and contrive, with varying motives and degrees of hypocrisy, to visit the Fair; what each discovers there is, in a sense, him- or herself, and this process of self-discovery fittingly comes to a climax with the puppet-play, when the characters themselves become an audience, passing judgement on a piece of drama.

Jonson cannot, of course, expect the experience of the Induction to last with the audience throughout the play, until it is specifically re-invoked in the puppet-play; so he augments it throughout the action of *Bartholomew Fair* by playing a kind of double game, apparently offering total verisimilitude, but always remaining shadowily in the background (as the Stage-Keeper literally feared) for those alert enough to see. This duality informs every feature of the play, as the opening speech of the play proper underlines in a virtuoso piece of juggling with dramatic artifice: 'Bartholmew[6] upon Bartholmew! there's the device!' exclaims Littlewit, 'who would have mark'd such a leap-frog chance now? A very . . . less than ames-ace, on two dice' (I. i. 8–10). It is pure Littlewit – who indeed would have 'mark'd' it but he? It is precisely the kind of small-minded witticism that would appeal to the author of the puppet-play which is eventually inflicted on the audience. But there is, of course, no real 'chance' about 'Bartholmew upon Bartholmew'; Jonson chose to write about the Fair, to give Cokes that name and, moreover, to 'inspire' Littlewit to comment on the coincidence. What emerges is thus a kind of double-bluff, Jonson playing on the conscious limitations of art in order to exploit the tensions between surface naturalism and artistic control. The scope of this can be gauged from the 'impudence' with which he repeats the 'joke' later in the play:

COKES: I call't my Fair, because of Bartholomew: you know my name is Bartholomew, and Bartholmew Fair.
LITTLEWIT: That was mine afore, gentlemen: this morning, I had that i'faith, upon his licence, believe me, there he comes, after me.

(I. v. 65–70)

Bad jokes, like bad coins, have a habit of turning up again. In allowing it to happen, however, Jonson does not simply reproduce an example of eminently credible uninspired wit; he obliquely acknowledges in the 'coincidence' his own role as the shaping artist and puppet-master (a term I use deliberately, thinking of the final scene). He also establishes that Cokes and Littlewit share a small-mindedness which is associated with the Fair; and, finally, ironically (since only the dimwitted could fail to see the connection for themselves) he spells out the fact that Bartholmew Cokes embodies the spirit of the fair. The 'joke' on stage is thus also a joke for the 'understanding' members of the audience, at the expense of the 'littlewits' there: it distinguishes those who appreciate the artistry from those whose wit falls below such things.

It would be tedious to rehearse all the ways in which Jonson maintains this dual perspective on his characters, though it is the essential ingredient which prevents the play froms lipping into the formless naturalism that apparently threatens it. One central example will suffice to demonstrate how pervasive the technique is. Zeal-of-the-Land Busy is one of the most significant figures in the play and his importance is indicated by the care with which Jonson prepares for his entrance – he is discussed some 350 lines before he appears on the stage. From the outset he is labelled as a 'hypocrite' – a common charge against Puritan pretensions to be holier-than-thou – but, as the scholar Jonson well knew, the root sense of 'hypocrite' is an actor on a stage. So Busy constantly straddles the line between being a credible Jacobean 'type' and an acknowledged element in a theatrical illusion, and this makes him a crucial figure in the various attempts to judge the Fair and its activities. Quarlous notes how he 'derides all antiquity; defies any other learning, than inspiration; and what discretion soever, years should afford him, it is all prevented in his original ignorance' (I. iii. 143–6). This is a witty if wilful parody of Puritan doctrine, particularly of their claims to acquire perfect truth by inspiration and to have escaped, by divine election, the taint of the Fall and original sin. In Jonson's hands, this is projected as the epitome of falsely conceived judgement, a licence for arbitrary and capricious behaviour; against such irrational zeal Jonson quietly allows Quarlous to oppose his own standards – antiquity, learning, discretion: a mature application of seasoned wisdom. Thus his mockery of a representative Jacobean 'type' grows into an appraisal of wider critical standards. This is typical of what I have called the artful realism of the play, which takes us beyond a mere image of contemporary society and into a calculated critique of it.

Busy's judgement is falsely grounded from the outset, but it becomes hypocritical (in the usual sense of the word) when he fails to judge himself by the standards which he applies to other people; it is clear that he worships in himself the very passions he denounces elsewhere. Littlewit finds him gluttonously 'fast by the teeth, i'the cold turkey-pie, i'the cupboard, with a great white loaf on his left hand, and a glass of malmsey on his right' (I. vi. 34–6). The evidence of self-indulgence is only compounded by the suggestions of Holy Communion (a sacrament rejected by many Puritans) in the bread and the wine – again a particular character-detail is set in the context of a broader analysis. These dubious standards are at their most evident and comic in the bombastic speeches which Busy gives in order to invest his own passions with an aura of sanctity. Having firstly rejected the Littlewits' idea of going to the Fair to eat pork, he relents and allows his own appetites to get the better of his spurious moral principles: 'In the way of comfort to the weak, I will go, and eat. I will eat exceedingly, and prophesy; there may be good use made of it, too, now I think on't: by the public eating of swine's flesh, to profess our hate, and loathing of Judaism, whereof the brethren stand taxed. I will therefore eat, yea, I will eat exceedingly' (I. vi. 92–7). His knowledge of man's sensual nature and the threat it poses – 'let not your eyes be drawn aside with vanity, nor your ear with noises' (III. ii. 31–2) – all derives from the animal side of himself, which he denies and tries to hide behind pious cant, but which keeps bursting through as it does when, searching for pork, 'Busy scents after it like a hound' (sidenote, c. III. ii. 80). His major attack on the flesh and the Fair, in the person of Ursula, is thus vitiated from the start by his failure to admit that it is also an attack upon himself: 'But the fleshly woman, (which you call Urs'la) is above all to be avoided, having the marks upon her, of the three enemies of man, the world, as being in the Fair; the devil, as being in the fire; and the flesh, as being herself' (III. vi. 33–7). Beneath the straight-lacing of the Puritan, the habit of his old profession of baker is only too visible; bakers were notorious for over-indulgence. This refusal to acknowledge himself in what he attacks makes him the perfect agent of the climax when, as Quarlous comments, 'I know no fitter match, than a puppet to commit with an hypocrite' (V. v. 50–1), cutting through all the layers of illusion and 'hypocrisy' to remind the audience of their responsibilities as true 'understanders', in opposition to the false understanding which Busy has demonstrated throughout. It is the essence of the artful realism of *Bartholomew Fair* that this quasi-naturalistic portrait of a typical Jacobean character should be so thoroughly integrated into the play's critical structure, and available to the audience on so many different levels.

It has been established, in ways we have noted, that Ursula (flesh) and Cokes (foolishness) are the polar symbols of the Fair; everyone who enters the Fair is subject to weakness that derive from one or the other, if not both. It is Cokes's curiosity and a feigned lust of the flesh – the pregnant Win's unaccountable desire to eat Bartholomew pig (and no other) – that draws most of the characters, including their 'guardians' and observers, into the Fair; it is appropriate that Win's 'appetite' is not even genuine but an excuse forged by Littlewit's notable brain. Flesh and folly are thus joined from the start in their power to subvert rational and moral standards. This is taken up in the recurrent imagery of the play, which is largely given over to animals and animal functions in its depictions of the flesh, and to insects when it comes to folly. Knockem's habit of describing humans in animal terms is central here; he calls Ursula 'mother o'the pigs' (II. v. 75) and protests at the rough handling she receives: 'they'll kill the poor whale, and make oil of her' (129–30). His forte is horses and their diseases: 'body o'me, she has the mallanders, the scratches, the crown scab, and the quitter-bone, i'the tother leg' (179–81). In the context of the Fair, this ceases to be eccentric and becomes a norm for describing humanity, which is constantly depicted at a level of animal activity – eating, sweating, drinking, urinating, farting, vomiting, copulating. Ursula revealingly says, 'two stone a suet aday is my proportion: I can but hold life and soul together, with this' (II. ii. 81–2). The old formula about holding 'life and soul together' is singularly inappropriate since the only life we witness in the Fair is a matter of physical self-gratification and has no regard whatever for man's divine part, his soul. In this respect too, Cokes and Ursula prove to be complementary; Edgeworth, the cut-purse (of all people), says of Cokes, 'Talk of him to have a soul? 'heart, if he have any more than a thing given him in stead of salt, only to keep him from stinking, I'll be hang'd afore my time, presently: where should it be trow? in his blood? he has not so much to'ard it in his whole body, as will maintain a good flea' (IV. ii. 53–8). Cokes has earlier been described in terms of insects: 'he has a head full of bees!' (I. iv. 81); 'he looks . . . like one that were made to catch flies, with his Sir Cranion-legs' (I. v. 98–100). In Edgeworth's words the implications of this become explicit: Cokes's empty-headed existence, drawn like an insect to the fleshpots of the Fair, is as soulless as Ursula's, without any spiritually redeeming dimension. That this 'soulless' condition applies not only to these individuals but is general in the Fair is made clear in the way that the language returns constantly to talk of animal functions, insects and disease. The 'pretty insect', Waspe, is as responsible for this as anyone, with his intemperate and foul-mouthed outbursts: 'A plague o'this box, and the pox too'; 'turd i'your teeth'; 'let your little wife stale in it'; 'you are an ass' etc. (I. iv. 48; 53; 63–4; 70). But the implications also run through the cries of the traders:

CORN-CUTTER: Ha'you any corns i'your feet, and toes?
TINDER-BOX MAN: Buy a mouse-trap, a mouse-trap, or a tormentor for a flea.

(II. iv. 6–8)

Nightingale's ballad titles, similarly, are either suggestively derisive or grotesquely obscene: 'A preservative again' the punk's evil'; 'the windmill blown down by the witch's fart' etc. (II. iv. 13; 18). There is a cumulative impression conveyed of man as an ungainly creature, subject to disease, animal functions and parasites, with dubious tastes and appetites: 'What do you lack, gentlemen? what is't you buy? fine rattles? drums? babies? little dogs? and birds for ladies? what do you lack?' (III. iv. 3–5). The ironic running together of babies (even if it means 'dolls'), little dogs and 'birds for ladies' – sentimental and procreational, human and animal – tells its own tale. 'What do you lack?' The call goes up time after time,[7] but the answer is only implied: what they lack, money will not buy. Like Cokes, who wants to buy everything, the people who are distracted by these baubles are nothing but children, without wit or understanding. Nor have the fair-folk any cause to feel superior to those who fall for their wares: the flesh that draws the insects is just as degenerate, just as lacking in the possibility of redemption.

This is a post-lapsarian world, as Ursula makes clear when she says 'I am all fire, and fat, Nightingale, I shall e'en melt away to the first woman, a rib again, I am afraid' (II. ii. 50–1). She thus stands alongside Overdo – Eve with her Adam, the primal mother and the self-appointed guardian of the Fair-as-world. But she has become the 'mother o'the pigs' and he has become so self-important in his role that he cannot tell true 'enormities' from false, even under his nose. No one has escaped the taint of the Fall, but two groups of characters significantly claim to have done so, and much of the play is devoted to examining their claims. On the one hand there are the Puritans, and on the other there are Quarlous, Winwife and Grace Wellborn. As we noticed earlier with Busy, the Puritans claim to be 'elect', to have been singled out by Providence, and so not subject to original sin and the other consequences of the Fall. When Win Littlewit pretends to have a longing to eat pig, Dame Purecraft assails her: 'Look up, sweet Win-the-fight, and suffer not the enemy to enter you at this door, remember that your education has been with the purest, what polluted one was it, that nam'd first the unclean beast, pig, to you, child?' (I. vi. 5–8). To her mother, Win is always 'child', 'my dear child', 'good child, sweet child', even though she is a grown woman, has quite literally been 'entered' by her husband and, as she puts it herself, 'I ha'somewhat o'the mother in me' (I. v. 168). Denying the natural weaknesses of the flesh, which would equate them with the 'polluted ones', leads the Puritans to refuse to accept the same standards of conduct and morality as apply to other people; they promote 'inspiration' over rational discretion and deny responsibility for anything that happens, since everything is in the hands of God (hence, for example, Dame Purecraft's whim to marry a madman). Jonson's satire against the Puritans consistently attacks their irresponsible, anti-social hypocrisy, underlining the fact that no one has escaped the consequences of the Fall and that, as Win's pregnant condition graphically displays, we are all equally subject to the weaknesses of the flesh.

This fundamental 'equality' is reflected in the 'pretty gradation' which Overdo learns from his beating: 'I begin now to think, that by a spice of collateral justice, Adam Overdo deserv'd this beating . . . the care I had of that civil young man, I took fancy to this morning, (and have not left it yet) drew me to that exhortation, which drew the company, indeed, which drew the cut-purse; which drew the money; which drew my brother Cokes his loss; which drew on Waspe's anger; which drew on my beating: a pretty gradation' (III. iii. 2–3; 14–20). No one is absolutely innocent in the Fair, the dimly perceived fact of which leads various characters to half-truths about themselves and their condition. 'I will be more tender hereafter', reflects Overdo, faced with his responsibility for Trouble-All's madness. 'I see compassion may become a Justice, though it be a weakness, I confess; and nearer a vice, than a virtue' (IV. i. 82–4). Similarly, it finally dawns on Waspe that 'he that will correct another, must want fault in himself' (V. iv. 99–100). The realisation that we are all equal and, in a sense, guilty, need not lead to a modern sense of the relativity of standards and the conclusion that any judgement of human behaviour is impossible. The failure of the authoritarian figures, like everything else in the play, falls within the dual pespective of Jonson's artful realism; the audience's responsibility to judge and understand is, if anything, increased by the failure of these characters to do the job properly.

This is demonstrated most fully in the career of Quarlous and his rivalry with Winwife over Grace Wellborn. Like Overdo, Busy and Waspe, Quarlous considers himself superior to the Fair and its inhabitants, but unlike them his pleasure lies not in denouncing its enormities but in sporting with them. The reason he and Winwife give for following Cokes and the others to the Fair is revealing:

WINWIFE: These flies cannot, this hot season, but engender us excellent creeping sport.
QUARLOUS: A man that has but a spoon-full of brain, would think so.

(I. v. 140–3)

The double-edged 'but a spoon-full of brain' is the key to Jonson's reservations about Quarlous; there is no doubt but that he is a man of genuine intelligence and perspicacity – qualities which earn him Ursula's abuse and Knockem's mock-deference: 'Duke Quarlous',

'Prince Quarlous'. But he consistently misapplies and abuses his talents – as, for example, when he insists merely out of conceit on joining in the crazy game of vapours. He is a dilettante, 'sporting' with the other characters and not facing up to his own responsibilities or indeed to the implications of what he sees. It is irresponsible of him to take advantage of his discovery that Edgeworth is the thief, rather than denouncing him to the authorities, and it leads him eventually to the realisation (albeit brief and in Latin) that *'Facinus quos inquinat, aequat'* – crime levels those it pollutes; typically, he tries to shrug it off, saying, 'But, it was for sport' (IV. vi. 29–30). His adoption of the madman's cloak implies a similar cross-contamination, which he does not recognise himself, and his decision to marry Dame Purecraft (an ambition for which he had previously mocked Winwife, with good reason) fully reveals his limitations: 'Palemon, the word, and Winwife the man?' (v. ii. 37). Contrary to his spirit of bland assurance, the Fair does not bestow its chief prize on his supposed merit; in stunned disbelief he repeats himself, faced with both the inequities of fortune and the limitations of his own wit. Like Trouble-All, or the game of vapours, the world itself seems mad, devoid of sense; man is not only fallen but beyond the scope of a providence that rewards merit. Idealism, therefore, is meaningless and it is this which Quarlous acknowledges in the cynical ease with which he switches his attentions from Grace Wellborn to Dame Purecraft: 'It is the money that I want, why should I not marry the money, when 'tis offer'd me? . . . There's no playing with a man's fortune! I am resolv'd! I were truly mad, an' I would not!' (v. ii. 80–5). This is doubly ironic in that he is wearing the madman's cloak as he says it, revealing himself (like Overdo) by his disguise, and it is this alone which disposes Dame Purecraft towards him. Instead of trying to beat the world at its own game, as he boasted to begin with, he accepts it on its own terms, which are those of the market-place and cash-value: 'I were truly mad, an' I would not.' In other words, he cynically makes do, identifying with the materialistic values of the Fair and being compromised by them. Like Lovewit at the end of *The Alchemist* he embodies a pragmatic wisdom which gives him the apparent authority necessary to close the play; but it would be a serious mistake not to see the ironic reservations with which Jonson qualifies such authority. His philosophy, like Lovewit's, is Mr Worldly-Wiseman's, and it is Jonson's most stringent test of his audience to see if they will swallow it as the last word.

Quarlous and Winwife are both versions of the wit, the omni-competent man-about-town which we encountered at the outset of

Jonson's 'select' career in Kno'well Jr and Wellbred in *Every Man In His Humour*; the guiding role of such characters in a play normally promotes assurance that sanity and stability both can and will be restored to the disordered world – albeit possibly by dubious means (this is part of Jonson's legacy to Restoration comedy). To some extent they remove the pressure of responsibility from the audience because they supply answers to the moral and practical problems raised by the play, and we feel less the need to work them out for ourselves. But the dubious fortunes of Quarlous and Winwife's entirely arbitrary victory deny this comforting pattern, giving the audience in the end more rather than less to do. Wit does not triumph, the marriage-arrangements offer something less than the genial resolution of the play's discord we might have expected.

The significance of this becomes more apparent when we recognise that the careers of Quarlous and Winwife form part of a parody of what was probably Shakespeare's last play, written in conjunction with John Fletcher. As Muriel Bradbrook puts it,

Ben Jonson parodied *Two Noble Kinsmen* in *Bartholomew Fair*. Rival suitors, whose fate is to be determined by drawing lots, chose the names of Argalus, out of *Arcadia*, and Palamon 'out of the play' . . . (IV. iii. 67–8). The puppeteer shows two faithful friends Damon and Pythias falling out for love of Hero, and abusing each other . . . *Bartholomew Fair*, with its puppets leaning out of the booth, must visually have evoked the two prisoners leaning out of their prison window; it testifies to the earlier show's success; for Jonson would not waste his satire on a failure.[8]

But there is more point to Jonson's satire than simply making fun of Shakespeare and Fletcher's success; anyone who knows *Two Noble Kinsmen* (not to mention its principal source, Chaucer's *Knight's Tale*) would suspect in advance that, when Grace Wellborn submits her choice between Quarlous and Winwife to the whim of mad Trouble-All ('because Destiny has a high hand in business of this nature' IV. iii. 51–2), that Winwife will capture Grace, as the true Palamon[9] captures Emilia – even though this runs contrary to expectations raised by Quarlous's more dominant personality.

Two Noble Kinsmen, like Shakespeare's other late plays, depicts characters governed by forces greater than themselves which they understand only dimly. 'Shakespeare is deeply aware in this play of the extent to which human life is dominated by forces outside human control – we should also take into account terms like "fortune" and "nature" – but although man must reverence and propitiate them, they often work in ways that cause bewilderment or suffering.'[10] When Jonson shows Grace Wellborn surrendering to fate ('Destiny') and Quarlous cynically concluding that 'There's no playing with a man's fortune!' he is parodying the whole concept of Shakespearean romance and the conventions associated with it, picking up from the scorn for 'Tales, Tempests and such-like drolleries' expressed in the Induction. The lives of Jonson's characters are determined not by numinous forces but by their own intrinsic natures, more or less governed by reason; if Winwife wins the best wife, Jonson implies, that is a fact of art, not of mystic providence. It is an inherent prerequisite of Jonson's outlook that we may all be held responsible for our own actions and choices, that we should all be required to exercise our own judgement. The only allowable exception has to be a true madman, like Trouble-All.

Louis MacNeice speaks of a Shakespeare who, in his last phase, turned to

> tapestried romances, conjuring
> With rainbow names and handfuls of sea-spray
> And from them turned out happy Ever-afters.[11]

Such a formula may not do full justice to the sense of loss-in-gain which is so poignantly part of the effect of Shakespeare's last plays (and never more so than in *Two Noble Kinsmen*) but it does express a quality which *The Winter's Tale* and *The Tempest* in particular have, allowing as they do the possibility – however painful and hard-won – of repentance, redemption and regeneration: in short of the purposeful entry of divine grace into men's lives. *Two Noble Kinsmen* varies the pattern somewhat in projecting a clear pagan sense of the jealous gods, but even here a kind of providence may be detected in that Palamon, disciple of Venus, is the right man to marry Emilia, and that, while Arcite dies, he does so as a disciple of Mars would wish, honourably and after a great triumph. In *The Winter's Tale* the very word, 'grace', is one of the most dominant threads of the 'tapestry'; it recurs, in one derivative or another, time after time in the play,[12] almost invariably associated with Hermione or Perdita, forging the pattern by which at least partial redemption is made possible after seeming tragedy.

It is significant that Jonson consistently denies himself this pattern in his plays.[13] But in *Bartholomew Fair* he does not simply ignore the question of grace; he subjects it to a critical scrutiny. It is a key issue with both the groups of characters who claim a superiority over the Fair. For the Puritans, their 'election' is (to them) a sign of grace, purportedly manifested in their pure and godly behaviour – such as their ostentatiously pious prayers. Littlewit avows that Busy 'says a grace as long as his breath lasts him' (I. ii. 67–8), while Quarlous asks Winwife, then wooing Dame Purecraft, 'Dost thou ever think to bring thine ears or stomach, to the patience of a dry grace, as long as thy tablecloth? and dron'd out by thy son, here, (that might be thy father;) . . .?' (I. iii. 87–90). Hypocritical long-windedness is here compounded with the common Puritan heresy of confusing God the Father and God the Son; these jokes implicitly spell out the truth that these characters have no more claim to a special grace than anyone else, indeed rather less than most.

The issue is put to a different test in making *Grace* Wellborn the most coveted prize that the Fair has to bestow. She is universally acknowledged to be desirable (just as Overdo is universally acknowledged to be wise) but it is open to doubt from the beginning whether this is because of her inherent virtue or because of her social 'grace'; as Overdo's ward (he 'bought' her), she has the kind of market-value (as distinct from intrinsic worth) that makes Dame Pliant such an equivocal prize in *The Alchemist*. The ambiguities emerge in the sadly forced puns on her name which her suitors use; Winwife: 'How melancholy Mistress Grace is yonder! pray thee let's go enter our selves in grace, with her' (III. iv. 74–5); Cokes: 'and then I'll ha'this poesie put to'hem, *For the best grace*, meaning Mistress Grace, my wedding poesie' (III. iv. 164–5). She herself is characterised by a stand-offish, even priggish correctness: 'I am so secure of mine own manners, as I suspect not yours' (III. v. 298–9). But her certainty that she is 'above' the Fair ('Truly, I have no such fancy to the Fair; nor ambition to see it; there's none goes thither of any quality or fashion' I. v. 130–2) is as dubious in its own way as Quarlous's; it leads her to some capricious judgements, knowing what she does not want (Cokes) but unable to decide for herself what she does. Her preference for the *savoir-faire* of Winwife and Quarlous is understandable – they represent the 'quality or fashion' that interests her – but shows only superficial good taste (she might, for example, have given some thought to their impecuniousness) and the method she uses to choose between them is as irresponsible as it is near blasphemous. To submit her decision to the whim of mad Trouble-All is a travesty of the action of divine providence in its allocation of grace, equating it with insanity. Grace Wellborn thus parodies not only Emilia, who is unable to choose between Palamon and Arcite, but also the likes of Perdita and Miranda, who find their perfect lovers through the action of some divine providence; her social 'grace' is a disenchanted reflection of the innate nobility which characterises those heroines (who are all apt to be mistaken for goddesses) and their cherished virginities. Their is nothing mysterious or miraculous about the characters' birth or origins in *Bartholomew Fair*, as Win's pregnancy (and near-prostitution) demonstrates; it is a simple matter of copulation, with no magical or regenerative overtones. Grace's actual role – the whole scrutiny of 'grace' in the play – thus defies what the word promises; in so doing it parodies and refutes the tastes and expectations of audiences given over to romances and, specifically, Shakespeare's last plays. As Muriel Bradbrook puts it: 'The object of romance was to suspend the critical faculties; the audience was meant to reach a state of "delight" or "rapture" in which they were "charmed", a state of being thoroughly immersed and totally overwhelmed.'[14] Jonson clearly looks for such effects himself in the privileged context of his masques, but it is not something he will sanction on the public stage, where his 'artful realism' rejects both the style and the subject-matter of romance and demands that, however much the audience may suspend their disbelief, they must remain alert and critical. None of them is to be allowed to feel that he will be saved from his own limitations either by natural right or by a benign universe.

Ironically, as the play progressively reveals the limitations of its supposedly superior characters, the dignity – if that is the word – of the Fair passes, as it should, to Cokes. In spite of all the Fair does to him, he escapes essentially unscathed and undaunted. Some loving providence guides him through the Fair, losing his money and his fiancée but not his enthusiasm; he is blessed with a wide-eyed blindness and a copious forgetfulness, and his 'providence' only mocks the lack of divine ordinance elsewhere. He above all lacks those qualities of discretion and judgement for which Jonson has ironically probed ever since the Induction, and it is singularly appropriate that he should be the member of the stage-audience who most appreciates the puppet-play – just as Busy is the one most enraged by it; for the puppet-play is a crude distillation of Bartholomew Fair itself. In it the most famous, most heroic love poem of the age, Marlowe's *Hero and Leander*, is transposed with ineptly fluent vulgarity to contemporary London, and merged with the 'true friendly greeting' of Damon and Pythias which, as we have seen, mirrors the competition of Quarlous and Winwife for Grace Wellborn. The characters on stage are invited to see themselves as much in Littlewit's play as the audience are in Jonson's; the dialogue between the Puppet Dionysius and Busy takes us directly back to the Articles of Agreement in the Induction, to the distinctions between art and life, pretence and reality, morality and licence – to the fundamental question of judgement. Busy's mistake lies, not in judging the play, but in judging it for the wrong things on the wrong terms; his attack on licence and licentiousness combines typical Puritan objections to the theatre as a focal point of immoral activity, to the dramatic illusion as a wicked 'lie' and to the scripturally forbidden wearing of women's clothes by men: 'you are an abomination: for the male, among you, putteth on the apparel of the female, and the female of the male' (v. v. 99–100). This is just as perverse as Cokes's inability to comprehend that the puppets should not be talked to like anyone else. 'The puppet (Dionysius) takes up his garment' (sidenote, v. v. 107), revealing that he is sexless, and Busy is completely confuted; the puppet's forthright action not only makes nonsense of the attack on sexual confusions, but also answers the implied criticisms of the play-as-illusion. Yes, the play is an illusion, it seems to say, but an openly contracted one, which discriminating audiences (i.e. not Cokes or Busy) understand, license and so make valuable. In revealing itself, the puppet breaks through all the layers of 'hypocrisy': the puppet is a puppet, is an actor/ character in a play, is an actor/character in *the* play, is thus no different from Busy himself – and the arch-hypocrite is finally silenced, faced with his own reality and the sterility of his judgement. The charge is also implicitly laid at the door of the audience who have not the wit to understand the skill and resonance of Jonson's art.

The manner of Busy's confutation explicitly equates good judgement in its widest sense with the capacity to understand and appreciate drama; form and content merge as the play nears its conclusion and art prepares to give way once more to reality. A crucial if unspoken factor in this process of resolving the drama is the King to whom the play is dedicated and before whom it was performed. Even when not present in person, the Articles of Agreement acknowledge 'our sovereign lord, James by the grace of God King' (Induction, 69). A verse of Nightingale's song, moreover, tells of a cut-purse:

> Nay one without grace,
> At a (far) better place,
> At Court, and in Christmas, before the King's face.
> (III. v. 124–6)

(Cokes characteristically enthuses: 'That was a fine fellow! I would have him, now.') James is king 'by the grace of God'; the cut-purse is 'without grace'. Everything focuses on the role of the monarch as God's anointed agent in a fallen world, the fountain of all spiritual and temporal authority; as in the masques, his office embodies the concept of absolute judgement. Of course, the play is never as solemn

about it as that, particularly if (as seems very likely) James was
expected to see something of himself in the figure of Overdo, who
emerges as the central figure of the drama at its very end: a magistrate with pretensions to learning who lectures quite ludicrously on
the evils of tobacco ('who can tell, if, before the gathering, and
making up thereof, the alligarta hath not piss'd thereon?' II. vi.
26–7)[15] and ends his soliloquies sententiously 'in Justice' name, and
the King's, and for the Commonwealth' (II. i. 48–9; III. iii. 40–1). We
need not make heavy weather of the idea of Jonson satirising King
James to his face; it was no treason to remind the king that, however
divine the office, its occupant was only human – and this king had a
particular taste for what has been described as 'unbuttoned'
humour. The key point is that the concept of the king's two persons –
the office and the man – is a perfect mirror of Jonson's 'artful realism': the more degenerate seems the natural world, the greater the
need for authority and judgement.

> This is your power to judge (great Sir) and not
> the envy of a few. Which if we have got,
> We value less what their dislike can bring,
> if it so happy be, t'have pleas'd the King.
> (Epilogue, 9–12)

It is the dimension of understanding and critical judgement that
the King affords which gives the play its essential shape and purpose.
The last scene makes a gesture of reconciliation, after all the folly
and confusion, in the invitation to supper at Overdo's house.[16] It is
tempting but dangerous to romanticise the tone of the ending, to
construe it as a genial and indulgent repudiation of all attempts at
judgement and authority after the failures of Waspe, Busy and
Overdo. Quarlous's injunction to Overdo's to 'remember you are but
Adam, flesh, and blood!' (v. vi. 96–7) is sensible, but has no more
regenerative overtones than have the depictions of the human body
throughout the play; the flesh to which he is heir, and which he has
just rediscovered, is that of his wife who – in the most graphically
naturalistic incident in the play – has just vomited. If Overdo and
Quarlous are somewhat sobered by the realisation of their limitations and move towards more civilised standards in the invitation to
supper, this must be set against the totally unrepressed Cokes, whose
plea 'Yes, and bring the actors along, we'll ha' the rest o'the play at
home' (v. vi. 114–15), ironically underlines the difficulty of achieving Overdo's new resolution: '*Ad correctionem, non ad destructionem; ad
aedificandum, non ad diruendeum*' (v. vi. 112–13 – towards correction,

not destruction; to build, not to destroy). Implicit in Cokes's wish is the suggestion that the audience as a whole will find the world of the play waiting for them back in their homes. What price Overdo's new Horatian ideals there, with such as Cokes to build upon? The fact that he speaks in Latin, which the Cokeses of the world would not understand, suggests that even in this least carping and least self-satisfied of endings, Jonson still appeals to a genuinely critical element in the audience, who will recognise that nothing has been 'solved' by the play except that, through it, their own understanding has been challenged and advanced. The ending of *Bartholomew Fair* demonstrates most perfectly how criticism of art can at the same time be criticism of life.

The final irony is that all this should have been accomplished through a truly popular play – one with an adequate level of enjoyment even for those 'understanding gentlemen' who will never appreciate its full significance and who embody, in effect, the true objects of its satire. In that sense it is a triumphant *riposte* to those who hissed *Catiline* off the stage, to those who have never appreciated the serious dimensions of his 'artful realism', and it lives only too well up to the promise 'to delight all, and to offend none. Provided they have either, the wit, or the honesty to think well of themselves.' All of which also explains why Jonson should have chosen, for a play so often singled out for its geniality and good humour,[17] such a barbed inscription from Horace for its title-page: 'Democritus, if he were on earth, would laugh: for he would view the people more attentively than the plays themselves, as affording more strange sights than the actor; and for their writers, he would think they told their story to a deaf ass.' It is a challenge that all readers of the 1616 folio should recognise, and relish.

Notes

Introduction. The 1616 folio and its place in Jonson's career

1. See 'My Picture Left in Scotland' (*The Underwood* 9).
2. Thomas Fuller's account of those 'wit-battles' in his *History of the Worthies of England* (1662) is reviewed with proper scepticism in Samuel Schoenbaum, *Shakespeare's Lives* (Oxford, 1970), pp. 94–5.
3. T. S. Eliot, 'Ben Jonson' in *Selected Essays*, 3rd edn (London, 1951), p. 47.
4. J. P. Kenyon, *Stuart England* (London, 1978), p. 336.
5. J. B. Bamborough in a review of *A Celebration of Ben Jonson*, ed. W. Blissett *et al.* (Toronto, 1973; London, 1974) in *Yearbook of English Studies*, 6 (1976), 246.
6. *The Underwood* 23 and appended to *The New Inn* (H & S, VI, p. 492).
7. See the introduction to *Ben Jonson: A Collection of Critical Essays*, ed. J. A. Barish (Englewood Cliffs, N.J., 1963), pp. 1–13.
8. Barish, *Ben Jonson and the Language of Prose Comedy* (Cambridge, Mass., 1960); Orgel, *The Jonsonian Masque* (Cambridge, Mass., 1968).
9. *Love's Triumph Through Callipolis*, 2–7.
10. *Conversations with Drummond*, H & S, I, pp. 132–51, lines 239–41. Unless otherwise specified, all the anecdotes about Jonson's life and opinions in this book are from this source.
11. See A. R. Dutton, 'Jonson and David Copperfield, Dickens and Bartholomew Fair', *English Language Notes*, 16 (1979), 227–32, for the interesting parallels between Jonson and Dickens on the question of 'demeaning' early employment.
12. Great spoils gained in single combat.
13. Esmé Stuart, Seigneur d'Aubigné, commemorated in *Epigrams* 127; Jonson dedicated *Sejanus* to him.
14. It has generally been accepted this century that *A Tale of a Tub* is an early work which the ailing Jonson dusted off late in his career and made a vehicle for his attack on Inigo Jones. Dr Anne Barton has recently argued, with some conviction, that it really is a late play and that, like *The New Inn* and *The Magnetic Lady*, it nostalgically harks back to the Elizabethan era and its styles of drama – which would explain some of its undoubtedly 'early' characteristics. The argument is, as yet, unresolved.
15. That is, he gained exemption from the penalty of the law by proving

that he could read from the Bible, a hangover from the medieval privileges of the Church.

16. Presumably *Epigrams* 58, 'On Spies'.

17. Even Shakespeare was moved to mock 'an eyrie of children, little eyases that cry out on the top of question and are most tyrannically clapped for't' (*Hamlet*, II. ii. 332–4).

18. See 'The magnificent entertainment' in *Jacobean and Caroline Court Masques and Civic Entertainments*, ed. R. Dutton (Nottingham, 1981–).

19. In fact, Marston went into hiding.

20. Sir Robert Cecil was the younger son of Elizabeth's long-serving minister, William Cecil, Lord Burghley; he masterminded the smooth succession of King James to the English throne, became his chief minister and was made Earl of Salisbury in 1605. He remained the most powerful politician in England until his death in 1612.

21. Printed in H & S, I, pp. 194–6.

22. Jonson's letter, and the details of the warrant, are given in H & S, I, pp. 202–3.

23. See, for example, Keats's 'Lines on the Mermaid Tavern'.

24. See Schoenbaum, *Shakespeare's Lives*, p. 259.

25. The occasional sour note about some of these figures, recorded by Drummond, needs to be put in perspective. Jonson, the big name from London, was clearly showing off much of the time to his rather prim Scottish host and may well have said some things for effect (his tongue doubtless loosened by drink) which he never anticipated being heard by anyone else, much less preserved for posterity.

26. See W. David Kay, 'The shaping of Ben Jonson's career', *Modern Philology*, 67 (1969).

27. In his *Palladis Tamia, Wit's Treasury*.

28. As I shall suggest in chapter 1, Jonson's attacks on those styles of drama in which Shakespeare made his mark are a way of defining and advertising his own choices, and not merely sour grapes. This is a major tactic in the early sections of the folio – the 'humorous' satires – though it subsides somewhat later. This is another good reason for finding room to discuss *Bartholomew Fair*, since in that play Jonson renews the attack with vigour, spelling out in detail his objections to certain features of Shakespeare's later career.

29. See, for example, Edward Partridge, 'Jonson's *Epigrammes*: the named and the nameless', *Studies in the Literary Imagination*, 6 (1973).

30. Jonson told Drummond that 'he was Master of Arts in both the Universities by their favour not his study' (252–3), but no evidence of the Cambridge M.A. has survived.

31. 'His grandfather came from Carlisle and he thought from Annandale to it' (234–5). George MacDonald Fraser confidently marks Jonson a scion of the Johnstone clan in *The Steel Bonnets* (London, 1974), p. 45.'

32. That is, the office was to come to him after the death of its present holder

and of one other who held the reversion before Jonson; in fact, Jonson predeceased the latter.

33. There is a very useful general account of this masque in D. B. J. Randall, *Jonson's Gypsies Unmasked* (Durham, N.C., 1975).
34. See 'An Epistle Answering to One that Asked to be Sealed of the Tribe of Ben', *The Underwood* 47, written *c.* 1624.
35. See his 'Upon Ben Johnson' and ' An Ode for Him' in *Hesperides*.
36. Title-page, 1631 octavo.
37. See D. J. Gordon, 'Poet and architect: the intellectual setting of the quarrel between Ben Jonson and Inigo Jones', *Journal of the Warburg and Courtauld Institutes*, 12 (1949).

1. The early plays

1. W. Shakespeare, *Works*, ed. Nicholas Rowe (London, 1709) 1. xiii; quoted in Schoenbaum, *Shakespeare's Lives*, pp. 95–6.
2. See, for example, his elegy on Shakespeare (*Ungathered Verse* 26) and *Discoveries*, lines 647–68.
3. Aristotle did not in fact insist that the so-called unities were essential in drama; it was the Italian, Castelvetro, who foisted them upon him in his 1570 edition of the *Poetics*. But Jonson would certainly have regarded Aristotle as an 'authority' against the 'mongrel' drama of his contemporaries.
4. Dryden, *Of Dramatick Poesie*, ed. J. T. Boulton (Oxford, 1964), lines 571–93.
5. See Richard Hosley, 'The formal influence of Plautus and Terence', *Elizabethan Theatre* (Stratford Upon Avon Studies, 9; London, 1966).
6. See the editions of the play by G. B. Jackson (London and New Haven, 1969), Appendix 2, and by J. W. Lever (London, 1972), Introduction, for a full account of the difficulties of dating the folio text.
7. A. C. Swinburne, *A Study of Ben Jonson* (London, 1889), p. 39.
8. *The Oxford Companion to English Literature* 4th edn, corrected (1975), p. 212.
9. See, however, Jonson's moving 'Epitaph on S[alomon] P[avy] a Child of Q.El[izabeth's] Chapel' (*Epigrams* 120). Jonson suggests that Pavy, who acted in *Cynthia's Revels*, played old men so convincingly that the Fates mistook him for one and took him before his time. But this is a tenderly playful conceit and cannot be read as a serious claim that boy-actors could be so convincing.
10. This scene is an adaptation of one of Horace's poems (*Satires*, 1. ix). Comic in itself, it is not all that well integrated in the play as a whole. See George Parfitt, *Ben Jonson: Public Poet and Private Man* (London, 1976), pp. 51–4.
11. Again, we may consider that this may not have been so obvious when acted by a child, but that is no justification of the published text.

2. *Sejanus* and *Volpone*: the defence of virtue

1. See chapter 6, below.
2. Sentence = *sententiae*, weighty comments or maxims arising from the action.
3. See J. A. Bryant Jr, 'The significance of Ben Jonson's first requirement for tragedy, "Truth of Argument"', *Studies in Philology*, 49 (1952); and G. Giovanni, 'Historical realism and the tragic emotions in Renaissance criticism', *Philological Quarterly*, 32 (1933).
4. See *The Prose Works of Sir Philip Sidney*, ed. A. Feuillerat (4 vols., reprinted Cambridge, 1963), III, pp. 12–19.
5. Dedication to *Volpone*, 108–9.
6. 'Cygnus' in *Jonsonus Virbius* (printed in H & S, XI, p. 314).
7. See E. M. T. Duffy, 'Ben Jonson's debt to Renaissance scholarship in *Sejanus* and *Catiline*', *Modern Language Review*, 42 (1947).
8. *Annals*, p. 162. References to Tacitus's *Annals* are to Michael Grant's Penguin translation (rev. edn, Harmondsworth, 1959).
9. Compare Tacitus, *Annals*, p. 111, with I. 124–56.
10. Robert Ornstein, *The Moral Vision of Jacobean Tragedy* (Wisconsin, 1960), p. 93.
11. A theme further explored in *Catiline*, where one of Cicero's few positive actions is to gather all men of good will around him.
12. Tacitus, *Annals*, p. 163.
13. But see M. L. Vawter, 'The seeds of virtue: political imperatives in Jonson's *Sejanus*', *Studies in the Literary Imagination*, 6 (1973), 41–60. He cites Jean Bodin ('whose works Jonson knew') as the potential source of a political philosophy which, while based on Christian morality, still sanctioned a more pragamatic approach to the control of vice than was traditionally acceptable. But perhaps we should bear in mind that it is the asinine Sir Politic Would-be in *Volpone* who is given to citing 'Nick. Machiavel and Monsieur Bodin' (IV. i. 26) – hardly evidence of Jonson's admiration.
14. See chapter 6 on this point, in respect both of *Sejanus* and *Volpone*.
15. Perhaps the closest contemporary parallel to Jonson's dramatic technique in *Sejanus* is not a tragedy but Marlowe's provocatively black comedy, *The Jew of Malta*, another play about a would-be Machiavel finally outwitted by a true one. Marlowe and Jonson have a lot in common and the parallels between these two plays may help us to appreciate the links between *Sejanus* and *Volpone*, the most Marlovian of all Jonson's comedies.
16. I discuss 'Come, my Celia' at greater length in chapter 5.
17. See 'The double plot in *Volpone*', *Modern Philology*, 51 (1953), reprinted in Barish's own collection of critical essays (see Introduction, note 7).
18. See I. Donaldson, 'A note on Jonson's tortoise', *Review of English Studies*, 9, n.s. (1968).

19. S. T. Coleridge, *Miscellaneous Criticism*, ed. T. M. Raysor (London, 1936), p. 55.
20. Harry Levin, 'Jonson's metempsychosis', *Philological Quarterly*, 22 (1943).

3. Rare poems and rare friends: Jonson's *Epigrams*

1. *Epigrams* 94, 'To Lucy, Countess of Bedford, with Mr. Donne's Satires', line 6.
2. Swinburne, *Study of Ben Jonson*, p. 9.
3. See Introduction, note 5.
4. George Parfitt, 'The poetry of Ben Jonson', *Essays in Criticism*, 18 (1968), 31.
5. *Ben Jonson and the Language of Prose Comedy*, p. 87.
6. See Partridge, 'Jonson's *Epigrammes*' (pp. 153–4), for a history of criticism on this point.
7. Quoted in G. P. V. Akrigg, *Jacobean Pageant* (London, 1962), p. 51. I have modernised the spelling.
8. It seems to have been almost a turn of mind on Jonson's part not to praise even those he respected most in absolute terms: 'he esteemeth John Donne the first poet in the world *in some things*' (*Conversations*, 117–18); 'I lov'd the man (Shakespeare), and do honour his memory (*on this side idolatry*) as much as any' (*Discoveries*, 654–5). My emphases.
9. The 'epigram' is printed as *The Forest* 7: 'Song, That Women Are But Men's Shadows'.
10. This is itself a typically Jonsonian pun. Ordinary has its usual modern sense (normal, unremarkable), but could also mean a tavern or fashionable gambling house: it is also the title of a judge. Hence we have the cumulative implications of a 'normal' reader, who is a man in a fashionable, probably self-indulgent crowd, passing judgement. Jonson's 'wit' is not spectacular, like Donne's, but it can be remarkably incisive.
11. J. G. Nichols, *The Poetry of Ben Jonson* (London, 1969), p. 65.
12. The doctrine is spelled out in detail, in relation to Jonson's masques, in W. T. Furniss, 'Ben Jonson's masques', in *Three Studies in the Renaissance: Sidney, Jonson, Milton* (New Haven, 1958).
13. *Sidney*, ed. Feuillerat, III, p. 19.
14. See D. Wykes, 'Ben Jonson's "Chast Book" – the Epigrammes', *Renaissance and Modern Studies*, 13 (1969), in which he makes the point that 'There is nothing random about the volume' (p. 84); Partridge, 'Jonson's *Epigrammes*', p. 170, draws an interesting parallel: 'as in *Bartholomew Fair*, order and pattern gradually appear and control the vivid bustle without dampening the energy of its life'.
15. Partridge, 'Jonson's *Epigrammes*', p. 173.
16. Probably the famous 'Letter from the Country', printed in H & S, XI, pp. 374–6.
17. See I. Donaldson (ed.), *Ben Jonson: Poems* (London, 1975), notes on p. 313.
18. See Introduction, p. 20 and note 37. Evidence for these poems being attacks on Inigo Jones is given in H & S, Appendix XXIV, vol. X, pp. 689–92.

19. See T. K. Whipple, *Martial and the English Epigram from Sir Thomas Wyatt to Ben Jonson* (reprinted New York, 1970).

4. The masques and *Epicoene*

1. *Hall's Chronicle*, ed. H. Ellis (London, 1809; reprinted New York, 1965), p. 526.
2. There were those, of course, who mocked what they saw as Jonson's pretentiousness in this sphere, just as they mocked his seriousness elsewhere. Samuel Daniel, one of his chief early rivals for the post of Court masque-writer, all but openly attacks him in the Preface to his 1610 masque, *Tethys' Festival*, for 'that disease of ostentation', proudly refusing 'to make an Apology of what I have done' since it will only convince those who agree already and 'may . . . render a good cause suspected by too much labouring to defend it'; he shrewdly insists that 'none hath gotten so high a station of understanding, but he shall find others that are built on an equal floor with him' and that if his 'figures do not come drawn in all proportions to the life of antiquity . . . yet I know them such as were proper to the business, and discharged those parts for which they served, with as good corresponding as our appointed limitations would permit'. He explicitly states that Inigo Jones as stage-designer deserves more credit for the masque than he does as writer, and later in the text makes much play of the fact that his show was performed by courtiers for courtiers. It is as calculated a riposte to Jonson as could be imagined, and it is useful to bear in mind when trying to assess the extent of Jonson's originality in, and personal contribution to, the form.
3. See *The Winter's Tale*, IV. iv. 35.
4. Son of the 'Actaeon' mentioned in *Cynthia's Revels* (see chapter 1, p. 46). The family largely blamed the Cecils for his death.
5. *Hymenaei* is one of the most fully annotated of all Jonson's masques, attempting in many ways to educate his readers in how to read any such text.
6. *Masque of Blackness*, 7–8. Apparently the spectators were allowed to strip the scenery of its rich clothes and semi-precious stones.
7. See Evelyn Simpson, 'Jonson and Dickens: a study in the comic genius of London', *Essays and Studies*, 30 (1944).
8. This was not actually the same company as Jonson had written for earlier. See Andrew Gurr, *The Shakespearean Stage 1574–1642*, 2nd edn (Cambridge, 1980), pp. 47–54.
9. Some idea of just how engrossing and disorientating consistent paradox can be will be available to anyone who has read Lewis Carroll's *Alice Through the Looking Glass*. See also W. W. E. Slights, '*Epicoene* and the prose paradox', *Philological Quarterly*, 49 (1970).
10. It is perhaps not surprising that the Earl of Essex became a leading Parliamentary general in the Civil War, considering what he and his family had to put up with from the monarchy.

11. Astraea (Justice) lived on earth and was a blessing to men in the Gold and Silver Ages, but their impiety drove her to heaven in the Bronze and Iron Ages.

5. *The Forest, The Alchemist, Catiline*: 'manners, arms and arts': a Renaissance ideal

1. The title represents the Latin *silva*, often used for collections of occasional poems.
2. Line 14 is also amended from 'Thus removed' to 'So removed'. The earlier version is a stage-gesture, referring to Volpone's handling of Celia's husband, Corvino; the later version is more generally anonymous – it can be any concerned person who has been beguiled (a father, brother, friend), not necessarily a husband.
3. See, for example, John Donne's 'Good Friday, 1613. Riding Westward': 'There I should see a Sunne, by rising set, / And by that setting endlesse day beget' (11–12, in *The Divine Poems of John Donne*, ed. H. Gardner (Oxford, 1964), p. 31).
4. Jonson develops the ironies of being an ageing lover in *A Celebration of Charis in Ten Lyric Pieces* (*The Underwood* 2.)
5. See J. T. McCullen, 'Conference with the Queen of Fairies', *Studia Neophilologica* 23 (1950–1).
6. There is also a pun on the sense of 'natural' meaning 'a half-witted person'.
7. William Empson, '*Volpone*', *The Hudson Review*, 21 (1968).
8. Coleridge reckoned it one of the 'three most perfect plots ever planned', along with *Oedipus Tyrannus* and *Tom Jones*.
9. See William Empson, '*The Alchemist*', *The Hudson Review*, 22 (1969).
10. T. S. Eliot, 'Ben Jonson', p. 149.
11. W. D. Wolf, *The Reform of the Fallen World: the Virtuous Prince in Jonsonian Tragedy and Comedy* (Salzburg, 1973), p. 27.
12. W. F. Bolton and J. F. Gardner, eds., *Catiline* (London, 1973), p. xvi.
13. Ornstein, *Moral Vision of Jacobean Tragedy*, p. 102.
14. H & S, II, p. 122.
15. Dedication to *Aureng-Zebe* in *Dryden: Poetry, Prose and Plays*, ed. D. Grant (London, 1952), p. 500.

6. Covert allusions: state decipherers and politic picklocks

1. See *Bartholomew Fair*, Induction, 136–45.
2. J. A. Symonds, *Ben Jonson* (London, 1886), p. 100.
3. Swinburne, *Study of Ben Jonson*, p. 9.
4. See Gurr, *Shakespearean Stage*, pp. 71–6.
5. One contemporary observer actually referred to it as 'our famous play of

Gondomar' (*The Letters of John Chamberlain*, ed. N. E. McClure (Philadelphia, 1939), II, p. 578).

6. Letter dated 8 Feb. 1609/10, *Calendar of State Papers Venetian* (1864), XI, no. 794, p. 427.
7. The rest of the sorry tale is told in Akrigg, *Jacobean Pageant*, chapter 11.
8. John Palmer, *Ben Jonson* (London, 1934), pp. 71–2.
9. J. A. Barish (ed.), *Sejanus* (New Haven and London, 1965), pp. 17–18.
10. Quoted in Sir John Neale, *Queen Elizabeth* (London, 1934), p. 342.
11. See Neale, *Queen Elizabeth*, p. 378, and the famous libel 'Little Bossive Robin', quoted in Akrigg, *Jacobean Pageant*, p. 110. Akrigg's chapter on Salisbury is called 'The Fox of Hatfield Chase'.
12. Quoted in B. N. de Luna, *Jonson's Romish Plot* (Oxford, 1967), p. 18 footnote.
13. See P. M. Handover, *The Second Cecil* (London, 1959), pp. 34, 57.
14. Quoted in D. H. Willson, *King James VI and I* (London, 1956), p. 187.

7. Bartholomew Fair

1. John Dryden, *A Defence of an Essay of Dramatique Poetry*, in *Dryden: Poetry, Prose and Plays*, ed. D. Grant (London, 1952), p. 442.
2. This must have been dispensed with, or radically rewritten, for Court performances.
3. *Ieronimo* or *The Spanish Tragedy*, by Thomas Kyd, *Titus Andronicus*, by Shakespeare; they were two early and enduringly popular revenge tragedies.
4. See, for example, C. G. Thayer, *Ben Jonson: Studies in the Plays* (Norman, Oklahoma, 1963), pp. 144–5. More soberly, D. McPherson, 'The origins of Overdo. A study in Jonsonian invention', *Modern Language Quarterly*, 37 (1976).
5. Professor Muriel Bradbrook charitably describes the tone as 'banter rather than spleen' in *The Living Momument: Shakespeare and the Theatre of His Time* (Cambridge, 1976), p. 111.
6. 'Bartholmew' is Jonson's consistent spelling for the Fair, Cokes's name and the title of the play; it doubtless reflects contemporary pronunciation (something like 'Bartle-mew'). I have followed the modern habit of using 'Bartholomew' for the title of the play, but retaining the contracted form for direct quotations.
7. See II. ii. 29; II. iv. 3; II. v. 4; III. ii. 34.
8. Bradbrook, *Living Monument*, p. 241.
9. Shakespeare and Fletcher give the name as Palamon; Jonson gives it as Palemon. I have remained consistent to the originals.
10. *The Two Noble Kinsmen*, ed. N. W. Bawcutt (Harmondsworth, 1977), p. 26.
11. Louis MacNeice, 'Autolycus', in *Collected Poems* (London, 1966), p. 233.
12. See, in particular, *The Winter's Tale*, I. ii. 67–82; also III. i. 22; IV. i. 24; V. ii. 105–6; V. iii. 121–3.

13. See, however, the episode of Sordido's conversion in *Every Man Out of His Humour* (III. vii; viii), commented on in chapter 1 (p. 40). This is an anomaly within that play and out of tune with Jonson's practice elsewhere.

14. Bradbrook, *Living Monument*, p. 188. See chapter 4, pp. 95–6.

15. This would inevitably remind people of James's *A Counterblaste to Tobacco* (1604).

16. This might have been meant literally at the Court performance; entertainments, like the masques, were usually followed by a banquet. This would further identify James with Overdo.

17. See, for example, J. B. Bamborough, *Ben Jonson* (London and New York, 1970), pp. 101, 104.

Reading list

Bamborough, J. B., *Ben Jonson* (London and New York, 1970)

Barish, J. A., *Ben Jonson and the Language of Prose Comedy* (Cambridge, Mass., 1960)

—— *Ben Jonson: A Collection of Critical Essays* (Englewood Cliffs, New Jersey, 1963)

Beaurline, L. A., *Jonson and Elizabethan Comedy* (San Marino, 1978)

Blissett, W., Patrick, J. and Van Fossen, R. (eds.), *A Celebration of Ben Jonson* (Toronto, 1973; London, 1974)

Boughner, D. C., *The Devil's Disciple* (New York, 1968)

Brock, D. H. and Welsh, J. (eds.), *Ben Jonson: A Quadricentennial Bibliography, 1947–72* (Metuchen, New Jersey, 1974)

Bryant, J. A., Jr, *Ben Jonson: The Compassionate Satirist* (Athens, Georgia, 1972)

Chan, M., *Music in the Theatre of Ben Jonson* (Oxford, 1980)

de Luna, B. N., *Jonson's Romish Plot* (Oxford, 1967)

Dessen, A. C., *Jonson's Moral Comedy* (Evanston, 1971)

Donaldson, I., *The World Upside-Down: Comedy from Jonson to Fielding* (Oxford, 1970)

Duncan, D., *Ben Jonson and the Lucianic Tradition* (Cambridge, 1979)

Enck, J. J., *Jonson and the Comic Truth* (Madison, Milwaukee and London, 1966)

Evans, W. M., *Ben Jonson and Elizabethan Music* (1929, reprinted New York, 1965)

Gibbons, B., *Jacobean City Comedy* (London, 1968; second edition, 1980)

Gilbert, A. H., *The Symbolic Persons in the Masques of Ben Jonson* (1948, reprinted New York, 1965)

Gordon, P. J., *The Renaissance Imagination*, ed. S. Orgel (Berkeley, California, 1975)

Grene, N., *Shakespeare, Jonson, Moliere: The Comic Contract* (London, 1980)

Jackson, G. B., *Vision and Judgement in Ben Jonson's Drama* (New Haven and London, 1968)

Knights, L. C., *Drama and Society in the Age of Jonson* (London, 1937)

Leggatt, A., *Ben Jonson: His Vision and His Art* (London, 1981)

Nichols, J. G., *The Poetry of Ben Jonson* (London, 1969)

Noyes, R. G., *Ben Jonson on the English Stage* (New York, 1935)

Orgel, S., *The Jonsonian Masque* (Cambridge, Mass., 1968)

—— *The Illusion of Power: Political Theater in the English Renaissance* (Berkeley, California, 1975)

Orgel, S. and Strong, R., *Inigo Jones: The Theatre of the Stuart Masque*, 2 vols. (London, 1973)

Parfitt, G., *Ben Jonson: Public Poet and Private Man* (London, 1976)

Partridge, E. B., *The Broken Compass* (London, 1958)

Peterson, R. S., *Imitation and Praise in the Poems of Ben Jonson* (New Haven and London, 1981)

Sackton, A. H., *Rhetoric as a Dramatic Language in Ben Jonson* (New York, 1948)

Savage, J. A., *Ben Jonson's Basic Comic Characters* (Mississippi, 1973)

Swinburne, A. C., *A Study of Ben Jonson* (London, 1889)

Symonds, J. A., *Ben Jonson* (London, 1886)

Tannenbaum, S. A., *Ben Jonson, A Concise Bibliography* (New York, 1938; Supplement, 1947)

Thayer, C. G., *Ben Jonson: Studies in the Plays* (Norman, Oklahoma, 1963)

Thomas, M. O. (ed.), *Ben Jonson: Quadricentennial Essays, Studies in the Literary Imagination* 6 (Atlanta, Georgia, 1973)

Trimpi, W., *Ben Jonson's Poems: A Study of the Plain Style* (Stanford, California, 1962)

Index

(The more substantial references are indicated in bold type.)

INDEX